The Challenge of Tradition

The Challenge of Tradition
Discerning the Future of Anglicanism

John Simons

editor

Anglican Book Centre
Toronto, Canada

1997
Anglican Book Centre
600 Jarvis Street
Toronto, Ontario
M4Y 2J6

Canadian Cataloguing in Publication Data

The challenge of tradition

ISBN 1-55126-163-4

1. Anglican Church of Canada. 2. Church renewal — Anglican Church of Canada.   3. Montreal declaration of Anglican essentials.
I. Simons, John, 1946 –

BX5614.C42 1996   283'.71   C96-932434-0

Contents

Foreword   7
Michael G. Peers, Primate, Anglican Church of Canada

Introduction: Recovering Authenticity in Anglican Faith and Practice   9
John Simons

1. **Feminism and the Church:** Challenge and Grace   19
   Susan L. Storey

2. **Naming and Glorifying the Trinity:** A Response   26
   to the Declaration's Stricture
   John Simons

3. **Towards a Biblical Church:** A Plea for Accountability in the   51
   Way We Use Scripture
   Paul Jennings

4. **The Word of God and "God's Word Written":** The Montreal   71
   Declaration on the Authority of the Scriptures
   Stephen Reynolds

5. **Humanity is One and History Is One**: Anglican Social Thought   98
   and the Montreal Declaration of Anglican Essentials
   Andrew Taylor

6. **Anglicanism and the Church's Global Mission:** A Critique of the   117
   Montreal Declaration of Anglican Essentials
   Terry Brown

7. **Faithfulness and Change:** Moments of Discontinuity in the   136
   Church's Teaching
   Gregory Baum

8. **Reflections on the "Anglican Ethos":** The Dialogical Middle Way   148
   Eileen Scully

Study Guide   *160*
  Paul Jennings

Appendix: The Montreal Declaration of Anglican Essentials   *179*

Contributors   *186*

Foreword

In June of 1994, over seven hundred Anglicans from across Canada gathered in Montreal in a conference called Essentials '94. They met, listened to addresses on a wide variety of topics, engaged in conversation about their faith and witness, and worshipped and prayed together with the purpose of discerning God's will for the Anglican Church of Canada. One immediate outcome of the conference was The Montreal Declaration of Anglican Essentials—an affirmation of participants of the ground on which they invite our church to take its stand. That Declaration, together with a collection of addresses given at Essentials '94, has been published in the book *Anglican Essentials: Reclaiming Faith within the Anglican Church of Canada*.

One of the most profound benefits of the conference has been the conversation and dialogue it has promoted among Anglicans about the nature of our faith. Anglican people of many points of view are speaking with one another in a more focused way about matters of faith and doctrine, about their own journeying to God. These conversations—in forums, Bible study groups, parish vestry and council meetings—are often full of energy (even fire!), and I rejoice at that. When accompanied by a will to listen, and to "speak the truth in love," then conviction and passion give life and energy to the church.

This volume is a collection of essays offering a response to the Montreal Declaration. It furnishes a critique that is thoughtful and tempered, potent and vigorous. The several authors often reveal an appreciation for the theological conversation that has been developing out of the Declaration—in fact, they have been profoundly absorbed in that conversation. However, when they examine some of the specifics of the Declaration, they find them severely wanting as an expression of Anglicanism or, indeed, of the fullness of the Christian faith. As editor John Simons states in his introduction, this book "is issued as a challenge" to the Montreal Declaration. It is a lively challenge indeed! While there is great respect shown for those who put together the Declaration, there is a thoroughgoing willingness to take issue with the claims and principles that inform much of it. This is a work that enters the dialogue seriously. Here you will find considerable food for thought, discussion, and prayer.

The reader might do well to think of this volume of essays as a "companion piece" to *Anglican Essentials*. At first glance, that may seem a strange suggestion, for the two books do not offer the same vision of the church—they are clearly distinct. However, they are companions in two important ways. First, both issue out of a love for God and for the church, and out of a desire to be faithful to the gospel we proclaim. Second, the writers of the chapters in this book intend to engage in genuine dialogue with those involved in the Essentials movement and the church as a whole. The word *companion* literally means "together in bread." And in the end, all our thinking, all our discussion (even argument and debate), and all our prayer must lead us to the table where we meet one another in the Lord. In the midst of our diversity and our tensions, we intend to remain one in Christ.

For certainly there are tensions in the church, and that is not at all a bad thing. Without tension, the strings on a violin could not be made to produce a single sweet note, let alone a melody. Without the tension that we call gravity—that tug that enables us to stand, and keeps the planets and the sun in relationship to one another—life on earth, and in the solar system itself, would collapse. Life depends on and flourishes when there is give and take, draw and pull. I would say the same of our life-in-faith: tension is the rule, not the exception. Our unity as Christians, and as Anglicans, is not one that is found in like-mindedness, in our being all the same. It is found in the generosity of God who created and loves us in our variety, in Christ who, lifted up on the cross, draws all people to himself, and in the gift of the Holy Spirit whose presence within us and among us creates the bond of peace.

It is in this spirit of companionship in faith, of dialogue and healthy tension, that I commend this collection to you. And I do so with much gratitude to its contributors. The challenge offered is substantial, the vision of church set forth is searching, and the hope expressed is truly heartening.

Michael G. Peers, Primate,
Anglican Church of Canada

Introduction
Recovering Authenticity
in Anglican Faith and Practice

JOHN SIMONS

The essays collected in this volume are issued as a challenge—they invite the reader to think through divisive issues in the contemporary church with candour and openness. Though they are written in particular for Anglicans in Canada, the essays will have relevance for English-speaking Christians of other denominations in North America and throughout the world, for they offer new perspectives on questions widely and hotly debated in our fin-de-siècle Christianity: the critique of feminism, the names of God, the authority of Scripture, liturgical renewal, the social and political dimensions of the gospel, evangelism, the church's global mission, homosexuality, and the nature and limits of tolerance.

The event which prompted the writing of these essays was the publication, in the summer of 1994, of the Montreal Declaration of Anglican Essentials. It was the fruit of a conference entitled Essentials '94, held at Ste-Anne de Bellevue, Québec. The conference brought together seven hundred Christians (mostly Anglicans) from across Canada. The lectures, speeches, and homilies presented at the conference were subsequently published in a book entitled *Anglican Essentials: Reclaiming Faith within the Anglican Church of Canada*.[1] The Declaration, appended to this volume, invites its readers to affirm its contents as "essentials of Christian faith, practice, and nurture today."

The Declaration, set out in the form of fifteen Articles, has, for Anglicans, the recognizable features of an erstwhile love. But the appearance of the classical Anglican consensus reiterated and updated proves to be only skin-deep. Hence, the authors of the essays collected here have felt that they must decline the invitation to affirm the Declaration. These essays are offered, therefore, as explanations for a refusal; and they are offered as counter-invitations to think about the issues along trajectories that, while faithful to the same standards of authority, are free of the defensive and rigid postures in which the Declaration would fix Christian orthodoxy.

If it is objected that the Declaration is not intended to fix Chistian ortho-doxy, one can only wonder why the document is called a "declaration." Declarations are usually issued in times of crisis precisely in order to foreclose debate. A declaration of independence is something more than a position paper inviting discussion of the desirability of political sovereignty; a declara-tion of war is not an argument in a debate about whether or not to engage in hostile action, but a solemn proclamation initiating such action. Is it a mistake to suspect that the Declaration intends to enunciate the non-negotiable terms of Christian orthodoxy?

Moreover, the Declaration states that its various Articles express the es-sentials of Christian faith. In its usual sense, the word *essential* is used to designate something that is absolutely necessary or requisite. An essential step in a therapeutic procedure, for example, is one that absolutely must be taken if the procedure is to be followed. An essential part of a building's structure is a part that must be there if the bricks, glass, and steel are to be structured as a building. Thus, an essential of Christian faith is a belief or practice that is absolutely required to be believed or practiced by an individual or community claiming to be Christian.

Consequently, when the authors of the Declaration call their document a declaration of essentials, and claim that it sets forth the essentials of Christian faith, they are apparently making a very strong claim. An ingenuous reader might be forgiven for thinking that its fifteen Articles are meant to state positions that must be accepted by all who hold the Christian faith. But surely, if this is the intention of the Declaration, it is far too brash. I cannot imagine that the authors of the Declaration seriously believe, for example, that Baptists, Lutherans, Presbyterians, and Roman Catholics should accept *The Book of Common Prayer* as the norm for all alternative liturgies.

There is, in fact, an unacknowledged ambiguity in the language the docu-ment uses to describe itself. It is a declaration of *Anglican* essentials, and it affirms the essentials of *Christian* faith. The ambiguity may be insignificant; or it may not be. The Declaration seems to ignore the ecumenical context of contemporary Anglicanism. Do we not suspect those churches of sectarianism that, without qualification or reference to a wider tradition of faith, simply assume their doctrinal stance is identical with the Christian one? Surely the authors of the Declaration do not wish to promote a sectarian Anglicanism, but the document's rhetoric—the elision of Anglican (as understood by the Declaration) and Christian, the definitive tone, the dismissal of variant views without dialogue or debate, the curious omissions—suggests the desire to create, at least in thought if not in reality, an ideal church defined by its doctrinal and moral purity. But what, we may wonder, is the relation of this "ideal" church to the actual society of the baptized? What is its relation to the church that lives and witnesses, sins and repents, grows and suffers in history? And what is the connection of this "ideal" church to the world for whose sake the church exists?

Let us assume, in any event, that what we have to do with is a declaration of *Anglican* essentials. What, then, might be the purpose of such a declaration? The most natural response would be that it sets forth a criterion of Anglican identity. That is, it specifies those beliefs and practices that must be affirmed by a church that claims to be faithful to its Anglican heritage. No church (province, diocese, parish) may propose variations in worship, doctrine, or discipline that are inconsonant with the Declaration without thereby forfeiting its claim to be Anglican.

In fairness, however, it must be said that the Declaration apparently intends to accomplish something more than to state a criterion of Anglican identity. It has the renewal of the church in mind, and declares that "this fullness of faith is needed ... for the effective proclamation of the good news of Jesus Christ in the power of the Holy Spirit." The essentials thus refer, not only to those beliefs and practices that are necessary for Anglican identity, but also to those beliefs and practices that are jointly sufficient to establish the church in the fullness of faith.

Sufficiency, too, is a mark of essentiality. Generally speaking, essentials are the set of properties that are individually necessary and jointly sufficient to define an entity or constitute its identity. Hence, the Declaration is saying to the church: This is what you need to believe and no more than you need to believe. Or, to put it in the first person, we need to believe the contents of the Declaration in order to be faithful Anglicans and to bring about the renewal of the church. Moreover, we need not concern ourselves with questions that have been settled by the Declaration, or undertake projects not licensed by it, for the beliefs and practices authorized by the Declaration are alone sufficient to specify the fullness of faith.

If this is indeed the two-fold intention of the Declaration, namely, to enunciate the criterion of Anglican identity and demarcate the fullness of faith, then the present volume may be taken as a cumulative argument demonstrating that the Declaration fails on both counts. The Declaration asks the church to accept certain restrictions as necessary elements of Anglican identity (for example, the prohibition of innovation in religious and theological language, and an unrevisable Prayer Book) that were never before imposed on the church; and it fails to mention other elements of belief and practice that arguably do contribute to the fullness of faith: the ecumenical vocation of the church, an emerging consensus on Christian initiation and the eucharist, a rediscovery of the church's prophetic role in issues of justice and peace, the witness our church has rendered in ordaining women to all three orders of ministry.

In its first Article, the Declaration declines proposals to modify or marginalize the classical triune Name; that is, Father, Son, and Holy Spirit. The intention is evidently to disenfranchise recent attempts to expand the repertoire of the church's linguistic resources in speaking of or to God. In the second chapter of this volume, I develop an argument for an expansion of the divine Names. I suggest that it is, in fact, the Declaration that tends to ignore or marginalize certain essential marks of a living trinitarian faith, and that the power of the classical Name to communicate the mystery of God to the church is not taken seriously enough by the Declaration. An analysis of the logic of the triune Name shows that the church which consciously lives that logic may well find itself multiplying its praises of the triune God.

It is no secret that the contemporary church owes its awareness of the limitations of masculine names for God to the feminist critique of the Christian tradition. Feminism is not an academic fashion; it is one of the most significant cultural movements of our time. Lamentably, the Declaration makes no explicit mention of the feminist critique and avoids engagement with it altogether, opting, rather, to pretend that the essentials of Christian faith can be articulated in our day as if the radical intellectual and existential struggles of the last thirty years simply haven't happened. Hence, Susan Storey's opening chapter, "Feminism and the Church: Challenge and Grace," is a necessary introduction to the chapters that follow. She argues that the church cannot avoid asking whether or not patriarchy is divinely revealed and sanctioned. If it is, then the Bible cannot bear good news for women and function salvifically for them. Nor can it function salvifically for men. Feminism, therefore, challenges the church to think in new ways about its foundational texts, and it recalls us to "the fundamental insight of the incomprehensibility of God."

There is nonetheless widespread fear among Christians that feminist perspectives introduced into preaching, teaching, and liturgy represent a dangerous departure from biblical Christianity. Furthermore, it seems to many that the authority of Scripture in matters of faith and morals is effectively denied by a church unwilling to enforce Jesus' prohibition of divorce, or the condemnation of same-sex relations in Leviticus and the Pauline writings, or Paul's teaching on the subordination of women in the church. The Declaration trades on this fear when it asserts in Article 6 that the canonical Scriptures are "'God's Word written,' inspired and authoritative, true and trustworthy, coherent, sufficient for salvation, living and powerful as God's guidance for belief and behaviour" and that the "church may not judge the Scriptures, selecting and discarding from among their teachings. But Scripture under Christ judges the church for its faithfulness to his revealed truth." Paul Jennings and Stephen

Reynolds, in chapters 3 and 4 respectively, directly address the fear, felt by many, that the contemporary church, in formulating new approaches to ancient issues, ignores or undermines the authority of Scripture.

Jennings objects to the Declaration's strategy. It is no use asking the church to reaffirm its belief in the authority of the Bible when the real issue that divides Christians has to do, not with whether we accept the authority of Scripture, but with how we understand the Bible to be authoritative. In "Towards a Biblical Church: A Plea for Accountability in the Way We Use Scripture," Jennings argues that we must reject a biblicist view of Scripture; that is, one that has no regard for the human context of the scriptural word. In answer to the Declaration's pronouncement that the church may not judge the Scriptures, Jennings replies that "we must learn, not to judge the Scriptures, but to discern the human and the divine voice in Scripture, to discern what spirit is speaking through a passage and through our understanding." This process of discernment is guided by the recognition that Scripture is not primarily a repository of doctrine, nor a law by which human behaviour is judged, but a witness to the living Word, Jesus Christ. The Bible speaks to us as a story, addressing our emotions and imagination as well as our intellect, and calls us into encounter with the living Word.

Jennings warns against the tendency to impose a false unity on Scripture by interpreting it in the light of a system of doctrine. Doctrine, he says, should "serve to balance and enable our encounter with the Word, not to replace it." The problem with the Declaration, he believes, is that it confuses faith and doctrine. The Bible is authoritative not only for doctrine but more fundamentally for faith, which he characterizes as "our communal yet intensely personal way with God." Consequently, a number of contemporary movements viewed by the Declaration as threats to orthodoxy—namely, liturgical renewal, liberation theologies, feminism, relational views of sexual ethics, an environmental understanding of the creation, and so on—can be understood to be profoundly biblical in inspiration and direction.

Stephen Reynolds notes that the Declaration's understanding of the authority of Scripture is expressed in the form of a metaphor, the metaphor of magistracy, inasmuch as Scripture is said to *judge* the church. In analyzing the metaphor, Reynolds concludes that it entails its own reversal: "it is not the Scriptures that 'judge' (in a judicial sense) the church; it is the church, as a community of living, personal agents, that 'judges' (in a judicious sense) the Scriptures." Examining the scriptural citations subjoined to Article 6 as "prooftexts" of its understanding of the authority of Scripture, Reynolds finds that none of them refers unambiguously to "God's Word written," and hence that none can be invoked to bolster the metaphor of magistracy. On the other hand, Reynolds argues that the concept of living word or speech attributed to God is something more than a metaphor. Since speech, rather than the written word, entails the presence of one to another, the Word of God, as living utterance, is God's living, particular presence to the people with whom God chooses to be in communion. In the Incarnation, God's particular presence to the community of Israel became "the living utterance of God's presence in all the particularity of human being itself." The primary, constitutive Word of God is thus not to be identified with "God's Word written." Still, the Scriptures may be understood to have a sacramental relation to the Word of God, and Reynolds concludes his essay by exploring the sacramental event as a model by which to understand the relation between the Word of God and "God's Word written." He finds that the relation of Scripture to the church is more complicated than the metaphor of magistracy suggests, and that the Declaration's failure to observe the distinction between "God's Word written" and the Word of God leads to the Declaration's "attributing unto Scripture more than it can have."

Andrew Taylor's chapter, "Humanity is One and History is One," presents a critique of the Declaration from the standpoint of what he calls "a critical orthodoxy." He begins with an analysis of the factors in Canadian Anglicanism that have led to the Essentials alliance and the publication of the Declaration. While sympathetic to many of their concerns—the evasion of sin in liberal Christianity, and the pop-psychology approach to spirituality—he is critical of the traditionalists' uncritical acceptance of the social and theological principles embodied in *The Book of Common Prayer,* and of their ideological distortion of the Bible in the condemnation of gays and lesbians. The problem with the Declaration, he argues, is that its soteriology is effectively bipartite (Fall and Salvation) rather than tripartite (Creation, Fall, and Redemption).[2] He then traces the ruinous consequences of this theological mistake and shows how they are illustrated in the Declaration. The Declaration, for example, is unable to articulate the "essentially social and universal significance of the acts of God in Christ," and this failure underwrites a sectarian understanding of salvation and the church.

A critical orthodoxy, on the other hand, affirms the re-creation of humanity as a whole accomplished by God in the Incarnation and Paschal Mystery. A church founded on this affirmation will have the resources to engage secular culture in a dialogical way, making clear from the outset its preferential option for the poor and outcast. A commitment to social, economic, and political justice is not simply an "implication" of the gospel, as the Declaration suggests; it is an inescapable dimension of the gospel, and social action "is an integral part of the gospel itself."

A retrieval and contextualization of the ancient traditions of the church in the contemporary Anglican Church, together with the influence of the inter-church faith and justice movement, has given Canadian Anglicanism, Taylor believes, a profoundly biblical, catholic, and orthodox direction. The Declaration, by contrast, represents a reactionary attempt to create a sectarian church.

In chapter 6, Terry Brown argues that the so-called essentials of Christian faith set out in the Declaration carry with them such excessive cultural baggage that they cannot be expected to function as seeds for the church's global mission. He locates the root difficulty of the Declaration in its "virtually fundamentalist" view of Scripture, and its affirmation of *The Book of Common Prayer* as the standard of Anglican doctrine and norm of Anglican worship. The classical Anglican understanding that the Bible is fundamentally about the divine revelation of God's love in the life, death, and resurrection of Jesus Christ, and the well-established Anglican respect for a critical approach to Scripture, has enabled the church in its mission to take into account the complexity and dynamism of the various cultures in which the church has been planted. The Declaration's view of Scripture, on the other hand, would seem to encourage an evangelism ill-equipped to foster the indigenization or inculturation of the gospel. Furthermore, Anglican missions influenced by the liturgical movement, ecumenism, and indigenization have produced new Prayer Books quite different from *The Book of Common Prayer* in theological orientation and cultural ethos. The Declaration's wish to impose an unrevisable Prayer Book on the Anglican Church of Canada is simply out of step with global Anglicanism.

Brown notes that the ecumenical movement has one of its roots in the missionary movement. The close link between mission and ecumenism has meant that Anglicans in the southern hemisphere have in some cases entered into new united churches, and have, in general, been able to contribute to the development of a post-denominational Christianity. In ecumenical relations, Brown suggests that the four clauses of the so-called Lambeth Quadrilateral continue to offer "a more than adequate summary" of Anglican essentials.

The situation of the church in Asia, Africa, the Middle East, Latin America, and the South Pacific, where interfaith relations are part of everyday life, has led many Anglicans in those parts of the world to re-think their understanding of evangelism. Brown suggests that the Declaration, as the product of an almost entirely white, middle-class Canadian Anglican gathering, and in its assumption of a proselytization model of evangelism, is unable either to provide a resource for or receive insight from the re-thinking of evangelism in the interfaith context of southern Anglicanism. Moreover, the Anglican Communion's reflections on mission, summed up in the "Ten Principles of Partnership," do not seem to inform the Declaration's understanding of global mission. Brown argues that the Ten Principles assume a different ecclesiology from that of the Declaration. The difference is not of merely academic interest, for the mission strategies of Canadian institutions and agencies inviting the support of Canadian Anglicans are such as to undermine the intentions and efforts of Anglicans seeking to observe the Ten Principles. This is an instance of a more general problem with the Declaration, which, Brown suggests, is its "sectarian Canadian Anglicanism isolated from developments in the Anglican Communion over the past fifty years."

In chapter 7, Gregory Baum, a Roman Catholic theologian who has taught, among others, Anglican ordinands and graduate students at McGill University, addresses one of the most contentious issues in the church today, that of the church's teaching on homosexuality. The Declaration's position is clear: "homosexual unions are intimacies contrary to God's design.... The church may not lower God's standards of sexual morality for any of its members, but must honour God by upholding these standards tenaciously in face of society's departures from them." Unfortunately, the issue does not seem so clear for growing numbers of Christians. In "Faithfulness and Change: Moments of Discontinuity in the Church's Teaching," Baum suggests a way out of the impasse of mutual incomprehension, imperious certitude, and indecisive ambivalence that characterizes the debate in contemporary Canadian Anglican circles. He begins from the observation that there have been moments of discontinuity in the church's teaching, and he cites the change of teaching introduced by Vatican Council II in regard to Jews and the Jewish religion. Following the theologian Juan Segundo, he suggests that there are five steps taken by the church in the movement from a particular doctrinal stance to its contrary. These are: (1) the discovery of a contradiction between doctrine and love; (2) the search for the root of this contradiction; (3) the re-reading of scripture and tradition to find hints for resolving this contradiction; (4) a turn to Christian experience as experiential verification of the new perspective; and (5) the development of a systematic theology capable of overcoming the contradiction.

Baum illustrates how the "hermeneutical circle" has worked in the case of the church's official attitude toward other world religions, and then asks whether it might likewise be employed to encourage greater official openness toward homosexual love. He emphasizes that these moments of discontinuity are not inspired by a cowardly wish to become conformed to the world, but involve grace-filled events, repentance from evil, searching the Scriptures, and a new commitment to love of the neighbour.

In chapter 8, Eileen Scully also endeavours to carry us beyond the polarized options of doctrinal debate. Our task, she believes, is not to set out a system of doctrine or define the essentials of Anglicanism, but to develop a method that will allow the fullness of the tradition to meet with the fullness of contemporary wisdom. Theological reflection requires us to keep a series of dialectics alive: the inherited story and the lived story, tradition and experiment, the remembered past and retrieval of the forgotten past, and so on. The tendency to affirm one side of the dialectic while negating the other, or to privilege one at the expense of the other, leads not only to intellectual dessication but to a betrayal of the catholicity of the gospel which, precisely because it is catholic, challenges us "to bring it anew in every age."

Scully also demonstrates that the development of a theological method is not simply a logical exercise; it is equally a moral one, demanding "humility and hospitality on the part of ... [the] bearers of tradition to create the context for mutuality and open dialogue." She finds adumbrations of such a method in the tone of Richard Hooker's sixteenth-century masterpiece of Anglican divinity, *Of The Laws of Ecclesiastical Polity*, and further resources in recent philosophical attempts to understand the ethical dimensions of dialogue. Her fear is that the theological challenges that are most pressing face increasing polarization "not because people are not well-grounded in Anglican 'essentials' but because we are poorly equipped for dialogue." Her hope, however, is that the Anglican virtues of reasonableness, tolerance, and openness will be taken up again in a new intellectual and social context.

The essays collected here thus give expression to hope. Our proximate hope is that the church will not, out of loyalty to narrowly conceived essentials, disenfranchise those of its members who seek to renew and expand our worship of the triune God, our witness to God's coming reign of justice and mercy, our freedom in Christ, and our reliance on God's living Word. Our ultimate hope, of course, is that the issues we debate with one another and with those who subscribe to the Declaration are issues that matter, and that the discussing of them may be taken up into the providential activity of the One who raises up things that are cast down, and makes new the things that have grown old, and brings all things to their perfection in Christ.

As editor, I wish to thank the contributors to this collection who, in the midst of already committed work schedules, responded with generosity and amazing alacrity to the invitation to submit essays. Thanks are due to the administrative staff of the Montreal Diocesan Theological College—Mrs. Cynthia Hawkins, Mrs. Patricia Hammond, and Mrs. Mary Fox—who bore my absences and absent-mindedness with their usual patience and helpfulness, while I pondered over manuscripts or tracked down references. I owe, too, a special debt of gratitude to Mr. Robert Maclennan of the Anglican Book Centre, who first approached me with the idea of the book, and who gently encouraged, prodded, and advised me over what proved to be a longer association than he had originally anticipated.

Endnotes

1. George Egerton, ed. (Toronto: Anglican Book Centre, 1995).
2. The Declaration does affirm the goodness of God's original creation (Article 2). Taylor's point, however, is that only "a passing nod" is given to creation as the necessary background for the drama of salvation. The continuity between God's creative grace and God's saving grace is lost.

1

Feminism and the Church
Challenge and Grace

SUSAN STOREY

It is becoming increasingly clear that one of the essentials for the church at the end of the second millennium is to come to terms with the feminist critique in all its aspects. For many Christians, including some Anglicans, feminism is perceived as a threat, a movement or point of view to be attacked or, alternatively, simply dismissed and passed over in silence. It is evident that this latter approach is the one chosen in the Montreal Declaration of Anglican Essentials.[1] However, neither of these two responses seems adequate or helpful.

To be sure, feminist analysis presents a major challenge to the church. Some feminists have come to view this challenge as unanswerable, Scripture and Christian tradition as irredeemable, and have left the church for the sake of their own integrity and spiritual health. Others, however, find not only damaging but also liberating elements in Scripture and tradition, and see Christian feminist thought not only as a challenge but also as a gift of grace given to the church in our time. This is Anne Carr's view:

> Christianity and feminism are not only compatible but they are, in fact, integrally and firmly connected in the truth of the Christian vision. While feminism presents a challenge to Christianity today, it is a challenge that is a powerful grace in its call for the church to be faithful to its own transcendent truth, to the deepest meaning of its symbols, its great tradition, and the new experience of over half its faithful members.[2]

Not all Christian feminists would take such a benign view of Christian symbols and Christian tradition. Nevertheless, in coming to terms with the feminist critique, it is useful to focus on both the challenging and the grace-filled aspects of feminist thought. First, however, we will need to define some basic terms from feminist analysis: "sexism," "patriarchy," and "androcentrism."

Margaret Farley has defined sexism as the "belief that persons are superior or inferior to one another on the basis of their sex. It includes, however, attitudes, value systems, and social patterns which express or support this belief."[3] Elizabeth Johnson notes the "twin faces" of sexism evident throughout Scripture and tradition; namely, patriarchy and androcentrism. She defines patriarchy, literally "father rule," as

> a form of social organization in which power is always in the hand of the dominant man or men with others ranked below in a graded series of subordination.... Religious patriarchy is one of the strongest forms of this structure, for it understands itself to be divinely established, consequently, the power of the ruling men is said by them to be delegated by God (invariably spoken of in male terms), and exercised by divine mandate.[4]

The other face of sexism, androcentrism—literally "man-centred"—is a pattern of thinking that assumes the male to be the human norm and sees the female as other, deficient, or auxiliary. "In theology, androcentrism assumes that ruling men will be the norm for language not only about human nature, but also about God...."[5] With these definitions in mind, let us now turn to ways in which feminism is indeed both a major challenge and a powerful grace to the church in the present era.

The challenge of feminist consciousness has probably been most evident to Anglicans in the advent of inclusive language liturgies and translations of Scripture. *The Book of Alternative Services*, following the recommendation of General Synod in 1980 to use inclusive language wherever possible, has, for the most part, reflected this norm with respect to human persons.[6] *The New Revised Standard Version of the Bible*, which is now used for the lectionary printouts from the Anglican Book Centre, has endeavoured to do the same. The intent in such Scripture translations and liturgical texts has been to refrain from using "words that make women disappear"[7]; that is, words that assume and perpetuate androcentric linguistic patterns. Part of the challenge has been to find felicitous ways of rewording existing texts and composing new material. The more difficult challenge has been in raising the consciousness of congregations to the significance of the inclusive language issue.

Nevertheless, progress has been made over the past fifteen years. In a discussion of personal pronouns in English usage, Gail Ramshaw notes that "the argument that *he* is generic is becoming extinct.... Whether one believes that the generic masculine ever existed, one must conclude it is now nearly dead, and current attempts to employ it often create unclarity."[8]

It is more difficult to claim insignificance for the other challenge of inclusive language, language about God and addressed to God. The most basic way of facing the challenge has been simply to avoid masculine pronouns when speaking of God. Sometimes this involves repetition of the noun "God," unless some other grammatical construction is employed. In giving the invitation to confession on page 191 of *The Book of Alternative Services*, many presiders, using participles and a demonstrative pronoun instead of masculine personal pronouns, reword the text declaring, "God is steadfast in love and infinite in mercy, welcoming sinners and inviting us to this table."

Another strategy is to minimize the use of male-gender-linked names for God, such as "father" and "king." Gail Ramshaw traces the origins of the name "father" for God to the ancient notion of the king as God's son, to a Greco-Roman title for the emperor, and to a misunderstood biology that supposed the father alone to be the active source of a child. In the New Testament, father is both loving nurturer (Matt. 6:25–33), and harsh disciplinarian (Heb. 12:5–11).[9] In spite of theological disclaimers, the title "father" for God came to be anthropomorphized as a "personalized masculine authority figure."[10] Ramshaw's preferred solution to the androcentric and patriarchal bias of traditional anthropomorphic metaphors for God is to emphasize in public worship "objectifying metaphors" for God, such as tree of life, light, fountain, living water, fire, wind (ch. 9). She also suggests a more creative liturgical use of verbs for the God who acts (ch. 10).

Other feminist writers, such as Elizabeth Johnson, advocate the use of female metaphors in addition to the male ones as a much-needed corrective in Christian God-language. Johnson notes the temptation to focus on the Holy Spirit as a feminine aspect of God, but rejects this approach for several reasons. In the first place, introducing gender polarities in the Trinity only emphasizes sexual differences, which is far from the intent. There is also a clear danger, especially when hierarchical patterns of thought and social organization are still creditable, of a feminine Holy Spirit seeming a fitting third, having her source and origin in the still-male father. Johnson suggests drawing on biblical sources for a "naming towards God" (Mary Daly's phrase), freeing us to use female metaphors for all the Persons of the Trinity. This is possible, in part, because "all three hypostases of the Trinity transcend categories of male and female."[11]

The overriding question is always "What is the right way to speak of God?" Or, to phrase the question more modestly, "How can we formulate less inadequate speech about God?" Johnson answers that one way is by using female images and metaphors:

> It is not essential for the truth of God's triune mystery to speak always in the metaphors of father, son, and spirit, although virtually exclusive use of these names over the centuries in liturgy, catechesis, and theology has caused this to be forgotten. At this point in the living tradition I believe

that we need a strong dose of explicitly female imagery to break the unconscious sway that male trinitarian imagery holds over the imagination of even the most sophisticated thinkers.[12]

Her suggestions for female images, metaphors, and names include Sophia, Holy Wisdom, She Who Is, "God as a woman in the labor of childbirth; God as a woman courageously engaged on behalf of justice; God as a woman angry against what harms and destroys...."[13] More than that, she eloquently links the suffering of women who are tortured, abused, and humiliated with the suffering of God: "The suffering body of Christ includes the raped and denigrated bodies of women."[14]

If one highly visible challenge of Christian feminist thought is seen in the growing use of inclusive language, the feminist challenge does not end here. The challenge to Christianity is a fundamental question of the revelatory status of the Scriptures. Sandra Schneiders notes that the problem with the Bible goes beyond the presence of sexist images (such as the comparison of unfaithful Israel to a whore, for example, in Hos. 2), misogynist narratives (such as the rape and murder of the concubine, in Judges 19:22–30), and patriarchal directives (such as the banning of women from liturgical leadership, for example, in I Cor. 14:34–35). It even goes beyond the pervasive masculine language for God.

Schneiders raises a fundamental question: "How can a text that contains so much that is damaging to women function authoritatively in the Christian community as normative of faith and life?"[15] Clearly, the possibility of Scripture functioning authoritatively depends on "whether or not the Bible teaches the maleness of God and the inferiority of women." In other words, it depends on whether patriarchy is divinely revealed and sanctioned or not.[16] If the Bible does teach that God is male and women are inferior, these texts cannot bear "Good News" for women or function salvifically for them. I would add that they cannot do so for men either, in the long run, because living under patriarchy distorts self-image and relationships for men as well as for women.

Here the depth and seriousness of the challenge of feminism for the church and for Christian faith is evident. The problem is in the founding texts themselves, in the human situation—the patriarchal context—of their human authors, and in the ongoing androcentric traditioning of the faith in subsequent generations. Acknowledging the difficulty and the gravity of patriarchal roots and an androcentric tradition is an important first step in engaging the feminist critique. Answering this challenge demands new ways of thinking about ancient texts, about their authors, and about ourselves as their readers and interpreters. Here we can begin to recognize some of the graces, the gifts to the church, that feminist analysis offers.

Some of the earliest and ongoing work of feminist scholars has been to bring to light obscured images and accounts of women in the Scriptures and in

Christian tradition. To be sure, what is reported about women in the Bible is presented from the androcentric viewpoint of the human authors, and reports on women living under patriarchy. Nevertheless, there are women who emerge as active agents, people of wit and courage, expressing their own interests and convictions.

Elisabeth Schussler Fiorenza has highlighted two such women in the titles of two of her major works.[17] In *In Memory of Her*, Schussler Fiorenza points to the unnamed woman whose anointing of Jesus will be told throughout the world, as Jesus says in Mark's Gospel, "in memory of her." Focus on this story brings to light its variations within the four Gospels. In Mark and in Matthew, the woman anoints Jesus' head, a symbol of kingly office (Mark 14:3–9; Matt. 26:6–13). In Luke's version, the woman becomes a "sinner" who anoints Jesus' feet, not his head, and the prophetic dimension of the anointing, placed shortly before his death by the other three evangelists, is erased by Luke. Here her memory is not honoured.[18] In John's account, this anointing precedes Jesus' death; it is again an anointing of his feet, here by Jesus' friend Mary of Bethany (John 12:1–8). This time, however, the woman is not a forgiven sinner, but one who does a service to a friend comparable to Jesus' own washing of the disciples' feet (John 13:1–20).

Another of Schussler Fiorenza's works, *But She Said*, owes its title to the story of a foreign woman who asks Jesus to heal her daughter (Matt. 15:21–28; Mark 7:24–30). Fiorenza uses this story primarily to draw a parallel between this foreign woman and those who enter into theological discourse and biblical interpretation from the standpoint of feminist consciousness. Feminists enter this arena, she says, as "resident aliens," with a different perspective than that from which the biblical text was written and from which it has subsequently been interpreted.[19] Reading this story from a feminist rather than an androcentric perspective, however, can open up new levels of meaning and provide bread even for the marginalized, for the "dogs under the table," for those who are outsiders—for women. By her willingness to enter the private house where Jesus is (with his disciples, according to Matthew), by her wit, by her boldness in using Jesus' own words to turn around what he is saying to make her case, by her perseverance, the foreign woman gets what she came for, the healing of her daughter. The point is that a liberating and healing word can still be heard, even in androcentric texts.

More generally, feminist scholars are evolving theories of interpretation that may allow biblical texts to speak in ways that transcend the limitations of their human authors. Sandra Schneiders has compiled a list of hermeneutical approaches to biblical texts developed by feminist biblical scholars. The list includes the following: criticizing oppressive biblical material through the use of liberating traditions (for example, the prophetic tradition and the original intention of the creation of male and female in God's image); re-telling misogynist stories as "texts of terror"[20] in memory of their victims, not as acceptable parts of salvation history; pressing the silences of the text for hidden stories of women; analysis of oppressive texts (for example, disciplinary injunctions against women) to establish women's actual roles in early Christianity.[21] This ongoing work is, in itself, a great gift to the church.

Finally, the work of feminist theologians offers a powerful grace to Christian discourse about God in recalling us to the fundamental insight of the incomprehensibility of God. Elizabeth Johnson speaks of the idolatrous consequences of allowing "the exclusive centrality of the male image and idea of God."[22] She notes the "dangerous situation" that results when "words becom[e] too clear and ideas too distinct," when we suppose God's self-revelation has removed God's ultimate unknowability.[23] Furthermore, the all-too-clear words and distinct ideas about God in male terms and images denigrates the human dignity of women, "banning female reality as suitable reference points for God."[24] Recognition of these two failings, found in Scripture, in Christian tradition, and still extant can recall the church to two Christian essentials: speaking rightly of God, insofar as we can, and promoting the dignity of women, as well as that of every other human person.

Although these two points are not explicitly named in the Declaration, perhaps they are intended as too obviously essential to need mentioning. One fears, however, that what is passed over in silence is missing because it does not fit easily within the vision of the church that inspired the Declaration. That vision perhaps becomes most clear in its final section where we find the statement: "God helping us, we resolve to maintain our heritage of faith and transmit it intact." A feminist vision of the church would not be of an institution charged with transmitting intact what it has received from the past, as entrusted wealth buried in the ground. It would be, rather, a vision of a community that remembers its history, for better and for worse, and opens itself to the wind of the Holy Spirit, to the breath of new life and the taste of new wine.

Endnotes

1. Feminism as such is not mentioned in the Declaration. Possibly the statement in Article 1, "we decline proposals to modify or marginalize these names [Father, Son and Holy Spirit]" is directed against suggestions by feminists, along with many others, to expand the repertoire of scripturally based names of God in common Christian usage. In Article 15, the Declaration does include "sexist domination" along with divorce, child abuse, domestic violence, rape, pornography, parental absenteeism, abortion, common-law relationships, and homosexual partnerships in a list of realities that "reflect weakening of the family ideal." Presumably, Anglicans

are being urged to speak out against, or even work for the eradication of, all of the above.

2. Anne E. Carr, *Transforming Grace: Christian Tradition and Women's Experience* (San Francisco: Harper and Row, 1988), 1–2.
3. Margaret Farley, "Sexism," in *New Catholic Encyclopedia* (New York: McGraw Hill, 1978), 17, 604.
4. Elizabeth A. Johnson, *She Who Is: The Mystery of God in Feminist Theological Discourse* (New York: Crossroad, 1992), 24.
5. *Ibid.*
6. See Michael Ingham, *Rites for a New Age: Understanding the Book of Alternative Services* (Toronto: The Anglican Book Centre, 1986), 95.
7. This is the title of an article by Alma Graham in *Redbook Magazine* (March 1977), which was reprinted by the Ontario Status of Women Council.
8. Gail Ramshaw, *God Beyond Gender: Feminist Christian God-Language* (Minneapolis: Fortress Press, 1995), 26–7.
9. Here, as Ramshaw points out, "the New Revised Standard Version's use of 'parent' [instead of 'father'] disguises the original meaning." *Ibid.*, 81.
10. *Ibid.* See her entire discussion "The Word Father," 77–81.
11. Johnson, She Who Is, 211.
12. *Ibid.*, 212.
13. *Ibid.*, 259.
14. *Ibid.*, 264.
15. Sandra M. Schneiders, "The Bible and Feminism" in *Freeing Theology: The Essentials of Theology in Feminist Perspective*, ed. Catherine M. LaCugna (San Francisco: HarperCollins, 1993), 31–57, 36.
16. Sandra M. Schneiders, *Beyond Patching: Faith and Feminism in the Catholic Church* (New York: Paulist Press, 1991), 37.
17. Elisabeth Schussler Fiorenza, *In Memory of Her: A Feminist Theological Reconstruction of Christian Origins* (New York: Crossroad, 1983), and *But She Said: Feminist Practices of Biblical Interpretation* (Boston: Beacon Press, 1992).
18. See Jane Schaberg, "Luke," in *The Women's Bible Commentary*, ed. Carol A. Newsom and Sharon H. Ringe (Louisville, Ky.: Westminster/John Knox Press, 1992), 275–92, 286.
19. See Schussler Fiorenza, *But She Said*, 170, for her use of the term "resident alien."
20. This term is from Phyllis Trible, *Texts of Terror* (Philadelphia: Fortress Press, 1984).
21. Schneiders, "The Bible and Feminism," 50.
22. Elizabeth A. Johnson, "The Incomprehensibility of God and the Image of God Male and Female," *Theological Studies* 45 (1984), 441–65, 443.
23. *Ibid.*, 441.
24. *Ibid.*, 443.

2
Naming and
Glorifying the Trinity
A Response to the Declaration's Stricture

JOHN SIMONS

Introduction

Over the past twenty-five years, the church has been finding new language to address and glorify and confess the one God of creation and redemption. The range of this linguistic creativity finds expression in a recent hymn of Brian Wren's to be included in the new hymn book of the Anglican Church of Canada.[1] In successive stanzas, God is called, "Strong mother God," "Warm father God," "Old aching God," "Young growing God," and "Great living God." Not surprisingly, the classical trinitarian Name of God, "Father, Son, and Holy Spirit," has not been immune to revision. In place of "Father," locutions like "Source and Partner of the Eternal Word," "Eternal Giver of Love and Power," "Fountain of Life and Source of All Goodness," "Author of Life Divine," and even "Parent" and "Mother/Father" are being used to address the First Person of the Trinity. One may likewise hear the Son addressed as "Word" or "Child" or "Servant." And, of course, the classical trinitarian formula is often replaced by such formulae as "Creator, Redeemer, Sanctifier" and variations.

To many in the church, this burgeoning of new images and names for God feels uncomfortably chaotic. As Bishop Rowan Williams points out, however, "talking of God can be chaotic."

> The first event in the public history of the Christian community was an outbreak of baffling, noisy, exuberant talk in diverse languages; and the great moments of the Church's renewal have all been associated with new words for praying and singing, new images, a new liberty to open one's mouth in confidence. From the Reformation to the Methodist Revival to the charismatic movement to the bible study in the Latin

American base community, renewal has meant people, all sorts of people, finding authority to talk *of* God and *to* God. We may find their words odd ... but the moment at which a person senses for the first time that he or she has the liberty for such speech should be for us a moment of revelation, of truth-telling about a God who risks the divine truth in opening the mouths of fallible people; because to be God *is* to be the generosity of self-communication.[2]

Unfortunately, Williams' positive assessment of the chaos is not shared by many Canadian Anglicans. If one may take the Montreal Declaration of Anglican Essentials as a statement of the position held by substantial numbers of Anglicans in this country, then we are an especially nervous and defensive church. The first Article of the Declaration begins with these words: "There is one God, self-revealed as three persons ... the Father, the Son, and the Holy Spirit. For the sake of the Gospel we decline proposals to modify or marginalize these names and we affirm their rightful place in prayer, liturgy, and hymnody." If the Declaration had wished to be a merely conservative document, it might have urged caution and discernment in the face of the "new liberty" of which Williams speaks. But it doesn't. It is uncompromisingly restrictive; the intent of its opening statement is to limit without exception our naming of the Trinity to the classical formula, "Father, Son, and Holy Spirit."[3]

In this essay I will argue that the Declaration's stricture on the triune Name cannot be justified. My argument will be set out in three parts. First, I will show that the church's affirmation of the triunity of God is fundamentally a living phenomenon concretely expressed in the various activities of Christian witness; namely, worship, service, fellowship, mission, evangelism, and so on. Affirmation of the Trinity is a property of these ecclesial activities in the essential shape and contour given them by God's grace; it is not the exclusive property of a privileged expression. To think that the triune God is truly confessed and worshipped only if the correct linguistic formula is used is not only to fail to appreciate the generosity of God's self-communication; it is to hold a particularly abstract notion of the church's communion in the life of the Trinity. When this abstractness is coupled with a failure to affirm the importance of such fundamental marks of the church's life as baptism, eucharist, and ministries of compassion and justice, there is, I believe, a greater threat to trinitarian orthodoxy than that posed by the new linguistic creativity.

Secondly, I will argue that even if we acknowledge the representational value[4] of the classical Name, and accept its normative character in naming the God of Christian faith, fidelity to the Bible and catholic tradition demands that we also acknowledge the intrinsic limitations of that Name. The church that fears to discover and use other names for God has failed to grasp something important about God. The God of the Bible is a different kind of being from anything or anyone else in our experience. "To whom then will you compare me, or who is my equal? says the Holy One" (Isa. 40:25). In speaking of or to God, then, we can never adequately represent the Holy One. This does not mean that we cannot speak truly of God or truly name God. It *does* mean that we cannot assume that the words we apply to God mean the same when used of God as when used of other items to which they may also refer. The divine being exceeds the representational value of the terms that are truly applied to God. Therefore, we should not be surprised if even the language sanctioned by divine revelation for witness and prayer has a tendency to de-stabilize itself and announce its own limitation. I will show how this tendency to de-stabilization is illustrated in the case of the classical trinitarian Name.

There is another kind of de-stabilization that also affects the representational value of words and formulae like the classical Name. As the cultural context in which they are used changes, so does their significance. Not surprisingly, the new cultural context in which the Western church finds itself, however we may choose to describe that new context, has had an influence on the meaning of the Name. I will argue that the traditional representational value of the classical Name cannot be preserved unless it is located within a wider repertoire of divine names.

Finally, I will suggest that the danger of idolatry is not lessened by an insistence on the exclusive use of the classical Name. One sometimes hears defenders of the Declaration claim that alternative formulations of the classical Name underwrite a shift in the church's consciousness towards a new or alternative religion to that of biblical Christianity. Unless we address the triune God by his proper Name, which is Father, Son, and Holy Spirit, we cannot be sure we are speaking to the only true God. To name God otherwise is to name another God, one of our own invention, and thus to fall into idolatry. I will suggest that this argument is not only unconvincing, but naively uncritical of the potentiality for idolatry in the religious outlook apparently condoned by the Declaration.

The Church's Affirmation of the Trinity

The doctrine of the Trinity as expressed, for example, in the Nicene and Athanasian Creeds, is based on the New Testament (NT) witness to the trinity of agents who bring about the divine work of salvation. The Father sends the Son who is anointed by the Spirit and does the Father's will, offering his life on the cross for the sake of the world. The Father accepts the sacrifice of the Son, exalting him as Lord and, with him, bestows the Holy Spirit who makes it possible for creatures to become children of God and co-heirs with the Son of the Father's blessing. The principle guiding the development of the orthodox doctrine of the Trinity is that this distinction of Persons in the work of salvation reveals an eternal triunity in God. The existence of three divine Persons is compatible with the unity of God because the distinction of Persons is eternally produced within God and by God. God, one might say, is self-distinguishing. At least this is what the creeds, following scriptural leads, suggest; the Father eternally communicates the fullness of divine existence to another—that is, the Son—who is therefore described as "God, from God," and the Spirit eternally proceeds from the Father (and the Son) and thus "with the Father and the Son together is worshipped and glorified." The three are one because the same divine existence is fully communicated and shared among them. But the full sharing of divine existence equally entails that the one God is not a sheer self-identity. God subsists as three Persons who distinguish themselves from one another. And, in the optique of classical Christianity, this dynamism of reciprocal self-distinction is not something inessential to God; it is not the unfolding of a more fundamental divine unity, nor simply the way God appears to the finite human mind. Dynamic triunity is God's way of being God. God is the One in whom deity itself is given, affirmed, and recognized in the distinction of the Persons from one another.[5]

If a lesson may be drawn from this cursory look at credal statements, it is that the doctrine of the Trinity is not merely a revealed truth about God. It is, no doubt, a revealed truth. For Anglicans that has meant that the affirmation of the consubstantiality and equal glory of the three Persons in the classical creeds "ought thoroughly to be received and believed: for [it] may be proved by most certain warrants of holy Scripture."[6] In other words, the church teaches, on the basis of the NT witness, that God is "self-revealed," as the Declaration says, as a triunity of Persons. Affirmation of the Trinity, in this view, is an ecclesial achievement and an ecclesial duty. The Scriptures contain revealed truths about God that are authoritatively expressed in the church's creeds. I am suggesting, however, that this is only part of the story, and, indeed, not the most interesting part. For if we take seriously the credal way of speaking about God, then before the church's affirmation of the Trinity, the Trinity affirms itself. The divine Persons eternally distinguish themselves from one another and recognize the fullness of deity in one another. The church's affirmation of the Trinity, I will argue, is fundamentally an entry into this same dynamism of triune life, a dynamism articulated—that is, revealed— in the deeds and gestures of grace as much as in sacred words or privileged formulae.

God's triune self-affirmation is concretely articulated in the events to which the NT bears witness, and it is to those events that we must return in order to fill in the dynamism only sketched in the creeds. That triune dynamism, we see, is one of mutual glorification. The mission of Jesus is to seek the glory of the One who sent him (John 7:16–18). His identity as the Son is manifest in his having been sent by an Other whose deity and unique goodness he affirms, and whose lordship he establishes.

> To establish the lordship of God is the chief content and primary goal of the mission of Jesus, and as his whole life is his mission he shows himself to be the Son who serves the will of the Father (cf. John 10:36ff.). The title "Son" reflects Jesus' message of the Father. The reflection of the content of the message falls on his person.[7]

At the same time, the Father glorifies the Son, for the Father identifies the Son as the One in whom divine authority is vested, to whom the divine work of renewing the creation has been handed over, and upon whom universal lordship has been bestowed. The Spirit, in turn, glorifies the Son by empowering his earthly ministry, raising him from the dead (Rom. 1:4), and extending his post-resurrection ministry (John 15:26, 16:14). The Spirit glorifies the Father and the Son by bearing witness to their mutuality and bringing creatures into its fellowship (Rom. 8:14–17; Gal. 4:6). And, inasmuch as the Father and the Son entrust the completion of their saving work to the Spirit who vivifies, fulfils, and bears witness to their divine cooperation, they glorify the Spirit.

My argument, then, is this: If the Son affirms the deity and lordship of the Father, then so, by grace, does the church. If the Father glorifies the Son, then so does the church. If the Spirit manifests the deity of the Father and the lordship of the Son, then so does the church. If the Father and the Son affirm the deity of the Spirit, then so does the church. And it is only to the degree that the church participates in, that is, enacts, with the Son, the Son's glorification of the Father, and, with the Father, the Father's glorification of the Son, and, with the Father (and the Son), their affirmation of the deity of the Spirit, that the church glorifies the Trinity. Only so does the church articulate God's triune self-affirmation. This ecclesial activity of glorification, it seems to me, is as essential to the church's trinitarian faith as the act of naming God, and, indeed, more essential than exclusive devotion to a privileged formula.

Glory to the Father...

In his high-priestly prayer, Jesus says that the Son has glorified the Father on earth by finishing the work he was sent to do, and he asks that the Father glorify the Son with the glory that he had with him before the foundation of the world (John 17:1–5). What is the earthly work of the Son through which he has glorified the Father? That work comes to its completion in the self-oblation of the Son on the cross. But to isolate the cross from the ministry that precedes it, and to place the whole weight of the Son's ministry on the passion and death, is evidently to miss the larger narrative context that gives the cross its significance.

One important theme in that larger context is Jesus' association with outcasts and sinners, and his table fellowship with them (Mark 2:15, Luke 15:2, Luke 19:7, Matt. 11:19 = Luke 7:34). It is clear that this practice aroused criticism. Some scholars have even argued that it was the principal reason why Jesus was handed over to the Romans for crucifixion.[8] Whatever the case, the practice provides us with an insight into the nature of Jesus' ministry, which was, at least in part, to renew Israel. In contrast, however, to what has been described as "the politics of holiness" in the Judaism of his time; namely, the attempt to realize the priestly people of God by creating a righteous remnant, a community of those deemed worthy to belong to the people of God in virtue of their strict obedience of the Law and observance of purity—Jesus reaches out precisely to those who are proscribed by the righteous. The religious and social significance of his eating with outcasts and sinners is summarized by Marcus Borg in this way: "It became a vehicle of cultural protest, challenging the ethos and politics of holiness, even as it painted a different picture of what Israel was to be, an inclusive community reflecting the compassion of God."[9] This is a central aspect of Jesus' ministry, one reflected also in his teaching—namely, the breaking down of the wall that keeps religiously and socially unacceptable persons outside the covenant of grace.

Fellowship with sinners is an aspect of the ministry by which Jesus inaugurates the kingdom of God, a ministry summarized by him in his application of the Isaianic text to himself: "The Spirit of the Lord is upon me, because he has anointed me to bring good news to the poor. He has sent me to proclaim release to the captives and recovery of sight to the blind, to let the oppressed go free, to proclaim the year of the Lord's favor" (Luke 4:18–19). The Son glorifies the Father by showing what the world is to be under the Father's deity. And so the Son at once announces the mercy and compassion of the Father and confronts the material conditions that immobilize human beings, that blind them, and that deaden human potential. The healing miracles dramatically illustrate Jesus' intention in this regard. But social and political miracles are likewise evinced. It has been suggested, for example, that in announcing good news to the poor, Jesus had in mind the Jubilee Year legislation of the Old Testament (OT), according to which, every fifty years, the land was to be redistributed to the poor. This was to prevent the growth of a landless class in Israel, and entailed, in effect, the elimination of poverty.[10] If the deity of the Father is affirmed in the liberation of a demoniac from possession; if the Father's goodness is felt in the body of the woman whose haemorrhage is stopped, felt in the skin of the leper who is cleansed, and in the legs healed of lameness; why not also in the sharing of bread with the hungry crowds, in the banquet prepared for the poor, the crippled, the lame and the blind, and, in the undermining of the religious and social subordination of women?[11]

One wonders to what extent the church as envisaged by the Declaration is committed to glorifying the Father as the Son glorifies the Father. While one may laud its call to the church to "work out the implications of biblical teaching for the right ordering of social, economic and political life, and for humanity's stewardship of creation" (Article 13), the only illustrations of such "right ordering" are the regulation of sexual behaviour and the preservation of the family ideal (Articles 14 and 15). And here the Declaration is frankly disappointing. It is difficult to see how its pronouncements on these issues can be construed as continuous with the spirit and substance of Jesus' ministry. To be sure, Jesus calls the church to a higher righteousness than that of the scribes and Pharisees (Matt. 5:20). But that higher righteousness evidently consists in a radical, interior obedience (Matt. 5:21–30), and it expresses itself in a generous (Matt. 5:43–48), humble, patient (Matt. 5:41), non-possessive (Matt. 5:28), non-condemnatory (Matt. 7:1–5) active seeking of the genuine good of others (Matt. 7:12). The religious need to divide the human race into the righteous and the unrighteous, the orthodox and the heretical, the pure and the impure is contrary to the spirit of the higher righteousness. In universalizing and interiorizing sin, Jesus robs the category of "sinner" of its ancient classificatory power. By contrast, the Declaration seems to come close to encouraging the classification of certain identifiable groups within society, especially those in common-law relationships and homosexuals living in partnership, as sinners. The authors of the Declaration might well ask if they are not unwittingly supporting the reinstatement of a politics of holiness—the very thing against which Jesus stood.

The Declaration's idealization of the family is likewise puzzling. One scholar has remarked that, "One of the most striking features of Jesus' teaching ... is the way in which he distanced himself from contemporary culture in his estimate of the importance and value of the family."[12] Indeed, sayings and episodes like those recorded in Matthew 10:34–36 and 12:46–50 suggest that the Declaration has missed what seems to be central in the message of Jesus. In the world in which the Father's deity is acknowledged and affirmed, there is a profound re-ordering of familiar values, even of religiously sanctioned ones. It could be argued that in the perspective of evangelical values, the family has been usurped as the primary vehicle of divine blessing. Similarly, the family is no longer the model for the society in which God shares divine life with the people of God; rather, the reverse. The covenant community, that is, the community of those who do the will of the Father in heaven, is now the model for the family, and the norm against which the family and other societies are to be measured.

The church envisaged by the Declaration would evidently be terribly concerned to regulate our affective choices and identify and eschew unacceptable alternatives to the family. But it would seem to have no good news for the poor, nothing to learn from outsiders and sinners,[13] and little serious interest in addressing the social and religious subordination of women.[14] To what extent could such a church be said to enact, with the Son, the Son's glorification of the Father?

It would be misleading, however, to suggest that the church's participation in the Son's glorification of the Father consists only in the imitation of Christ through the worldly enactment of his mission. The culmination of the Son's glorification of the Father is his self-oblation on the cross, a sacrifice that exhibits and finalizes the filial devotion that is present throughout the whole ministry. Hence the church that faithfully enacts Christ's mission in the world is the church that interiorizes his filial devotion and prays for the grace to be united to him in his sacrifice. The acts of remembering and proclaiming his sacrifice are evidently essential elements of this prayer. Without liturgical anamnesis, mission is easily cut off from its mystical root.[15] Thus it is not only by enacting and extending the Son's mission, but also by prayerfully identifying itself with the Son's self-oblation, that the church participates in the Son's glorification of the Father. The primary locus of this anamnesis, let us note, is the church's eucharistic gathering.

And to the Son...

Anamnesis is likewise at the heart of the church's participation in the Father's glorification of the Son. The Father affirms the Son's deity in entrusting to him the divine work of redeeming humanity and renewing creation. The Son inaugurates this work through his incarnation, ministry, teaching, and death on the cross. The Father responds to the Son's life of radical obedience by accepting his sacrifice and exalting him as universal Lord. The atoning and renewing work of the Son, accomplished once for all on Calvary, is thus given a permanent, universal, operative power. The Father bestows upon Jesus Christ, crucified and risen again, all the authority of deity.

How does the church enact, with the Father, the Father's glorification of the Son? Clearly, by affirming Jesus Christ as the saviour and redeemer of the world. On the necessity and primacy of this activity, the Declaration is unambiguous. Article 11 on The Priority of Evangelism is a strong reminder to the church of the importance of proclaiming Christ as "divine Saviour, Lord, and Friend." The Declaration also points to a connection between the church's proclamation of Christ and its worship: "No form of worship can truly exalt Christ or draw forth true devotion to him without the presence and power of the Holy Spirit" (Article 10). To all of this, one must say, Amen. What is puzzling is the Declaration's failure to note the principal resource given by God to the church for this proclamation and worship, namely, the eucharist. The ARCIC Agreed Statement on the Eucharist (1971) speaks of Christ's institution of the eucharist as a memorial "of the totality of God's reconciling action in him" and indeed asserts that "God has given the eucharist to his Church as a means through which the atoning work of Christ on the cross is proclaimed and made effective in the life of the Church." To be sure, evangelism and worship are by no means confined or reducible to the church's eucharistic celebration, but it seems odd that a document setting out Anglican essentials would overlook the connections of the former to the latter.

If we think of the eucharist as the primary locus of the church's participation in the Father's glorification of the Son, we will, I think, have a somewhat different understanding from that of the Declaration of the church's evangelistic task. Consider the implications of Christ's being proclaimed as Lord by a church that thinks of itself as a supernatural society (Article 7), engaged in training for persuasive outreach (Article 11), and possessing in the Bible (alone) a textbook of true beliefs, rules of correct behaviour, and guidelines for the right ordering of social, economic, and political life (Articles 6 and 13). Would it be unfair to characterize this proclamation as "triumphalist"? Is it not assumed that Christ's lordship is invested in the church that proclaims him in such a way that those who accept his lordship have the inside track on the form that the cultural, political, and moral life of society ought to take? Consider, on the other hand, Christ being proclaimed by a church conscious of its union with the incarnate Lord and of its need to be, like him, in solidarity with the outcast; gives thanks on behalf of the world for the gifts of God in creation; with its High Priest and Intercessor, prays for the world's redemption; and joyfully celebrates the meal that anticipates the coming of his kingdom. A eucharistically based evangelism, one suspects, would have a different flavour from that apparently endorsed by the Declaration.

Surprisingly, the Declaration doesn't explicitly mention the eucharist at all. There is a reference in Article 7 to the church's ministry of word and sacraments, which presumably includes the eucharist. But one wonders to what extent the church as envisaged by the Declaration is a eucharistic community. The Declaration *does* speak of what God has done for us in creation and redemption, and emphasizes the importance of our grateful response through worship. There is mention of the loving unity of Spirit-filled Christians and churches as a powerful sign of the truth of Christianity, and there is an affirmation of healing, spiritual and physical, as welcome aspects of Anglican worship. This is well and good; but it makes it all the more baffling that there is no mention of the eucharist as the central act of the church's worship, the living and effective sign of Christ's sacrifice, the invocation of the Holy Spirit, and the real presence of the crucified and risen Christ giving his life for all humanity.[16] Why is the eucharist so noticeably absent from the text of the Declaration? To marginalize the eucharist is to marginalize the Trinity, for it is to ignore the God-given means by which the church articulates both the Son's glorification of the Father (through thankfully commemorating his incarnation, ministry and sacrifice, and receiving the sacrament of his life given for the sake of the world), and the Father's glorification of the Son (through proclaiming the mystery of faith—Christ has died, Christ is risen, Christ will come again—and distributing the gifts of his Body and Blood).

Nor does it seem that this marginalization of the eucharist could be remedied merely by re-asserting traditional Anglican teaching on the sacraments. In spite of the positive teaching of our catechism and the Thirty-Nine Articles, historically and practically Anglicans have tended to marginalize the eucharist; it is only in the last generation that we have recovered on a wide scale a sense of its centrality in the church's worship and life. There are signs, indeed, of a wider ecumenical recovery of eucharistic practice and spirituality. Such a recovery evidently requires something more than making the Prayer Book Communion Office the principal service on Sunday morning. It requires a liturgical renewal that places the paschal mystery at the centre of our worship and an ecclesial renewal of our corporate priesthood; that is, an active solidarity with human beings in their pain and passion, coupled with a representative ministry of thanksgiving and offering on behalf of the whole world. The Declaration explicitly proscribes liturgical renewal and apparently has little sense of the church's community with "outsiders."

And to the Holy Spirit

That the church is able to participate in the Son's glorification of the Father, and the Father's glorification of the Son, is due to the Spirit. The same Spirit who enabled the Son, in his earthly ministry, to show forth the deity of the Father is now given to the church so that it may be the body of Christ (I Cor. 12:13), have the mind of Christ (I Cor. 2:16), and extend his mission in the world (John 16:14, read with John 14:12; I Cor. 12:4–11). And the same Spirit by whom the Father raised Jesus from the dead and made him Lord of all (Rom. 1:4) now enables the church to confess that Jesus is Lord (I Cor. 12:3). The Spirit, indeed, works at every stage in the proclamation, reception, and confirmation of the gospel in the church. While the language of glorification is rarely used in these NT descriptions of the Spirit's work, it is clear that the Spirit's ministry is aimed at enabling the human race to come to a living faith in the deity of the Father and the lordship of the Son.

It could be argued that in handing over to the Spirit the work of drawing the world into their communion, the Father and the Son likewise glorify the

Spirit. Perhaps, however, an even clearer indication of the Father's (and the Son's) glorification of the Spirit is to be seen in the giving of the Spirit as the seal, pledge, and firstfruits of eternal glory (Rom. 8:22–23; II Cor. 4:14–5:5; Eph. 1:13–14). If the gift is an instalment and anticipation of divine life in its fullness, then the deity of the gift is affirmed in the act of its bestowal. The deity of the Spirit is manifest in the same act whereby the Spirit is given as a seal unto the day of redemption.

Now, the ecclesial act whereby the Spirit is given is baptism. Hence the church participates in the Father's glorification of the Spirit by ministering holy baptism, nurturing Christians in the baptismal life, and renewing the baptismal covenant. At the same time, the gift of the Spirit in baptism sacramentally re-enacts the Pentecostal origin of the church. Baptism signifies and brings about that conversion, pardoning, cleansing, and incorporation into the body of Christ that makes it possible for the church to glorify the Father through the Son and in the Holy Spirit. Baptism is therefore constitutive of the church's existence as the human society that participates in the triune dynamism of God's life.

Anglican liturgical and catechetical texts are clear in asserting that baptism signifies both the gift of the Holy Spirit as a pledge of eternal life and membership in the church. Perhaps this Anglican teaching is implicit in the Declaration's statement in Article 7 that "[t]hrough the church's ministry of the word and sacraments of the Gospel, God ministers life in Christ to the faithful, thereby empowering them for worship, witness and service." But the general impression conveyed by the Declaration is that baptism, insofar as it has any place at all, occupies a secondary position among those things that are deemed essential to Anglican Christianity. For example, when the Declaration speaks of the work and gifts of the Holy Spirit it makes no mention of baptism. Similarly, no mention of baptism or the baptismal covenant is made in the Articles on The New Life in Christ, The Priority of Evangelism, and The Challenge of Social Action, where one might have expected it. Here again, one wonders why baptism, like the eucharist, plays such a minor, not to say marginal, role in the text of the Declaration. The omission of baptism at critical points prompts one to ask whether the authors of the Declaration believe that membership in the church is effected by baptism in the Name of the Trinity.

The burden of my argument in this first part has been to show that when the Declaration refuses an expansion of the church's repertoire of trinitarian terms on the ground that "the Gospel invites us through the Holy Spirit to share eternally in the divine fellowship, as adopted children of the God in whose family Jesus Christ is both our saviour and our brother," it commits a whopping non-sequitur. The church's communion in the life of the Trinity does not entail the exclusive use of the classical Name, or, for that matter, of any special name. It *does* entail baptism into Christ, discipleship, eucharistic fellowship and spirituality, and prophetic witness to God's inclusive kingdom of mercy and justice.[17] The Declaration either ignores these identifying marks of life in the Trinity, or it marginalizes them, pushing them to the periphery of the essentials.

The Representation of Mystery[18]

The church's affirmation of the Trinity involves linguistic acts, and so I turn now to a consideration of the claim that the classical triune Name has an exclusive validity when it comes to talking about or to the Trinity. It is not my intention to call into question the normative status of the classical Name. There are strong warrants for retaining it in the baptismal formula, the creeds, and eucharistic prayers. But reverence for the Name should not distract us from a candid recognition of its limitations. In fact, I will argue, contrary to Article 1, that as a matter of fidelity to catholic tradition and integrity of faith, the classical Name *ought not to be* the only Name by which we address and glorify the triune God. If the church were to comply with the Declaration's insistence on exclusive use of the classical Name, our capacity to articulate the mystery of God would surely be diminished with stultifying effects on prayer, liturgy, and hymnody. The problem, moreover, is not just that the mystery of the triune God cannot be adequately signified by this Name. The problem is that the representational value—that is, the meaningfulness of the Name — cannot be safeguarded unless it is part of a larger trinitarian discourse. Thus, there are two questions to be addressed in this part of my argument: (1) What does the classical Name tell us about the Trinity? and (2) Why do we need to locate the classical Name within an expanded repertoire of divine names?

If someone were to use the terms "Father" and "Son" in reference to two persons, we would assume that the persons so designated had the properties of a male parent and a male child.[19] If our interlocutor were to reply, "Oh no, you misunderstand me; I am not using these terms to signify a male parent and a male child," we would feel justified in protesting, "But that's what the words mean. Can you explain why we should understand these terms differently in this case?" We can imagine our interlocutor answering, "I am using these terms as names. In this instance, I do not mean them to be understood as general terms that pick out objects possessing the properties in their definitions. The one I am calling 'Father' is not a male parent, and 'Son' is not a male child; it is simply convenient to call the one person 'Father' and the other 'Son.'" No doubt we would accept this explanation because we can readily understand the use of general or descriptive terms as names, and we acknowledge that there is usually no intrinsic connection between the meaning of a name and the properties of the person or object named. Danielle (see note 4) may at some time witness to the truth that God is judge, but, although that is the meaning of her name, she will not have the properties of the subject (God), nor necessarily those of the predicate.

To allay any lingering misgivings we may have about the gender of the persons named "Father" and "Son," our interlocutor might explain further. "I subscribe to the Thirty-Nine Articles of Religion, and according to Article I, 'There is but one living and true God, everlasting, without body, parts, or passions ... and in unity of this Godhead there be three Persons ... the Father, the Son, and the Holy Ghost.' So, when I call one divine Person 'Father' and the other 'Son' I am referring to incorporeal and everlasting Persons. Hence it would be a mistake to think the Father is sexually generative or older than the Son, or that the Son is younger than the Father and male in gender." This explanation may help us to see that the terms "Father" and "Son" can be used to designate the Persons of the Trinity without committing us to crude anthropomorphism. It is unlikely, however, to satisfy us completely. We may point out that in some contexts the power of a name consists in its capacity to convey the being or reality of the named object. The Name of God, in particular, represents and communicates the reality of God to the hearer and/or speaker.[20] The triune Name, then, has a representational or revelatory power; it is not "simply convenient" to call one Person "Father" and another "Son" and another "Holy Spirit." The Name is meaningful, and it is meaningful in virtue of its representational character. Still, we have agreed that the Name is not to be taken anthropomorphically, and so we may wonder in what precise sense it *is* representative and revelatory of God.

The Name, in the first place, represents a communion of persons. In the cultural environment of the ancient Near East, the names "Father" and "Son" suggest a relationship between two persons according to which one receives being and life from the other, is tutored to become like the other, is entitled to inherit the authority, status, and property of the other, and, in return, honours him and projects his name into the future. Since, in the case of God, we are talking about incorporeal, everlasting Persons, we must free this relationship from its biological and secular conditions in order to appreciate its representational power. We are left with the concept of one person communicating everything he is and has to another person: existence, dignity, wisdom, authority, and so on, and of the recipient returning honour and glory to the giver. This is, in fact, the direction in which the catholic tradition has developed the language of Father and Son.

In the second article of the Nicene Creed there is a distinction made between two kinds of divine production: begetting and creating. The Son is begotten of the Father, begotten not made. Heaven and earth, and all things visible and invisible are created by the Father through the agency of the Son and the Holy Spirit. But the Son is not created. The Son does not come into existence in time, but eternally receives existence from the Father. The Son is God, from God, Light from Light, true God from true God. There never was a time when the Father existed without the Son, there never will be a time when the Son exists without the Father, and there is no interruption or variation in the eternal communication of being and glory from the one Person to the Other. The Son receives everything he is from the Father, and returns honour and devotion to the Father. This eternal, internal mutuality in God's own life is the basis of our entry as creatures into a living relationship with our creator. We are made God's children by adoption and grace, conformed to the Son so that we may offer the same filial devotion to God, and be made fellow-heirs with Christ of eternal life.

To speak of God as Father, then, is to speak of God as the One who generates or produces divine existence in others—in the divine Son by nature, and in us by grace. To speak of God as Son is to identify Jesus Christ as the One who has a unique and eternal relationship with the Father, and who provides the eternally valid model for our creaturely attitude toward the One who is the source of our being and bestower of all good things. To speak of God as Holy Spirit is to evoke a fluid, energetic principle in God, one that is not only within God, searching the depths of God (I Cor. 2:10), but able also to be with the world that is "outside" God and interact with God from the side of the creature (Rom. 8:15–16, 26–27). The Nicene Creed speaks of the Holy Spirit as the "Giver of life," a description that we might think more appropriate for the Father. But if the term is interpreted in reference to the credal statements that follow, it suggests that the Spirit makes possible the world's living participation in the Father's glorification of the Son and the Son's glorification of the Father by speaking through the prophets, founding and animating the church, effecting the forgiveness of sins through baptism, and guaranteeing the resurrection life.

The representational value of the triune Name thus consists in its power to express an eternal communion within God—a communion for which the world is created and into which it is drawn. But the Name represents more than communion. Each of the names has a peculiar representational function, for each represents the distinctive mode of divine being possessed by one of the Persons of the Trinity: the first name represents an eternally generative and generous Person; the second, a Person who eternally returns glory to the First; and the third, a Person who eternally witnesses, shares, and mediates the glory of the divine life that is fully given and accepted in the mystery of the Godhead.

Notice, however, a further peculiarity of this triune Name. The Father is the Father in relation to the Son and in relation to God's adopted children, but not in relation to the Holy Spirit. If God were the Father of the Holy Spirit, would the Spirit not be a second divine Child, produced by a second act of divine begetting? But according to Scripture and the creed, the Son is the "only-begotten" Son of God. The credal tradition resolved this dilemma by affirming that just as in time there are two distinct divine missions—the sending of the Son, and the outpouring of the Spirit—so there are in the eternity of God's being two distinct acts of divine production. The Nicene and Athanasian Creeds distinguish the production of the Spirit from that of the Son by saying that the Spirit *proceeds from* the Father. Later theology will coin a new word to denote this distinctive divine production: spiration.[21]

How do these credal distinctions bear on the present discussion? They show that the representational value of the triune Name taken as a whole has a de-stabilizing effect on the representational value of each name taken individually. That is, the internal logic of the divine Name suggests that the Father is the Father in relation to the Son, but not in relation to the Spirit. Hence the Person who is the Father has a mode of divine being that is not adequately represented by the name Father. The Son is Son in relation to the Father, but not in relation to the Spirit; he is not the Son of the Spirit, but of the Father. Hence the Second Person possesses a mode of divine being that is not exhaustively signified by the term Son. Similarly, the Spirit is not the only Spirit, for the Father too is Spirit, and so is the Son. The Spirit is not the only Holy, for the Father too is Holy, and so is the Son. So, the Father is not only Father, the Son is not only Son, the Holy Spirit, insofar as he is a distinct Person, is not only Holy Spirit. In other words, each of the divine Persons has a mode of divine being not adequately represented by the proper triune Name. Moreover, as I have argued, the inadequacy of each proper name is itself represented in the Name! If we take seriously the Declaration's assertion that God is "self-revealed" as Father, Son, and Holy Spirit, then we must also take seriously the revealed limitations of the Name, for the Name itself announces its inability adequately to represent the Persons it names. Hence to suggest, as does the Declaration, that the Trinity's self-revelation is to be represented only or exclusively in the classical trinitarian Name is to miss something important about the revelation. It is to assume the adequacy of a particular representation or analogy when that very representation licenses the articulation of others. The First Person is not only Father, but Source, Fount, and Author; the Second is not only Son, but Word, Image, and Wisdom; the Third is not only Spirit, but Advocate, Witness, and Life-Giver. There is no good reason to decline proposals to integrate terms such as these—and why not others?—into the church's prayer, liturgy, and hymnody. Indeed, there are compelling reasons to expand the repertoire.

We all know that meanings are determined by contexts of use. If asked to translate a word from French into English, we will want to know about the context in which the word appears in order to be sure that our translation is consistent with the import of the discourse as a whole. And we know that the meaning or possible meanings of an expression, a conversation, or speech depend upon a multiplicity of contextual factors, including the social situation of the speakers and hearers.

As I have already indicated, the representational value of the names Father and Son in trinitarian discourse is at least partially determined by a socio-cultural context in which fathers and sons are viewed as the only true persons—that is, the male is the only agent of biological reproduction, the one who normally owns and inherits property, receives an education, exercises political leadership, gives the family its name, and so on. In a society where patriarchy is unquestioned, the language of Father and Son is eminently suited to represent, by analogical extension, the power, generativity, devotion, and communion of divine Persons. But patriarchy is no longer unquestioned. We know that the mother contributes as much as the father to the existence and genetic inheritance of the child; that women as much as men possess intelligence and wisdom, have the right to own and inherit property, can exercise authority, and be sources of blessing to others. The cultural assumptions that support the putatively unique meaningfulness of the Father-Son analogy no longer hold. This does not entail that the use of Father and Son in the Name of God is dépassé, for its analogical meaning can be explained and re-asserted. But the new cultural context does give the Father-Son dyad a quite different nuance from that of its traditional context. In speaking the divine Name, we no longer spontaneously evoke the personal generativity, devotion, and mutuality of the Persons who, with the Spirit, have created and redeemed us. The use of these names today brings to the fore the question of God's gender, and the relation of the Trinity to the social system of patriarchy. If we now wish the classical Name to represent what it represented for our ancestors, we must be able to show—in prayer, liturgy, and hymnody, and not just in academic theology—that it does not entail God's maleness, and is not inevitably linked to the cultural assumptions of patriarchy. And how, in our context, will the church be able to signify the Trinity who transcends the division of sex and who undermines systems of domination, if it is unable to re-situate the classical Name within an expanded repertoire of divine names?

There is also justification for including feminine imagery for God in an expanded repertoire. A strong case can be made that an androcentric bias has unconsciously directed our reading of the Bible and the church's selection of scriptural images and metaphors for God. It is curious, for example, that the psalmist's likening of the soul's peace in the presence of God to that of "a child upon its mother's breast" (Ps. 131) can have gone unnoticed by countless generations of hymn writers; and even those who make regular use of the psalms in their daily prayer are often surprised when they discover it. Admittedly, female images for God do not appear in the Bible with the same frequency as male ones, but they are there to be found.[22] Hence, if the Bible permits the use of feminine images to represent God and the one God of the Bible is the triune God of Christian faith, why should the church be prevented from using feminine imagery in signifying the divine Persons?[23] Using feminine names for God, however, raises for many the spectre of idolatry, and so I turn now to a consideration of this issue.

The Danger of Idolatry

The Declaration does not speak explicitly of the danger of idolatry, but at least one contributor to the book *Anglican Essentials*, and defender of the Declaration's stricture on the triune Name, has publicly justified the Declaration's position by stating that it represents a safeguard against the threat posed to biblical Christianity by "eco-feminist pantheism."[24] For such persons it is presumably not only feminine imagery that represents a threat, but also the attribution to God of putatively impersonal terms like "Source and Partner of the Eternal Word."[25] Since both feminine and impersonal terms are used in the Bible to signify God, the onus is on the exclusivist position to furnish an explanation as to why male nomenclature is valid and female/impersonal nomenclature dangerous. The Lutheran theologian Robert Jenson has offered such an explanation with regard to female God-language in his book, *The Triune Identity*.[26]

Jenson argues that the God of biblical revelation is not a projection onto eternity of the values established in nature and culture. Israel's God, unlike the gods of the nations, is not the divine personification of those finite and natural powers that shape the destinies of human beings. In particular, God's creativity is not a sexual creativity, for God transcends the division of sex. To avoid the misapprehension of God's creativity as sexual, it is more appropriate, according to Jenson, to call God "Father" than "Mother." The reason, he says, is that males are not as sexual as females. In the male, sensuality and reproduction can be separated; not so in the female. Jenson says that this makes the female "more ineradicably human" than the male who is therefore "ontologically inferior" to the female. The sexual fragility or ontological inferiority of the male is what makes the term "Father" (and presumably also "Son") more appropriate than "Mother" and other gynomorphic forms in speaking of or to God, for male God-language "is the only available way to satisfy the determination of Israel and the church to attribute neither [masculinity nor femininity] to God." An implication of Jenson's argument is that female representations of God are idolatrous. The chief divine gender will be female, he says, in those societies that have "an integral relation to the given ... structures of human life" and when deity is a projection or personification of those structures. Combining Father and Mother in language about God is even more objectionable, for "it repristinates the deepest fertility myth, that of divine androgyny."

It seems to me that there are three difficulties with Jenson's argument. Firstly, his claim that males are not as sexual as females, because sensuality and reproduction can be separated in males, is a non-sequitur. The case is not made that males are less sexual than females, only that male sexuality is different. Does male sexuality make the male less sexual or less human than the female? In the context of his argument, Jenson's talk about the ontological inferiority of the male is transparently gratuitous. Secondly, Jenson conveniently ignores the fact that the term "Father" means precisely "male parent." A father is a sexually generative male. If the term "Father" can also be applied to a celibate male who cares for others as a father (ideally) cares for his own children, this is no argument for the separability of spiritual parenthood and sexuality only in the case of males: it is no less true that the maternal role can be filled by a female who has no reproductive connection to her "children." In short, Jenson simply does not make the case that a heavenly Father is a more appropriate representation of a non-gendered deity than a divine Mother, or a divine Person with maternal qualities.[27]

Another difficulty with Jenson's position—one shared by supporters of the Declaration who fear idolatry—is the assumption that gynomorphic language about God is intrinsically more dangerous than andromorphic language in risking the pollution of Christian worship. Is the exclusive use of male God-language, including the classical triune Name, a prophylactic against idolatry? From a biblical perspective, idolatry is the worship of the creature instead of the creator: "they exchanged the glory of the immortal God for images resembling a mortal human being or birds or four-footed animals or reptiles" (Rom. 1:23). Idolatry, moreover, is the product of unconscious self-deception. Human beings fashion idols for themselves and worship them, forgetting that they have produced them.[28] An idol, therefore, is an unconsciously produced representation in the form of a god or goddess of a finite power, a natural phenomenon or a cultural force, that shapes the destiny of the worshipper: there are gods of sky, earth, fire, the tribe, fertility, war, and so on. So, in a biblical optique, idolatry is present when the humanly produced representation and the deity are in reality the same entity, and their identity is registered in the heart of the worshipper unconscious of the artifice. The living God, on the other hand, is different from the forms in which he is represented. He is not the fire or the rock, and he is not just a warrior, judge, or king. The images through which he is represented are icons—that is, cultural constructs that, by grace, reveal the One whom neither the heaven nor the heaven of heavens can contain. As cultural constructs, icons are just like idols, but whereas in the case of the idol the deity and the cultural construct are indistinguishable, both in reality and in the mind of the worshipper (who, as we have seen, forgets that the deity is constructed), not so in the case of the icon.

Could the classical Name possibly function as an idol rather than an icon? One of the conditions of idolatry would be met if the church forgot that the Name's capacity to represent the triune God derived from its culturally constructed meaning. The Declaration, therefore, seems to be on dangerous ground when it proposes the exclusive use of the Name because God is "self-revealed" as Father, Son, and Holy Spirit. Such a close linking of God's self-revelation with these names fosters the notion that the names are solely the product and gift of the divine revealer, and that their representational power has no foundation or location in the cultural history of the human race. To the degree that the Declaration assumes and promotes the belief that the divine Name is not also a cultural artefact, it obscures its status as a verbal icon and risks turning it into a conceptual idol.

Furthermore, the Declaration gives evidence of a latent pattern of thought that should disturb the consciences of any who are genuinely concerned about idolatry. According to the biblical criterion which is enunciated also by Jenson, the God we worship will be an idol if he is no more than the projection or divine personification of values established in nature and culture. Let us suppose, therefore, as a means of testing the authenticity of our worship, that God, as we conceive him, is in fact the projection onto eternity of the cultural values established in patriarchy. If that is the case, then our God will be thought to possess personal and social characteristics more like those attributed to men than those attributed to women. If God is thus more like a male than a female, then andromorphic God-language will not only be appropriate but also essential in order to safeguard an accurate picture of God. Moreover, if God is more like a male than a female, then men will be better equipped than women to represent for the church and the family the authority, dignity, providence, devotion, humility, and so on that we attribute to divine Persons. Finally, if men are better equipped than women for this role, then women should not, as a rule, assume positions in the church that have this representative function. At very least, the ordination of women should not be viewed as something essential to the life of the church.

The results of our test, then, are that the presence of a certain type of male-god idolatry will evince (1) an insistence on andromorphic God-language, and (2) little or no enthusiasm for the appointment of women to positions of spiritual authority or pastoral leadership. If we look at the Declaration, what do we find? There is, evidently, an insistence on andromorphic God-language. While this piece of evidence is no proof that the religious outlook of the Declaration includes an unconscious idolatry of the type in question, it should nevertheless encourage supporters of the Declaration to an honest examination of their motives in advancing their exclusivist position. But what about the second piece of evidence we might expect to find in case there is an idolatry of the divine Male? It does seem troubling that the same document that insists on the exclusive use of the classical Name in its first Article is also unable in Article 9 to affirm that God calls women to all orders of ministry. The Declaration is able to celebrate the introduction of charismatic healing into Anglican worship (an innovation that has become an Anglican "essential"); it is able to affirm the priority of evangelism (another essential that has only in this decade received the attention it deserves in the Anglican Communion); but it is apparently unable to celebrate the Anglican Church's ordination of women to all three orders of sacred ministry and their appointment to positions of pastoral leadership. The stricture imposed on the church in Article 1 hardly seems unrelated to the mute silence concerning women's ordination in Article 9. The upshot is that the Declaration betrays not one but two consequences of the hypothesis that assumes the presence of an idolatrous worship of the male-god. These evidences, I repeat, do not prove that the Declaration's religious attitude is idolatrous, but they do indicate that a possible explanation of the Declaration's exclusivist stance is the presence in our church of an unconscious idolatry of the God of patriarchy. At the very least, our authenticity test shows that insisting on the exclusive use of the classical Name is no safeguard against idolatry.

Conclusion

In this paper I have argued that there is no good reason to accept the Declaration's refusal to expand the church's repertoire of names for the triune God. The Declaration's assumption that the church's participation in the life of the Trinity depends on the exclusive use of the classical triune Name is unfounded. I have given an account of what it means for the church to affirm the Trinity, and have noted that it is, in fact, the Declaration that tends to ignore or marginalize certain essential marks of a living trinitarian faith. I have also argued that the power of the classical Name to communicate the mystery of God to the church is not taken seriously enough by the Declaration. The revealed Name reveals its own limitation, and thus urges the church to multiply its praises of the thrice-holy God. Moreover, because God's Word is always addressed to human beings for whom meaning is culturally conditioned, we simply cannot assume that the representational value of the classical Name will be invariant throughout history. In fact, as I have suggested, if we wish the classical Name to retain its revelatory power, we need to re-situate it within an expanded repertoire. Finally, I have argued that the church will not be preserved from idolatry if we insist on the exclusive use of the classical Name. Idolatry is the product of a less obvious and more ironic seduction.

Endnotes

1. See *The Hymn Sampler* (Toronto: Anglican Book Centre, 1993), Hymn 7.
2. "Teaching the Truth," in *Living Tradition: Affirming Catholicism in the Anglican Church*, ed. Jeffrey John (Cambridge, Mass.: Cowley, 1992), 31.
3. That this is indeed the intent of Article 1 was confirmed in a public lecture by Dr. Edith Humphrey held at the Montreal Diocesan Theological College on May 25, 1995, and sponsored by the local (Montreal) Essentials Committee. Dr. Humphrey was a participant in the Essentials Conference that adopted the Declaration, and contributed an essay, "Who Was Jesus? Re-envisioning the Historical Jesus and the Vision of God's People" to *Anglican Essentials*, ed. George Egerton (Toronto: Anglican Book Centre, 1995).
4. A word, concept, or semantic unit will have representational value if, in virtue of its meaning, it tells us something about the object[s] to which it refers. For example, when I say "Danielle is a young woman," the phrase "young woman" has representational value. It expresses and discloses an aspect of Danielle's being by representing the gender, age-range and/or level of maturity of the person I call "Danielle." Note that the name "Danielle" does not have a representational value. Its meaning (from the Hebrew for "God is judge") tells us nothing about the person it names. Nevertheless, it might be suggested that since we nowadays use the word "Danielle" as a name for a female person, it has a meaning or use that does indeed tell us something about the object[s] we address and refer to by means of it; namely, that they are female persons. Thus it could be argued the name "Danielle" does have representational value because, in virtue of an accepted use, it tells us that the person so named is female. The representational value of names is clearer in cultural contexts where they are assigned with such a value in mind. "Dances with wolves" tells us something about the history and character of the U.S. cavalry officer who was so named by his Aboriginal neighbours. I discuss the representational value of the divine Name in the section "The Representation of Mystery."
5. Historically, there have been two analogies or models for the Trinity. The dominant analogy in Western theology has been the so-called "psychological analogy," according to which the inner being of God is to be understood as analogous to the inner structure of the human mind. On this analogy, God is identical with one self, i.e., one centre of cognition, volition, and action, and this one self has three eternal aspects. The second analogy is the so-called "social analogy," according to which the divine being is to be understood as analogous to an inter-subjective society of distinct centres of cognition, volition, and action. David Brown, in *The Divine Trinity* (London: Duckworth, 1985), speaks of a Unity Model of the Trinity, and takes St Augustine as representative of its approach, and of a Plurality Model, deriving from the Cappadocians. The challenge for those who adopt a social model is, of course, to explicate the interrelationships of the divine Persons in such a way that the divine unity is preserved. The

psychological model, on the other hand, must face the difficulty of expli-
cating the three-foldness of God in such a way that the distinction of
Persons is preserved. It is beyond the scope of this essay to arbitrate
between these models.

6. See Article VIII of the Thirty-Nine Articles of Religion. The Article is
   concerned with the classical creeds and not with the doctrine of the Trinity
   per se. The substance of these credal statements, however, is the articula-
   tion of the doctrine of the Trinity.

7. Wolfhart Pannenberg, *Systematic Theology*, trans. Geoffrey Bromiley (Grand
   Rapids, Mich.: Eerdmans, 1991), 1:309. My explication of the doctrine of
   the Trinity is inspired by Pannenberg's treatment of it, as well as by
   Leonard Hodgson's in *The Doctrine of the Trinity* (London: Nisbet and Co.,
   1943), but developed, I believe, differently from theirs.

8. See, for example, Norman Perrin, *Rediscovering the Teaching of Jesus* (New
   York: Harper and Row, 1967), 102–103; and W. R. Farmer, "An Historical
   Essay on the Humanity of Jesus Christ," in *Christian History and Interpreta-
   tion*, ed. Farmer et al. (Cambridge: Cambridge University Press, 1967), 103.

9. *Jesus: A New Vision* (San Francisco: Harper, 1991), 133.

10. See John Yoder, *The Politics of Jesus* (Grand Rapids: Eerdmans, 1972);
    Sharon Ringe, *Jesus, Liberation, and the Biblical Jubilee* (Philadelphia: For-
    tress, 1985); Luise Schottroff and Wolfgang Stegemann, *Jesus and the Hope
    of the Poor* (Maryknoll, N.Y.: Orbis, 1986).

11. On Jesus' attitude towards women, see Joachim Jeremias, *New Testament
    Theology*, trans. John Bowden (London: SCM, 1971), 1:223–227; and Elisabeth
    Schussler Fiorenza, *In Memory of Her: A Feminist Theological Reconstruction
    of Christian Origins*, 10th ann. ed. (New York: Crossroad, 1994), 105–159.

12. L. William Countryman, *Dirt, Greed, and Sex: Sexual Ethics in the New
    Testament and their Implications for Today* (Philadelphia: Fortress Press,
    1988), 168.

13. In calling the church to work out "the implications of biblical teaching for
    the right ordering of social, economic, and political life," the Declaration
    gives the impression that the social task of creating a just order can bypass
    the cultural traditions of a given society, and the critique of secular thought.
    The Declaration also seems oblivious to the fact that the naming of various
    forms of oppression, the analysis of them, and effective strategies for
    combating racism, sexism, poverty, ethnocentrism, and indifference to the
    environment have come as much (perhaps more so) from secular reform-
    ers as from the guardians of biblical teaching. So far as its attitude towards
    "sinners" is concerned, the Declaration does not seem receptive to the
    notion that the church might have something to learn from the suffering of
    homosexuals.

14. The Declaration does denounce sexist domination, domestic violence,
    rape, and pornography, all of which it interprets as evidences of the
    weakening of the family ideal. The Declaration's logic suggests that it is in
    the family that women will find freedom from oppression, for the family
    provides the "divinely ordained focus of love, intimacy, personal growth,

and stability for women, men, and children." Indeed, the Declaration calls Christians to work for socio-political conditions that support the family. Since divorce and abortion are also counted among those factors that weaken the family ideal, one wonders whether the writers of the Declaration think that the socio-political conditions that will foster the well-being of women include legislation against divorce and abortion. The Declaration, finally, is unable to affirm that God calls women to all orders of ministry in the church.

15. I use the Greek term *anamnesis* because it has become a quasi-technical term in ecumenical discussions of the sacraments. In its Elucidation (1979) of its earlier Statement on Eucharistic Doctrine (1971), the ARCIC gives a brief history of the term and concludes: "The Commission believes that the traditional understanding of sacramental reality, in which the once-for-all event of salvation becomes effective in the present through the action of the Holy Spirit, is well expressed by the word *anamnesis*. We accept this use of the word which seems to do full justice to the semitic background." On the relation of liturgy and mission, it should be borne in mind that while the God of the Bible has been known to reject the liturgy of the people on the ground that they lacked justice, never does God reject works of justice on the ground that the liturgy is defective. This observation was made by John Dominic Crossan in a discussion at the Trinity Institute, entitled *Jesus at 2000*, held at Corvallis, Oregon, February 9 and 10, 1996.

16. My description of the eucharist here is derived from an ecumenical statement, i.e., *Baptism, Eucharist And Ministry,* Faith and Order Paper No. 111 (Geneva: World Council of Churches, 1982).

17. I am not denying the necessity of naming God in these forms of witness. My point is that these forms of witness are as essential to the church's identification and affirmation of the triune God as the name that is invoked in them.

18. In this essay I do not distinguish between metaphoric and analogous representation because the distinction is not crucial to my argument. Note, however, that the representational value of a word, name, or concept, i.e., its capacity to tell us something about the items to which it refers, may be literal, metaphoric, or analogous. There is literal representation when the meaning of the term expresses the same nature as that found in the item or subject of which it is predicated. Because Danielle actually is a female person in her twenties, "young woman" represents her literally. The same nature expressed in the meaning of the concept "young woman" is possessed in actuality by Danielle. Metaphoric representation, on the other hand, expresses a similarity or likeness rather than sameness. If I say "Danielle is a rock," I do not mean that she is a large mass of stone, but that her ability to offer emotional and/or intellectual support to others is similar to a rock's capacity to offer physical support. Technically, a metaphor is a type of analogy, namely, one of improper proportionality. The nature of rockhood is found just in large masses of stone and not in

persons; so Danielle in no sense possesses the nature of a rock. The ability to offer support, however, is found in both Danielle and a rock (in different ways), and so it (the ability-to-offer-support) is the properly analogous notion. A properly analogous representation, therefore, is different from a metaphoric one. Unlike a metaphor, it expresses a sameness of nature; but unlike a literal representation, that same nature is instantiated in different items in quite different ways. For example, it could be argued that "rock" is a metaphorical representation of God, as it is of Danielle, while "Father" is an analogous representation of God, since the personal generativity that defines paternity is found in different ways in both God and human fathers. Another way of stating the argument of this essay is that there is no justification for the exclusive use of the classical trinitarian analogy. Other analogies, as well as metaphors, may and should be used in prayer, liturgy, and hymnody addressed to the Trinity.

19. It is important to note that the difficulty I am describing arises whether or not the words are used as proper names and forms of address, or are predicated of persons who are known by other proper names. To claim, as some do, that the name "Father" is immune from criticism because it is a form of address and not a metaphorical description of God is simply evasive. Whether "Father" is understood as a metaphor, proper analogy, or a form of address, it is a meaningful name whose representational value can be articulated.

20. For a detailed discussion of the significance of the name in biblical thought, see the article entitled "Name" by R. Abba in *The Interpreter's Dictionary of the Bible*, ed. George Buttrick et al. (New York & Nashville: Abingdon Press, 1962).

21. Edmund Fortman, *The Triune God: A Historical Study of the Doctrine of the Trinity* (Grand Rapids, Mich.: Baker Book House, 1972) suggests the term was officially adopted at the Second Council of Lyons in 1274. It seems, however, to have been in use in Latin theology before the Council. See pp. 57, 202–220.

22. See, for example, Phyllis Trible's article on "God, Nature of, In the OT," in *The Interpreter's Dictionary of the Bible*, supp. vol. (Nashville: Abingdon Press, 1962).

23. I am not suggesting that any and all proposals would be equally felicitous. Given the place of Mary, the *Theotokos*, in the history of salvation, as well as Jesus' own way of addressing the One who sent him, it would seem inappropriate to address the First Person as "Mother." See Gail Ramshaw's balanced discussion of the appropriateness of Mother language in *God Beyond Gender: Feminist Christian God-Language* (Minneapolis: Fortress Press, 1995), 105–107. A good case might nevertheless be made for speaking in maternal terms of the First Person's work achieved through the Son and Holy Spirit. See, for example, Nicholas Lash's discussion of God's creativity in *Believing Three Ways in One God: A Reading of the Apostles' Creed* (London and Notre Dame: University of Notre Dame Press, 1993), 34–47.

Lash says, "I am inclined to say that the strong and central Jewish doctrine of the endlessly generous fidelity of God ... is, in the trinitarian development of Christianity, radicalized in the direction of a maternal understanding of how the Creator in due time brings the world to birth through the laborious bearing of her Son in love."

24. Dr. Edith Humphrey in a public lecture delivered at the Montreal Diocesan Theological College on May 25, 1995.

25. At the lecture mentioned in the preceding note, Dr. Humphrey rejected this circumlocution for the Father because it leads to a "de-personalization" of God.

26. Robert W. Jenson, *God According to the Gospel: The Triune Identity* (Philadelphia: Fortress Press, 1982). The argument is developed on pp. 13–16. Quotations are taken from pages 14, 15, and 16.

27. See my remarks on the appropriateness of Mother language in note 23 above.

28. See Romans 1:21. Isaiah gives a clear account of the self-deception involved in idolatry in Isaiah 44:9–20.

3
Towards a Biblical Church
A Plea for Accountability in the Way We Use Scripture[1]

PAUL JENNINGS

Defining the Problem

The relationship of the church to the Holy Scriptures remains a complex and divisive issue, but one vitally important for the health of the church. We live, it seems, in a time in which there is no clear vision or consensus about the nature of these Scriptures, and what their function is in our common faith. We are heirs of a two-hundred-year-old tradition of historical-critical study of the Bible. This has left us with a wealth of understanding and a fruitful array of tools with which to approach it, but it has also left us with a wide and growing gap between the academic study of the Bible and the use of the Bible in the church. If there is a kind of consensus taking shape, in the "mainline" churches at least, it is this: we cannot go back to a time before historical-critical awareness, but neither can we remain stuck on historical questions. The insights gleaned from the critical study of the Bible are useful, stimulating, and essential for our common faith, but only if we move beyond a merely intellectual encounter and allow them to address us with the basic questions of faith. The search for this second, post-critical "naiveté" is a characteristic of a new interest in the Bible in our churches.

This is the good news: we seem to be experiencing a proliferation of creative, experiential approaches to the Bible. These approaches—both powerful and superficial, theologically insightful and unhelpful—testify to a continuing hunger to hear something new for our lives in Scripture. In this context, I would suggest our common aspiration is becoming clearer; namely, to be a biblical church, a church in which our faith is vigorously informed by the living presence of God encountered in the witness of Scripture. Our practice limps behind this aspiration, but by God's grace, as we break and share the Word in our liturgy, preaching, and Bible study, we continue to be fed by flashes of the Spirit and unexpected revelation.

Yet, for all the evidence of a broad interest throughout the church in rediscovering the voice of Scripture, we Anglicans still seem hopelessly divided as to how we should go about being a biblical church. Debate within the church, particularly on theological issues, is hampered by mutual incomprehension. The familiar theological and political polarization in terms of liberal and traditionalist positions is alive and well; indeed it seems to be gaining new strength—fed by the general social and political trends of the 1990s. Yet these are categories, I would suggest, we have in fact already moved beyond. The extreme traditionalist position (such as is represented by Christian fundamentalism) is one which we as a community have left behind us, because we cannot see our understanding of truth as completely divorced from historical context. We recognize that our understanding is always in some way conditioned by our historical context.[2] But more than that, we have come to understand that the living, incarnate God meets us in the context of our lives and our times.

The inadequacies of classical liberalism,[3] on the other hand, have become equally apparent. Liberalism in this sense is the underlying, usually unconscious assumption that the language of faith is merely the symbolic representation of our own religious and moral sensitivities, that Scripture, doctrine, and liturgy can only express our innate spirituality, instead of informing it and nourishing it with something new. We feel the need for a theology and language that express the experience of a genuine meeting with a free and real Other. We are—many of us—growing suspicious of a God who says only what we feel a God should say. Inasmuch as few of us would wholeheartedly embrace either of these classical positions, they belong to the past. We are united in seeking a theology beyond these alternatives, but inasmuch as we continue to think and argue in terms of this false alternative, we remain trapped by the endless and unproductive debate of another age.

This liberal-traditionalist debate has always been centred on the issue of the interpretation of Scripture; so one might be tempted to look for the root of our present malaise in, say, our attitude to historical-critical study. But it seems fairly evident that our disagreements lie deeper than this. The place of historical-critical study may even be the one aspect of this debate we are close to resolving. Few Anglicans would want to approach the Bible as a timeless, noncontextual, verbally dictated book of instruction. And few of us would want to leave it as a mere edifying and moralizing storybook, ultimately passive and powerless in our hands. We approach the Bible critically *and* in faith.

The real problem lies, I would suggest, on another level, with the question of how Scripture functions in the church. What does it mean to be a biblical church? Here, it seems to me, our thinking is still clouded by the fruitless categories of an inappropriate alternative. In evangelical circles, the category of obedience seems central, both with respect to moral teachings and doctrine. What is emphasized is our duty to subject both our lives and our intellects to the Word of God; but this emphasis on duty threatens to make irrelevant the question of whether this teaching is comprehensible to our minds and our hearts, whether it can be a truly healing and converting gospel. At the other extreme, there is a liberal tendency to use a rather superficial conception of "relevance" as the criterion for judging biblical ideas and stories, rejecting anything that might challenge us as strange or offensive to our sensitivities, leaving us with those parts that can function as a kind of symbolic expression of our prior moral convictions.[4] The ongoing rhetoric which presents our theological options only in terms of evangelical or liberal serves to force us to choose between these two equally inappropriate models.[5]

At the bottom of this issue is an even more profound problem: our basic understanding of faith. This too continues to be coloured by an outmoded alternative. The evangelical wing of the church, with its primary emphasis on tradition, doctrine, and orthodoxy, seems to equate faith with an intellectual assent to certain authoritative doctrinal propositions. And undeniably, the liberal tendency to equate faith with a kind of diffuse religiosity is alive and well in the church, reducing faith to a symbolic system that reflects innate human feelings and aspirations. Some would have us believe we have no other option. It is my underlying assumption, however, that neither of these understandings is true to the biblical experience of faith, which is that of an ongoing relationship with a living God, a relationship marked by struggle and trust on our part, and by faithfulness and mercy on God's part. The primary function of Scripture is to nourish this faith. We are a biblical church inasmuch as we live this faith both in an ongoing encounter with the Bible and in our daily lives.

The Position of the Declaration

The preceding may serve to indicate the standpoint from which I approach the Montreal Declaration of Anglican Essentials and the conflicting impressions it called forth in me. I feel there is a genuine concern in the Declaration that the church be guided by God's Spirit. There seems to be a healthy awareness of the danger of simply deciding on other grounds what we think God should be like, and then arranging the tradition accordingly. There seems to be a corresponding concern that we should allow ourselves truly to be addressed by the reality of God in all aspects of our church life: in our reading of Scripture, in our relationship to the tradition, in our struggle with ethical and doctrinal issues, in our worship. If we believe God is real, then we can trust God to guide us and tell us something new. I believe the Essentials movement shares this concern, and I believe with them that it is truly *essential*.

I have, however, the distinct impression that I differ from the Declaration in my view of how this insight applies to the church today. Specifically, in many of the movements and ideas which I see as signs of God's presence in the church, the Essentials movement seems to see examples of politically correct compromise and concession to liberal society. I am thinking of a number of contemporary impulses: the liturgical renewal, the ecumenical movement; social justice concerns, liberation theologies, feminist perspectives; spiritualities which move beyond a preoccupation with sin as the exclusive determinant of the human condition; a relational view of sexual ethics; the environmental understanding of creation[6]—to name a few.

My impression on reading the document—and more so when I see the strategy and rhetoric of the movement as a whole—is that the Essentials ideology (in keeping with the inappropriate alternative outlined above) views these tendencies as liberal, and so finds it necessary to combat them as threats to traditional orthodoxy. The accusation is often made, both expressly and implicitly, that these movements in general tend to manipulate the Scriptures to make them inoffensive to modern sensibilities. There is certainly a need for constant vigilance, as the church has always tried and will always try unconsciously to manipulate Scripture to make it less offensive. There is also undoubtedly much flaky, superficial thinking in the liberal wing of the church. But the general condemnation of any or all of the above concerns—the direct result of thinking in an outdated and inappropriate liberal-traditionalist alternative—would be both offensive and mistaken. These movements are the signs of a living and faithful church, struggling to respond in truth to the issues of our present reality. They are gifts of the Holy Spirit to the church. And they are profoundly biblical, in that through them the richness and fullness of the biblical tradition is being opened in new and exciting ways.

To sum up my second impression: the Declaration fills me with a deep distrust, a suspicion that the techniques of Reform party politics[7] are being used to stifle the living presence of the Spirit and deny the challenge of our calling. This suspicion may be unjustified, but a lot of people share it, and it is perhaps important to state clearly where I'm "coming from."

In contrast to these strongly positive and negative impressions, my third impression is one of ambivalence. It seems to me that the Declaration in many places doesn't really say anything; that is, it uses traditional doctrinal language—language which most of us would agree with, but which remains ambiguous because we mean different things by it.

This impression is most pronounced in the Declaration's treatment of Scripture. That the Bible is "God's Word written, inspired and authoritative" is something Anglicans of all stripes maintain. There may still be a few Old Liberals who are uncomfortable with the terms (the result of a long tradition of fundamentalist abuse of the words); but it can be stated categorically that for committed Anglicans of all traditions the Scriptures are a source of strength, enlightenment, and guidance, a primary place where we encounter God. The difficulty, of course, is that we experience and understand the role of Scripture in very different ways, and so we mean very different things when we speak of "God's Word written, inspired and authoritative." What is dividing the church is not whether or not we take Scripture seriously enough (I'm sure none of us do), but the question of how Scripture nourishes our faith, how it is "God's Word written, inspired and authoritative." As I am sure that I for one mean something very different by this statement of belief than many in the Essentials movement, I find it singularly unhelpful to ask the church simply to repeat dogmatic formulas which hide the real issues confusing and dividing us. What the church needs—theologically and, even more importantly, pastorally—is a clear and open discussion about what we believe about the Bible, with the goal of greater mutual accountability in the Body of Christ.

With this in mind, it seems to me it would be most helpful to give an account of what I mean by the theological terms we apply to the Bible. I do this in hope of calling forth assent, disagreement, or correction, but in any case, in the hope of bringing some clarity to the question. And in so doing, I hope I am also by implication bearing witness to the power of the Scriptures.

The Bible as the Word of God

We believe that the Bible is God's Word; that is, we believe that God speaks to us through Scripture. And yet, because this is such a powerful and bold statement, we must be clear about what we mean by it. The sovereignty of God is at stake. There is a logic in our carefulness which is reflected in the first table of the Commandments: the moment we identify and worship God (the First Commandment), it is essential that we be on guard not to make graven images, nor to take God's name in vain. By the same token, we are told (awesomely) that God's voice speaks in Scripture; hence, we must be very careful that we do not identify something less as the voice of God. The fear of the Lord is indeed the beginning of wisdom.

This "something less" in Scripture is of course the human voice (or voices). Yes, it is God's Word, but these are human words as well, written in human language, coloured by the individual understanding of the writers, shaped by their culture and their times. As modern Christians, we have become more aware of the extent of the human voice in Scripture. We are more capable of understanding the human factors influencing the Bible, because we are heirs of the project of historical-critical study that was devoted precisely to clarifying the human aspects of Scripture: the language, the historical context, the culture, the issues and ideas.

The practical implication is that we must clearly and openly reject a biblicist view of Scripture, one in which we can simply choose a verse and say without regard for the human context: this is God's Word, this is God's teaching. We must reject this heresy not just on grounds of intellectual honesty (though that should be enough) but on profoundly theological grounds. The biblicist view of Scripture identifies without distinguishing the divine and human voice. This identification is profoundly idolatrous.

We all know this, at least on some instinctive level. No one takes a verse such as "Happy shall they be who take your little ones and dash them against the rock!" (Psa. 137:9) as God's guidance on how to treat your enemies. And yet we still hear, endlessly, that a verse in Romans is God's teaching on homosexuality, and that "Wives, submit to your husbands, for the husband is the head of the wife" is the Word of God. It is not particularly difficult to see, name, and understand the human motivations behind these and many other verses of Scripture. And yet we continue to invoke them as having the authority of God's absolute decree to solve the issues and challenges we face as a church. One wonders why we continue to abuse Scripture in this way, when we really should know better.

Certainly sin plays a role, as it does in all our human muddling: the very human reluctance (call it laziness or dishonesty or what you will) to face the anxiety of a lived struggle for truth, the willingness to exchange the integrity God calls us to for simple certainties we can control and with which we can control others. But besides these negative reasons, there is one factor in our habit of using Scripture unreflectively that should be answered with respect, as it springs from a genuine concern. It is the reluctance to think critically about Scripture because that implies looking down in judgement from the standpoint of a superior intellect, a position in which we can never really be touched or convicted by the Word. In the words of the Declaration, "The church may not judge the Scriptures, selecting and discarding from among their teachings."

The Declaration is expressing a genuine concern here, because it is pointing to a real problem. How can we be led and taught by Scripture if we are analyzing it? How do we, having started down the road of critical analysis, move beyond it to the point where we can again be addressed and challenged? How do we, who have learned to perceive the human word in Scripture so well, learn again to hear the Word of God?

This is the core question in our relationship to Scripture, and it is one for which there is no pat answer. It will guide our reflections for the remainder of this chapter. At this point, let it be said that the dilemma is real. We cannot make it go away just by pretending it doesn't exist. The Bible is God's Word, but it is God's Word incarnate in human words. And so we must learn, not to judge Scripture, but to discern the human and the divine voice in Scripture, to discern what spirit is speaking through a passage and through our under-standing.[8] This is a process that will sometimes not be as clear as we would like. It's not infallible; not because God's Word is not in itself infallible, but because no human understanding or method can ever be infallible. It is only the presence of God's Spirit that will lead us into all truth; we have to rely on that, to pray for it and seek it and test it in community, and to give up the kind of shortcuts to absolute certainty that we prefer. We have no choice—if we insist on ignoring the problem and grabbing what we like out of the Bible and declaring it to be the Word of God, we are rejecting the risk of trusting the living God and turning to the idols of human thoughts and opinions we have set up as absolute truth.

The Word of God and the Bible

The Bible is "God's Word written." How do we understand the Word of God? The briefest theological reflection should warn us to pay attention, because Scripture speaks of another Word of God: the Word who was in the beginning, through whom all things were made, the Word who became flesh. And so we must beware of carelessly referring to the Bible as the Word of God, without being conscious that we are using a name of the Second Person of the Trinity.

The Word of God is first and foremost Jesus Christ. This is the primary meaning of the expression. And if the word *Word* has not been chosen at random, then this confession says something about the nature of revelation. The revelation of God is not reducible to correct doctrines or a sacred book. It is not just information, as we may be tempted to suppose, in an age obsessed with it: God's revelation cannot be reduced to bytes and sent over the wire. If that were the case, Jesus would not have had to be born and crucified. God's revelation is a revelation in flesh and blood, in the life Jesus lived and the death Jesus died.

And so, the Bible is only secondarily the Word of God. Its authority does not lie in itself, but in its bearing witness to the living Word. This distinction, like the distinction between the human and divine word in Scripture, is not an irrelevant theological splitting of hairs. It is a basic question of the integrity of the God we worship. If we forget or ignore this distinction and speak abso-lutely about the Bible as *the* Word of God, then we are applying to a fashioned image an attribute which belongs to God. It may be a sacred and inspired image, but it is nevertheless an *image* which must not be confused with the fullness and sovereignty of God. "In *him* the fullness of God was pleased to dwell bodily"—not in a book.

The consequence is that our faith is not *ultimately* Bible based or Bible centred—it is Christ based and Christ centred. Yes, the Bible must be at the basis and centre of our faith, but only as window through which we see the real centre. If we keep staring at the window as the actual centre, then God in Jesus Christ will be out of focus. It is Jesus Christ, as he lived and died, who is the criterion by which we understand and discern God's Word in Scripture— in Luther's succinct wording, *was Christum treibt*; "whatever furthers Christ." In other words, the Christian Bible is ultimately about the revelation of God which is Jesus Christ. He is the revelation of God's faithfulness, mercy, and loving-kindness: not just because he, and the biblical tradition as a whole, talks about God in these terms, but because God came in person in Jesus Christ to prove that faithfulness by his solidarity with us unto death. He is the revelation also of our true humanity, not just by defining and ordering what human behaviour should be, but by living a full and righteous human life. The Christian Bible is about this God and this call to fullness of life; the life and death, the words and deeds, of Jesus of Nazareth are the key and criterion by which the church reads the whole Bible.

For example, in our attitude towards sin, we would do well to pay particular attention to the way Jesus approaches sinners, to that delicate, compassionate balance of judgement and grace, law and gospel. I say this in light of our current obsession with finding "biblical standards" to undergird our moral presuppositions. The Bible certainly offers a rich field for the human tendency to want life to be governed by rules.[9] But if the Bible is ultimately and primarily not about rules, but about the Good News of Jesus Christ, then these standards must be measured by Jesus' preaching and practice of grace. This is not to say that Jesus was always nice or soft on sin. On the contrary, we would do very well as a church to learn to hear the words of judgement and wrath more clearly and more often—most of them directed at the Pharisees. We shouldn't be soft on sin, not our own, anyway. But it is high time that this church bid farewell to the kind of legalism that addresses people primarily in terms of their sin, not in terms of the gospel of our righteousness by God's grace. There should be no room for the slightest doubt, either in our minds or in the minds of those watching the church from the outside, that the Bible which nurtures our faith is about the reality of God's grace in Jesus Christ. It is a gospel which announces the end of the old law, and substitutes the law of love. In Paul's words, for a Christian "all things are permitted," nothing is disqualified automatically as arousing God's anger; the criterion, what matters to God, is whether our actions are "beneficial," whether they contribute to the building of the Body of Christ and to a dignified human life. Christian morality is a matter of constant relevance to the church, but it is *Christian* morality only when it is sought in the light of this primary truth of the gospel.[10]

It is offensive to the gospel when the Canadian Bible Society targets a secular public with the advertizing slogan, "You can't play the game without reading the rulebook." And I am similarly troubled by the last sentence on

Scripture in the Declaration: "Scripture under Christ judges the church for its faithfulness to his revealed truth." Here again the primary function of Scripture is portrayed as judgement, as a test we have to pass. The same tacit assumption is betrayed, perhaps unconsciously, in the definitive sentence on the Bible in the same Article: the Scriptures are defined as "living and powerful as God's guidance for belief and behaviour." I believe this lapse in the phrasing is significant; it betrays a basic evangelical misconception that the fundamental nature of Scripture, the way in which the Bible is living and powerful (epithets referring directly to the presence of God) is as law. One misses here any reference to the fundamental nature of the Scriptures as *gospel*, as the Good News (truly news, and not to be taken for granted) of God's loving care for humanity. One wonders whether the *evangelion* (good news) in evangelical has been forgotten.

The Inspiration of the Bible

We have looked at the question of the human voice in Scripture, and at the role of Jesus Christ as criterion and key for our understanding. Yet the question still looms large: how do we read and hear Scripture as God's Word? The Declaration speaks of Scripture as inspired. In exploring what we mean by this term, we will perhaps begin to move closer to a clearer sense of the voice of God speaking through Scripture and addressing us.

Our understanding of inspiration has been confused by a vulgar tradition of verbal inspiration, which envisaged the process by which the Bible took shape as a kind of divine dictation to a passive human secretary. It must be clear from what we have said so far about the human voice in Scripture that this understanding of inspiration is inappropriate. It continues, however, to muddle our understanding of Scripture, so I believe we must attempt to say a little more about what it does mean positively.

I would suggest that inspiration is first of all a working of the Holy Spirit. It is that working of the Holy Spirit on men and women of biblical times by which she opened their eyes, hearts, and minds to perceive God at work in their lives and in their world; by which she moved them to praise God, remember, pass down, and record what they saw.

This means that what the Bible has to tell us is not only or even primarily ideas or doctrines. It is not a shelf filled with absolute truth, preserved in mason jars for our consumption. What it offers us is something more precious: the witness of men and women, not completely unlike ourselves, to the reality of God's gracious and creative presence. What it contains is the living faith of those who have been touched by God before us, a faith we can make our own. We can't just read it with our minds, extracting a simple moral, a fossilized truth, out of the living story of struggle and grace. We have to read it with our whole existence, because God is addressing our whole existence and only such a total response is adequate.

And this too is inspiration. This too is the work of the Spirit. The writing down of the Bible was only half the story. The other half of the inspiration of Scripture happens when we read it. Our understanding of inspiration, of how God speaks through Scripture, misses the mark if we are not fully aware of this action of the Spirit. When we open the Bible, and especially when we come together as a church to share the Word, we are dependent on the Holy Spirit to let this witness of God's deeds speak to our lives: to let us share in the experiences of the men and women of long ago; to see what they saw of God's great works; *and* to open our eyes to see God's presence in our lives and our world. This is not something we can arrange or control or direct. It happens when the Spirit moves. But by God's grace it comes again and again to feed us.

The Coherence of the Bible

Before turning to the question of how the Bible is an authority in the church, a word is necessary about the coherence of Scripture. To what extent does the Bible contain a coherent message and teaching, or to what extent does it speak with different voices, set different emphases, or even contradict itself? It is an issue arising directly from the historical-critical study of the Bible, a method which relies on perceiving subtle (or sometimes not so subtle) differences of language, tone, or content between various passages. The difficulty of integrating historical-critical questioning into the church's practical use of the Bible has led some Christians to protest against this emphasis on differences; the Bible's fundamental unity of teaching must be reasserted against all tendencies to portray it as a simple collection of fundamentally incoherent teachings.

The only honest and helpful answer to this dilemma is to recognize that both sides are true, as far as they go: historical-critical study is an invaluable help in perceiving the richness and complexity of the biblical witnesses, but the church, reading the Bible as Holy Scripture, believes, confesses, and seeks the underlying unity of God's purpose. We distinguish the various emphases and colourings of the human voices in the Bible, but we believe in the underlying coherence of God's voice speaking to us through Scripture.

However, we must beware of drawing a too-facile conclusion from this identification of diversity with the human voices in the Bible: the fallacy that we can safely ignore the diversity and differences as being irrelevant to our faith. We cannot automatically separate the divine and human voices in the Bible and pay attention only to the former. The Word of God comes to us only embodied in human words, and only by careful attention to the specific and distinctive features of the various traditions of Scripture can we be open to the fullness of God's presence within them. The most obvious example is that the life of Jesus comes to us not in one authorized biography, but in four Gospels, each with its own interests and emphases. Generally we tend to ignore this fact, as though it were an embarrassing lapse on the part of the Holy Spirit, and reconstruct our own authorized life of Jesus. May I suggest that we would do well to have enough faith in the inspiration of the canon that we take this diversity of tradition seriously, and trust that it is good.

This balance of coherence and diversity is important in our attitude as Christians towards the Hebrew Scriptures, our Old Testament. It is first of all the unity of the two Testaments which we must emphasize in keeping with the orthodox Christian tradition. Unfortunately, one still encounters in our church the widespread prejudice that the Old Testament as a whole is an inferior part of the Bible, bearing witness to a primitive and vindictive spirit. Having said this, we must be careful that our confession of the fundamental unity of Old and New Testaments does not lead us to ignore the specific accents of Old Testament texts. Here we find the principal witness to many biblical themes (creation, covenant, social justice, idolatry, and the honour of God, to name a few). In the Old Testament narratives, we find models of faith (Heb. 11) as a struggle and journey of men and women of flesh and blood—models we really can't afford to banish to the Sunday school. Yet too often we turn to the Old Testament only for snippets which reinforce our doctrinal preconceptions, instead of allowing ourselves to be informed and moulded by the whole witness of Israel's history with God, which by faith is our own.

At the root of the question of the diversity and unity of Scripture is the problem of how we read the Bible, how we go about "making sense" of what we read: the practice of exegesis. In his article in *Anglican Essentials*, Bishop Peter Mason suggests as an exegetical rule of thumb that we "assume a high degree of internal consistency within the whole range of Scripture."[11] I hope and trust that he is referring to the basic assumption of the unity of God's will throughout all of Scripture, but I am uncomfortable when this is formulated as an exegetical rule. I fear that it could be taken to mean that we should consciously ignore inconsistencies and overlook difficult passages, as is too often our practice. The trouble with this kind of consistency and unity, bought at the price of overlooking the seemingly unimportant details which don't fit our conception, is that it tends to be a very human unity, limited by the narrowness of our own understanding. We spoke above about the danger of our intellects so controlling Scripture that we do not allow it to address us. Nowhere, it seems to me, is that danger so great as in the order that we impose on Scripture in the name of consistency.

The tension between the coherence and diversity of the Bible is a factor in understanding the relationship between doctrine and Scripture.[12] Often we assign doctrine a normative function in our reading of Scripture; that is, we approach the Bible ready to hear only what we believe to be orthodox Christian doctrine. We either ignore or reinterpret any details which don't fit, and thereby effectively block any genuine encounter with the biblical text. It is no longer the Bible which shapes and informs our faith, but only our prior understanding of the doctrinal tradition. This understanding cannot grow or be challenged, because we only let the Bible confirm what we think we already know. In this way we block out, not only alternative understandings of the events of salvation history (and the Bible is full of these), but also the ways in which the Bible addresses us primarily as a story, speaking to our emotions and imagination.[13]

This observation corresponds to a tendency ingrained in the Western intellectual tradition: to look for the real meaning of a poem or narrative in an explanatory paraphrase, in a reader's attempt to translate it into the language of abstract ideas. The real meaning of a poem or narrative lies in the reader's encounter with the poem or narrative itself; in the same way, the real meaning of the Bible does not lie in its paraphrase as doctrine, but in our encounter with the story of the living God. Doctrine paraphrases and summarizes what the Bible teaches.[14] It has, as such, a clarifying function which leads us to a fuller encounter with a text by stating the larger theological context it stands in; it refers the specific emphases of the passage to the ultimate unity of God's presence in history. Doctrine should serve to balance and enable our encounter with the Word, not to replace it.

On the other hand, we all—at least all of us who preach or otherwise practice the discipline of exegesis—have the experience from time to time of encountering a text or verse which confuses us, repels us, or won't fit into our theology. But as we chew on it, do our exegesis more thoroughly, and see it perhaps from a slightly different angle, it begins to speak to us, to make sense in a new and powerful way, because our understanding of God's ways has been broadened. Or a text may come to life for us in a new way when we come to it from a new situation in life. The Scriptures speak powerfully and genuinely to us only when we approach them, not with an idea of what we think they should say, but with careful attention to what they really say, including all the apparent inconsistencies and ambiguities. None of us is as good at this as we should be. Not the liberals; not the evangelicals either—for all their claim to be a biblical tradition, they are bound by their strong commitment to a particular interpretation of the faith.[15] The coherence we can and must trust in Scripture is not the foreshortened coherence of our own systems of under-standing—it must be nothing less than the living unity of God's real presence as we read those pages, a unity always one step beyond our attempts to make sense of it, uncovering and challenging our limitations, leading us bit by bit to a fuller awareness of God's truth (John 16:13). There is nothing new or radical about this insight: it is simply the proper humility the church has always brought to Scripture.

The Authority of the Bible

The final epithet of Scripture we must examine is *authoritative.* In a sense our reflections have been leading to this central question: Where does the author-ity of Scripture lie? If we are to be a biblical church, how are we to be shaped and guided by Scripture?

There is a tradition which speaks about the authority of Scripture in the church in terms of a criterion and source for teaching. We turn to the Bible to seek doctrinal truth and moral standards. It is the canon by which we test and measure the traditions we have inherited, rejecting "anything which cannot be proved from Scripture." It is this tradition which seems to determine the Declaration's approach to Scripture. It is a good tradition, a necessary one. It expresses the experience of the church, throughout its history, that the Bible can and must be a uniquely powerful critical instance in our theology, cutting through the jungle of pious sentiments to address us with a genuine and relevant clarity. It is a central legacy of the Reformation, which no Christian theology can afford to ignore.

And yet this tradition, if it remains only a theological method, is limited. It is a necessary ingredient of responsible theology, but it is not, to use the traditional formulation, sufficient for salvation. It makes a biblical theologian (and the church needs them!), but it does not make a biblical church. If the Bible were authoritative only in this sense, then the Reformers could have resolved to leave its texts in Latin, even as they used it to support their theological revolution. Instead, it was critically important to them that the Bible be translated, be read and preached in the churches, and come into the hands of the people. Their project of a biblical church was not just one in which the *magisterium*, the theologians and teachers, are informed by Scripture; it is a vision of a church whose whole life is accompanied and shaped by Scripture. This vision is a central legacy of Anglicanism, perhaps our central legacy from the Reformation, expressed in the collect—not that we may use the Scriptures to prove our doctrine, but first and foremost "that we may in such wise hear them, read, mark, learn, and inwardly digest them, that by patience and comfort of thy holy Word, we may embrace and ever hold fast the blessed hope of everlasting life."

In other words, the Bible is authoritative not only in a regulative sense for our doctrine; it has authority in a creative sense for our faith.[16] Indeed this creative sense, calling forth and shaping our faith, is the *primary* way in which we are a biblical church, and it is only against this background that the use of Scripture as an authority to regulate doctrine makes sense. Doctrine is not faith—they are related, but they are not the same thing. This is a quarrel I have with the Declaration: it seems to me to confuse faith and doctrine in a very fundamental way, and thus reduce faith to an assent to a set of propositions.[17] Doctrine is a common interpretative framework to understand our tradition; faith is our communal yet intensely personal way with God, our own struggles, joys, and grief.

We have a long way to go towards becoming a biblical church, a church in which personal faith is nourished by Scripture in community. Taking part in Bible studies over the years, I have observed that there is nothing more difficult for many people than linking a Bible text to their own struggles. The art of encountering a biblical text with our whole person—of associating freely, of finding ourselves and our story in the text, of being addressed in our own life experience—is not an art we have taught in the Anglican Church. Instead we have taught our people to distrust their own thoughts and feelings, to be afraid of saying the wrong thing, to look to the clergy to tell them what they are supposed to think. We have taught them to look to Scripture only for the correct doctrine, and nothing else. As far as we have succeeded, we have destroyed the basis of a healthy biblical faith.

We have, for example, been taught as children what the sacrifice of Isaac was about: see how wonderful Abraham's faith is; we should be like that too. We have been taught the "right answer," and the right answer was usually about how we should be better Christians. We pull out a moral and learn to repeat it blithely. But is our faith really engaged? What do we do with the horror of this story? What do we do with the fears that this story must surely touch upon, deep down inside each one of us? Do we really ask ourselves seriously how we can deal with this God? And if we don't ask these questions, how will we ever deal with it if a time in our life comes when God seems to be heartless and uncaring? However, when we engage the story with our whole being, then we find that it speaks with a power and authority that is very different from our moralizing attempts to "make sense" of it. It is critical for the health of our personal faith, and for the future of the church, that we grow in the practice of living with Scripture, of finding our own struggles and joys in the biblical story, of sharing in the struggles and joys of others, and so together experience the reality of the biblical God in our world.

It is in this sense that the traditions I referred to at the beginning of this chapter—traditions often dismissed as liberal—are profoundly biblical. These traditions, or at least the best part of them, have turned to the Scriptures with particular concerns (as do we all), and they have found there something new. They have discovered that the Bible speaks with authority in ways we had not imagined. Various traditions of spirituality have rediscovered the power of biblical symbolism and biblical narrative to heal and convict the human heart. The liturgical reform has brought a greater fullness of the biblical tradition into our worship, and has given us eucharistic prayers which celebrate the whole biblical story of salvation, instead of just lecturing us on the atonement. Feminists have taught us to discover a whole world of women's experience in the Bible, and have taught us all to pay more attention to human experience in general. The ecological crisis has brought the meaning of the creation story to life, after decades in which it was tied up by the concerns of literalists.

By the working of the Spirit, we are discovering new worlds in the Bible, and our common faith is enriched and deepened. Some people can see in these directions only a threat to orthodoxy. But if orthodox doctrine really reflects what is in the Bible, and I believe it does, then orthodoxy should not be afraid of what we encounter in Scripture. These directions are simply examples, and they're not the only ones, of the power—the authority—with which the Bible still speaks to our concerns. The particular concerns I mentioned may not be everyone's, but they do point the way in their reference to Scripture to our common future as a church: a place where each community and parish truly lives with the Bible, experiencing God's presence in their midst as they break the Word together.

Living with the Bible

Let us briefly review the argument. I began by noting both a widespread hunger to be a more genuinely biblical church, and general confusion and disagreement as to what that might mean. I have attempted to clarify the problem by examining the most important attributes traditionally applied to the Bible: What do we mean when we call the Bible *God's Word*? What do we mean by *inspired, coherent*, and *authoritative*? Unpacking these terms, I have attempted to confront and clarify some subtle but very fundamental issues around the church's understanding of Scripture: the relationship of God's Word to the human words of biblical authors and biblical culture; the role of Jesus Christ as the central criterion; the role of the Spirit in both the writing and the reading of Scripture; the tension between the genuine coherence of God's wisdom and our attempts to foreshorten and "make sense" of Scripture; the creative authority of the Bible for our personal and collective faith.

As a church, we are confronted with the choice of three options. We can continue to apologize for Scripture, to use it as a vaguely quaint relic from the past, picking out helpful illustrations for our progressive viewpoint, distancing ourselves from the rest by consigning it to another age. This was the classic liberal option; it is bankrupt, because it leaves us no other authority but our own enlightened morality. Or we can treat the Bible primarily as a sourcebook for standards of belief and behaviour, as a reference tool to which we turn for answers to dogmatic and ethical issues. This is, if my analysis and impressions are correct, the Declaration's prescription for a biblical church. The difficulty with this model is that it reduces the Bible ultimately to a thing: an object we can interpret through the lens of our doctrinal position, seeing what we already know and leaving the rest. But if the Bible is going to be a sacrament of God's presence, then we must very consciously choose another model for how we treat it. We must learn, not simply to use it as a tool, but to live with it as a person might live with a beloved partner:[18] giving and receiving, being comforted by a familiar friend, but respecting its integrity, its mystery; never daring to think we know it so well that we cannot be surprised, confronted, challenged by the encounter with the Word. Only when we are clear about this approach to Scripture do we leave room in ourselves to let God be God, the mysterious, awe-inspiring, giving Other. Only if we are clear about not making Scripture perform for us can we find grace in the Word. Only in this way can we be a genuinely biblical church.

Endnotes

1. The following text is a revised and expanded version of a paper presented at the Montreal Diocesan Theological College on March 23, 1995, in the framework of a series of public debates on the Montreal Declaration of Anglican Essentials.
2. We are speaking of our understanding of the truth as being historically conditioned, not of the truth itself as being merely relative.
3. The use of the word "liberal" is one of the factors in our confusion. In North American churches it is used in a broad sense as a general term for "progressive" or "critical" theologies of many varieties. I am using the term here in a more specialized sense, referring to a trend in theology in the last two hundred years or so, characterized by specific assumptions about the priority of religious experience over tradition. Though largely discredited as an expression of nineteenth-century optimism, these as-

sumptions are still influential. A liberal theology (progressive, critical, responsive to contemporary concerns) is not necessarily "liberal" in this technical sense—it may be quite biblical in its foundations.

4. This is of course the common accusation against liberal Christianity, and I share in the opinion that this tendency to edit Scripture according to our prior convictions is fundamental to our difficulties in being truly nourished by the Word. I am in fact convinced that this is not only a problem for the liberal wing of the church, but at least as much so for the evangelicals, though their criterion is doctrine, rather than contemporary relevance. I can scarcely recall hearing an evangelical sermon where it was evident that the preacher was genuinely informed or even challenged by his or her text, rather than just using the text—whether it happened to fit or not—to bolster up his or her own particular theology.

5. Perhaps an example might be appropriate at this point. Bishop Burton, in his contribution to *Anglican Essentials*, centres his critique of the BAS on its alleged undermining of the primacy of Scripture: "[T]here appears to be an underlying difference between how the two books view the Bible. Is it the authoritative Word of God, as the BCP maintains, or is the Bible an incoherent collection of faith documents, inspiring tokens of the past belief systems of the people of God?" (ed. George Egerton [Anglican Book Centre, 1995], 150). The structure of the argument deserves close attention: (1) The BAS is accused of having an incoherent, relativist, in short, a *classically* liberal view of Scripture; (2) this view is contrasted with another view (allegedly that embodied by the BCP) in terms of an implicit absolute alternative (if it's not one, it must be the other); and (3) the second alternative is expressed primarily in language which is incontrovertibly true ("the authoritative Word of God")—but which remains ultimately ambiguous. Only in the context of the article as a whole does it become clear that Bishop Burton understands this authority primarily, if not exclusively, in terms of the teaching of doctrine. This seems to me a textbook example of how the argumentation in an absolute but false liberal-evangelical alternative distorts our collective thinking.

6. As I was fairly challenged on this point at the public presentation of this paper by an Essentials supporter with a passionate and proven environmental commitment, I can let this stand only with an explanatory note. I have no doubt that the theological concerns of the Essentials movement allow of a genuine *ethical* commitment to environmental issues, as I know they do to social justice concerns as well. Where I am not convinced is whether the movement's rigid insistence on traditional expressions of orthodoxy would allow the church to hear the *theological* critique and corrective which creation-centred theologies are bringing to our doctrinal tradition (often from a biblical standpoint). I am not advocating embracing Matthew Fox as the new orthodoxy, but only suggesting that theological work involves constant self-correction (*semper reformanda!*) and that our church and faith will benefit from an examination of how the tradition has

been distorted by a one-sided Augustinian concern with "God and the soul—nothing else!"

An example of this kind of self-examination is the excellent essay by Loren Wilkinson in *Anglican Essentials*. While being justifiably critical of the fallacies of the more superficial "nature spiritualities," Wilkinson none-theless takes seriously the distortions in our understanding and articula-tion of the faith in the modern Western historical tradition: "But, on the whole, the more 'evangelical' our theology, the more we have seen the incarnation not as 'the word without [whom] nothing was made' but only as a kind of divine rescue mission, necessary to save God's image-bearer, man, from a cursed and doomed creation, like a child from a burning house" (p. 235). Unfortunately, these insights found no place in the Decla-ration.

7. Some explanation of what I mean by this rather bitter expression is appro-priate. I am thinking of the implications of the fashionable expression "politically correct": the sense of a legalistic and rather stupid liberal elite dictating morality and curtailing freedom of speech and thought; the corresponding sense of speaking for a decent and long-suffering silent majority of ordinary folks; and—as though justified by this construction— the massive contemptuous disregard for the concerns underlying the positions so-labelled. This pathos—to my ears, anyway—infuses the rheto-ric of the Essentials movement. I don't wish to press the point further, except to point out that the accusation of conforming our theology to the trends of secular society can—always—cut both ways.

8. It will not be a coincidence that Paul lists the discernment of spirits along with the other charismata which serve the building up of the community through understanding: prophecy, tongues, and the interpretation of tongues (I Cor. 12:10).

9. For example, a fairly solid case can be made for the biblical teaching that Christians should not own or ride horses. In the Old Testament, they are almost universally objects of fear in possession of Israel's enemies, chiefly the Egyptians (Ex. 15:1) and later the Arameans. They have idolatrous associations (I Kings 20:23–25; II Kings 23:11). It is Solomon who, among his other sins, introduced horse trading into Israel (I Kings 10:25ff). Nu-merous references in the Psalms and prophets make it clear that "[the Lord] delighteth not in the strength of the horse" (Psa. 147:10) and "An horse [is] a vain thing for safety" (Psa. 33:17). Hosea's teaching gives us an unequivocal standard: "we will not ride upon horses" (Hos. 14:3). The superb passage in Job (39:19–25) does tend to resist moralizing, but we can at least say that it is not particularly encouraging. With the exception of their rather unpleasant associations in Revelation, they are scarcely men-tioned in the New Testament. All in all, it seems surprising that the church does not offer moral guidelines in this question by condemning horseback riding as displeasing to God.

10. To return to our example of the horse, in a less facetious vein: there may in fact have been a time (the Middle Ages, for example) when the conscience of Christendom ought to have been challenged by the biblical picture of the horse as a weapon of war. But the basis for ethical discernment would be a rejection of violence rooted in God's love for humanity and sealed by the outrage of crucifixion, and a recognition of the role of the horse as a weapon of war in biblical times and in contemporary society; in short, a response in faith, shaped by a relationship to God defined by Jesus Christ. As people tend to prefer rules to the personal responsibility of a faith relationship, the medieval knight tended to be more concerned with gaining the necessary indulgences than with the appropriateness of butchering and raping peasants.

   In the same way, it seems to me that there is a lot we could and should be saying as a church, from the standpoint of our faith in Jesus Christ, about the effects of consumerism in our society: the illusion of self-sufficiency and control which breaks down our communities and our trust in God, the human cost of an economic system based on mutual exploitation, the cheapening of sexuality by images of domination and possession, the breakdown of relationship in a world where everything is for sale. We have another vision of humanity which this world needs to hear; we have a standard of judgement and condemnation which needs to be spoken aloud. However, the human obsession with rules seems to be alive and well, and listening to many in the Anglican Church today, one might almost believe that the Christian response to the moral issues of our time is to tell couples they need a marriage licence if God is not to be angry with their relationship.

11. "On Track with the Word: The Authority of the Bible Today," in *Anglican Essentials*, 74.

12. By doctrine I mean quite broadly the whole tradition of the church in systematically interpreting biblical events and ideas, as expressed in creeds, catechisms, sermons, commentaries, and other theological tracts.

13. The most widespread and damaging example of this tendency is the absolute dominance of a satisfaction doctrine of the atonement in the evangelical understanding of the cross. This doctrine is an attempt to explain the meaning and necessity of the crucifixion, that event which the Gospels place at the centre of Jesus' life and mission. It interprets the cross as the just punishment of death which God must inflict on humanity for our sins; a punishment which He then graciously inflicts on his Son to spare us. This doctrine is an ancient tradition, present in John's Gospel and the letters of Paul, developed by such theologians as Augustine, Anselm, and Calvin to a central tenet in the tradition. It is a valid and productive understanding of the cross; but it is not that which evangelical theology makes it out to be: the unique and authoritative expression of God's grace, the all-sufficient and compulsory understanding of our salvation. This

obsession with one doctrine has led our common tradition to ignore or undervalue other insights into the meaning of the cross. One might name for example the exposure and condemnation of the concrete sin of violence and oppression inherent in human society; the overcoming of the power of death; the final solidarity of God's love in which the incarnation is carried to its final end in the crucified God. But it is not just this emphasis of one doctrinal interpretation to the exclusion of all others that is problematical; on a more profound level, *any* attempt to make a doctrinal explanation the object of our faith, rather than the events of the story itself, is profoundly troubling. Our intellectual explanations—however orthodox they may be—must not serve as ways of hiding from our horror and outrage and confusion in the face of the cross. The bottom line in the New Testament about the crucifixion is not the construction of a coherent theology of atonement, but simply the terrible and incomprehensible "must" of Mark 8:31, and the conviction in faith that this necessity was "for us."

14. For example, the doctrine of the Trinity gives us a framework to understand the unity in the diversity of the biblical witness to God; christological doctrines, as we find them in the Nicene Creed, are attempts to clarify the event of the incarnation in the language of another age; doctrines of the church (less successful in providing unambiguous norms) strive to find a unified vision of the meaning of the church from the various biblical witnesses.

15. Cf. above, note 2.

16. What else would we expect from a true witness to him who "taught with authority, and not as the scribes and Pharisees?"

17. I am particularly troubled by the use of the word "faith" in the conclusion to the document: "We resolve to maintain our heritage of faith and transmit it intact." This use of the word, clearly referring only to traditional doctrine and identified with the creeds, Thirty-Nine Articles, and the Prayer Book, is then even designated "fullness of faith." There is no apparent awareness of the biblical experience of faith as a wrestling with God (Isra-el) in the struggles of daily life, a trusting in God's mercy and love, a hope and reliance on God's power to transform our lostness into fullness of life. I see an ideological system; I do not see a witness to Jesus Christ as our "only confidence in living and in dying" (Heidelberg Catechism).

18. I am indebted for this image to my teacher D. J. Hall, who used it in a seminar to describe the Reformers' understanding of Scripture in contrast to that of many contemporary evangelicals.

4

The Word of God and "God's Word Written"

The Montreal Declaration on the Authority of the Scriptures

STEPHEN REYNOLDS

Whatsoever is spoken of God or things appertaining unto God otherwise than as the truth is, though it seem an honour, it is an injury. And as incredible praises given unto men do often abate and impair the credit of their deserved commendation, so we must likewise take great heed lest, in attributing unto Scripture more than it can have, the incredibility of that do cause even those things which indeed it hath most abundantly to be less reverently esteemed. I therefore leave it to themselves to consider whether they have in this first point or not overshot themselves; which God doth know is quickly done, even when our meaning is most sincere, as I am verily persuaded theirs in this case was.[1]

Richard Hooker, in the second book *Of the Laws of Ecclesiastical Polity* (1594), was responding to puritan ideologues within the Elizabethan Church of England, who held that "one only law, the Scripture, must be the rule to direct in all things, even so far as to the 'taking up of a rush or straw.'"[2] By one of those peculiar twists of Anglican history, Hooker could just as easily have been responding to a document issued four centuries later: The Montreal Declaration of Anglican Essentials. Article 6 of this Declaration concerns the authority of the Bible, and is evidently the stick with which the Essentials movement attempts to draw a firm line of Anglican faith and morals in the sands of contemporary life. As Hooker was persuaded about the puritan ideologues of his day, so too am I "verily persuaded" that the "meaning"—the intent—of the Essentialists "is most sincere." But what they say about the authority of the Holy Scriptures in Article 6 of their Declaration also makes me wonder "whether they have in this first point or not overshot themselves."

What the Montreal Declaration Says about the Authority of the Scriptures

First of all, it may be useful to place the text of the Declaration's sixth Article on the table. This Article consists of three paragraphs, with a catena of supporting references from the Scriptures and *The Articles of Religion*. The first two paragraphs read:

> The canonical Scriptures of the Old and New Testaments are "God's Word written," inspired and authoritative, true and trustworthy, coherent, sufficient for salvation, living and powerful as God's guidance for belief and behaviour.
>   The trinitarian, Christ-centred, redemption-oriented faith of the Bible is embodied in the historic ecumenical creeds and the Anglican foundational documents. To this basic understanding of Scripture, the Holy Spirit leads God's people and the church's counsels in every age through tradition and reason prayerfully and reverently employed.[3]

So far there would seem to be hardly any reason to think that Hooker's caveat about "attributing unto Scripture more than it can have" should be levelled at the Declaration. The Essentialists certainly do not go so far as the puritan ideologues with whom Hooker controverted. In no way does their sixth Article explicitly assert that the Scriptures constitute the *only* authority and the *sole* criterion in matters of "Christian faith, practice, and nurture." Indeed, the Declaration goes out of its way to make room for the authority of "the historic ecumenical creeds and the Anglican foundational documents" and even for "tradition and reason prayerfully and reverently employed."[4] It would be very difficult to find any divine in the Anglican mainstream, at least before the middle of the last century, who would have expressed qualms about these affirmations. The first two paragraphs, then, may be said to approximate an older Anglican consensus.

But this same Article of the Montreal Declaration has a third paragraph. It is here that the Article bares its teeth: "The church may not judge the Scriptures, selecting and discarding from among their teachings. But Scripture under Christ judges the church for its faithfulness to his revealed truth."[5] According to the Declaration, the Anglican Church does not and cannot have any discretionary power with regard to "God's Word written." If the Scriptures deliver an express ruling on any point of faith or morals—for example, Jesus' ruling about another marriage after divorce (Matt. 5:31–32; Mark 10:11–12; Luke 16:18), or Paul's rulings about the subjection of wives to their husbands (Eph. 5:22–24; Col. 3:18) and the subordination of women in the assembly of believers (1 Cor. 14:33b–36; I Tim. 2:11–15), or the rulings about same-sex relations in Leviticus and the Pauline writings (Lev. 18:22, 20:13; Rom. 1:21–28; I Cor. 6:9–11; I Tim. 1:8–11)—then the church has a positive obligation to teach and practise that ruling. One dire conclusion would seem to follow. If the church sets a scriptural ruling to one side, then it ceases to be faithful to God in Christ and thereby ceases to be *Christian*. The Declaration thus maintains that the judgement of the living community of the church is absolutely subject to the jurisdiction of those ancient writings which compose the canonical Scriptures.

The Metaphor of Magistracy

Such a position prompts one vital question. This question is *not* whether the Scriptures have or ought to have authority in the church. The canonical Scriptures do have and indeed ought to have such authority. But having granted this point, the real, the fundamental, question stands forth in these terms: What *kind* of authority do the Scriptures have?

The Declaration represents the authority of the Scriptures as a power "under Christ" to "judge the Church for its faithfulness to his revealed truth." A metaphor is at work here. In general, when we use a metaphor we are saying that one thing *acts like* another thing in one way or another (a similarity of action), even though it *is unlike*, or *is not*, the other in nature (a dissimilarity of being). For example, in John 6:35, Jesus declares, "I am the bread of life." As Thomas Cranmer and other sixteenth-century Reformed divines strenuously protested,[6] this is strictly speaking a metaphor: Jesus may be said to *act like* bread insofar as his passion and death, and therefore his body and blood, nourish and sustain the lives of those who believe in him; but of course Jesus himself *is not*, and therefore is *unlike*, bread.

In the present case, the Declaration uses what may be called the metaphor of magistracy. The basis for naming the metaphor thus is the verb in the statement, "Scripture under Christ *judges* the church for its faithfulness to his revealed truth." In this context, the verb "judge" can have one of two senses. The first and most obvious sense is judicial: it has to do with the administration of law and, more particularly, with the power of certain officers of the Crown to interpret the law in particular cases and to pronounce due punishment upon those convicted of breaking the law. The second sense has to do with the more general quality of judiciousness—the wisdom, the insight, the understanding which allows one to discern the truth of a matter and to state it with balance. The Declaration patently intends the verb "judge" in the first, judicial sense: the Scriptures are supposed to act like a living magistrate who has authority to hear and consider evidence, discretion to interpret the divine law which is promulgated in their pages, and power both to render a verdict and to impose due punishment on the church when it is shown to have violated that law.

I wonder whether the metaphor of magistracy, thus unconditionally asserted, does not "attribute unto Scripture more than it can have." For even if there is no need to express the dissimilarity of being between holy writ and a living magistrate, can it still be said that there is a similarity of action—that the Scriptures act like, *adjudicate* like, a magistrate? Judicial authority not only implies but also requires personal agency; that is, the discretionary powers of intellect and volition which enable one to interpret data (in this instance, constitutional and statutory law), and to apply its provisions to particular cases. But the Scriptures cannot be said to *act like* a living judge, even as they cannot be said to *be* a living judge. They are a collection of written works. As such they have no more real agency than any other written work; in themselves they have no personal discretion, no qualities of intellect and volition, to interpret various cases and then to determine their own responses or apply their own provisions to those various cases. In other words, the Scriptures cannot, of themselves, exercise any judgement or jurisdiction. Lacking such agency, the metaphor breaks down, for there is no similarity of action on which to base a metaphorical comparison.

It is still possible to affirm the authority of the Scriptures and perhaps even their jurisdiction "under Christ." But such authority and jurisdiction as they possess has to be mediated. They require the agency of living persons to interpret, proclaim, and apply their message. Such mediating activities are themselves acts of judgement—not only in the judicial sense implied by the Declaration's metaphor, that of rendering a verdict and pronouncing due punishment, but also in the judicious sense of seasoned wisdom which seeks meaning and truth. Since this is the case, we end up having to reverse the metaphor of magistracy: it is not the Scriptures that "judge" (in a judicial sense) the church; it is the church, as a community of living, personal agents, that "judges" (in a judicious sense) the Scriptures.

The Constitutional Analogy

All things considered, it might be another act of simple judiciousness to abandon the Declaration's metaphor of magistracy. Nevertheless, it is still possible to maintain the legal bias of the Declaration's position and to uphold what it contends for; namely, the paramount authority of the Scriptures. In place of the metaphor of magistracy, I suggest, we may resort to an even stronger kind of comparison, that of analogy—and specifically, the analogy of intrinsic attribution. An analogy of this sort differs from a metaphor in that the basis of comparison between two entities is not only similarity of action but also similarity of being. The two terms of the comparison *act like* one another because they can be said to *be like* one another.[7]

One analogy in particular preserves the legal bias of the Declaration and its contention for the paramount authority of the Scriptures. It is what I shall call the constitutional analogy. In a secular state, such as Canada, a constitution ordains the structures of government and the mutual relations of those structures, and may even identify and guarantee the rights of the nation's citizens. We might not be able to say in every case that a constitution actually *makes* the nation and its government what they are, but we can certainly say that it *defines* what they are. Now, the various branches and agencies of government—legislature, military, judiciary, police, and so forth—possess and exercise authority proper to their offices in order to administer and apply the provisions of the constitution. At the same time, these agencies do not possess and exercise authority or jurisdiction *over* the constitution; they possess and exercise authority or jurisdiction *under* and *by virtue of* the constitution. It is the constitution which gives them their jurisdiction, their authority to act, in the sectors allotted to them. By the same token, it might be argued, the living community of the faithful does not have authority or jurisdiction *over* "God's Word written," but *under* and *by virtue of* that written word. Thus it would appear that the Scriptures not only *act like* a constitution, but also *are* the constitutional standard to which the living community of the church can and must be held accountable, if it is to continue to exist and cohere as a community.

We may narrow the analogy still further and seek to maintain some links with the Declaration's original metaphor of magistracy by focusing on the constitutional functions of the judiciary. But once more we run up against the problem posed by the metaphor of magistracy. For though a constitution authorizes some officers of the Crown to adjudicate civil and criminal cases, yet that constitution, of itself, does not and cannot act as the judge. If we follow through on the analogy, we would have to say that, though the Scriptures might authorize the church to adjudicate the world, its own members, and even angels (I Cor. 6:2–3), yet the Scriptures themselves do not and cannot act as the judge. The principle of personal agency implicit in the original metaphor of magistracy is once again lost, for we are forced to appeal to agents outside the actual pages of the Scriptures for the enforcement of the constitutional standard they are supposed to embody.

Questions Arising

The Constitution of the Canon

The Essentialists may be willing to concede the principle of personal agency (and so the original metaphor of magistracy itself), if the constitutional analogy provides greater security to their more fundamental principle, that of the Scriptures' paramount authority. And the constitutional analogy would indeed seem to offer some measure of greater security to the more fundamental principle.

But as soon as the analogy is framed, a difficulty arises. It is, at first sight, a question of political theory: how does a constitution have authority in the first place? As several recent Canadian governments have learned to their cost, this question does not inhabit the realm of theory alone; it has a way of entering the game of practical politics. In the constitutional debates, accords, and referenda which have preoccupied Canadians in recent years, politicians have been forcibly reminded, several times over, that the will of the electorate has something to do with the ratification of the constitution. That is to say, a constitution's authority is not grounded in itself. It is grounded in the popular consensus which ratifies it and then chooses to abide by its terms.

If the constitutional analogy holds, we are obliged to ask how the Scriptures have authority in the church. It cannot be asserted that their authority as "God's Word written" is self-evident or self-authenticating. For we know that portions of the early church included several writings in the New Testament which were subsequently excluded, such as The Didache, The First Letter of Clement, and The Shepherd of Hermas, and that some churches either excluded or relegated to a quasi-apocryphal status other writings, such as the Letter to the Hebrews, the Letter of James, and the book of Revelation, which were subsequently received.[8] We do not know how or for what reasons the latter three writings were finally accepted. Nor can we say for certain why The First Letter of Clement was finally excluded, even though its canonical status and authority were accepted in the fourth century. We may guess that the fact its author was not an apostle had something to do with it[9]—which, needless to say, is not itself a scriptural principle. Neither is the reason given in the so-called Muratorian Canon for the exclusion of The Shepherd of Hermas; namely, that it lacked the note of "antiquity."[10] So how, and even more importantly *by whom*, was it determined that the writings actually included, and none other, are indeed God's Word?

I should argue that the judgement of the church (in the juridical as well as the judicious sense) had something to do with it. The various writings subsequently included in the canon of the Scriptures were all written to and for an already existing community of faith. It would take a staggering naïveté to presume that the Pentateuch was written (or compiled) to create the religion of Israel, rather than to consolidate that religion. And the earliest segments of the New Testament, Paul's letters, were not written to create churches where no churches yet existed. The Apostle wrote to "edify," to build up and consolidate, churches which already existed. The same must be said, only more so, of the other writings in the New Testament canon. Hence, the church existed prior to the apostolic and evangelical writings it recognizes as "Scripture," just as the community of Israel existed prior to the writings it acknowledged as "Scripture."

In dealing with this point of recognition and acknowledgement, we are of course talking about the issue of canonicity; and here the analogy with a constitution's ratification holds true almost with a vengeance. The canon of the First Testament was determined by a consensus of Jewish rabbis, first those who produced the Greek version of the Hebrew Scriptures known as the Septuagint, and later those who produced the so-called Masoretic text of the Hebrew Bible itself. A consensus of the Christian churches, forged over three or four centuries, endorsed the Septuagintic consensus and subsequently determined the canon of the Second Testament. It was the community of believers, not the Scriptures themselves, that decided which writings would be included in the canon and which would be excluded, such as The Gospel of Thomas, The Protevangelium of James, The First Letter of Clement, The Didache, and The Shepherd of Hermas. In other words, the church judged the Scriptures, selecting and discarding not simply among its teachings but among those writings whose teachings it would acknowledge as genuinely "inspired of God." There can be no more basic exercise of jurisdiction than the church's historical act of constituting, or establishing, the canon of the Scriptures.

If the consensus of the church once established the canon of the Scriptures, we must also acknowledge that it is the consensus of the church which even yet maintains the canon. The consensual basis of the canon is acknowledged in that "Anglican foundational document," *The Articles of Religion*: "In the name of the holy Scripture we do understand those Canonical Books of the Old and New Testament, *of whose authority was never any doubt in the Church....* All the Books of the New Testament, *as they are commonly received,* we do receive, and account them Canonical."[11] In other words, this Article does not appeal to the Scriptures themselves for the establishment of the canon; it appeals to the mutual agreement of the whole church, which was reached in times past ("of whose authority was never any doubt") and still continues ("as they are commonly received").

The Validity of the Analogy

A second question arises from the historical issues which the constitutional analogy has tendered. Indeed, it tests the validity of the analogy itself. Can the Scriptures be truly called the constitution of the church? Or, to put it another way, do the Scriptures constitute the church; that is say, do they make the church what it is, or at the least define that which makes the church what it is?

Chronologically speaking, the answer to this question has to be No for the reason I have stated; namely, the church both pre-existed the writings included in the New Testament canon and determined that canon itself. But this does not settle the question by any means. The appeal to history can prove embarrassing to those who fail to press it far enough. For it has to be admitted that, even as the church was forging a consensus about the canon, the Scriptures had already assumed a constitutive authority with respect to the church. Classical Anglican divinity appealed to the theological literature of the first five centuries as the norm of tradition; and one has only to read the sermons, catechetical discourses, and controversial treatises of those centuries to see that the Scriptures were given a unique authority in the development of the catholic faith. Ancient Christian teachers, heterodox as well as orthodox, felt compelled to anchor nearly every point of their arguments on appeals to the Scriptures in order to secure the divine authority of God's Word for their own words.

Needless to say, the Scriptures of themselves did not develop and define the catholic faith. But the theological appeal to the Scriptures may be characterized as constitutional, in that ancient teachers of the faith looked to the Scriptures for the terms of the church's calling, even of its existence, as a community of believers. And liturgical history seems to confirm theological history. It would be very difficult to find a Christian liturgy, regardless of communion or sect, in which the reading and expounding of the Scriptures has not formed (at least in principle) a necessary event. That very fact also argues for the constitutive role of the Scriptures: in liturgical celebration, as in theological discourse, the church has looked to the Scriptures for the terms of its calling, of its very existence, as a community of believers.

What Do We Mean by the Word of God?

The constitutional role of the Scriptures is tied to the faith of the church that the terms of its calling and existence are set by nothing other or less than God's own Word. So far I cannot argue with the Essentialist position in Article 6 of the Montreal Declaration. But what are we talking about when we refer to "the Word of God"? The Declaration itself seems to assume that this "Word" is simply identical with "God's Word written" in the Holy Scriptures. At least, such is the assumption which governs the catena of scriptural citations subjoined to the Declaration's sixth Article. These citations are designed to act as scriptural "proof-texts" of the Article's points. We need to ask ourselves, however, whether the citations really serve the Declaration's purpose. Do they support the sixth Article's identification of "the Word of God" all but exclusively with the Scriptures?

The catena subjoined to the sixth Article of the Declaration contains eleven citations. Two of these citations do indeed appear to lend credence to the Essentialist position. Let us consider them first.

1. Matthew 5:17–18

Do not think that I have come to abolish the law or the prophets; I have come not to abolish but to fulfill. For truly I tell you, until heaven and earth pass away, not one letter, not one stroke of a letter, will pass from the law until all is accomplished.

This passage opens that section of the Sermon on the Mount in which Jesus assumes the role of the new Moses and delivers a new, revised standard version of "the law and the prophets." The saying cited here, taken in isolation, clearly equates "the law" with its written form in the Scriptures of the Pentateuch. *Prima facie*, then, it serves as a "proof" of the Article's assumption that "the Word of God" is identical with the Scriptures.

But the "proof" becomes more complicated when we return this one saying to its larger Matthean context. It introduces a sequence of pronouncements, each of which begins with Jesus declaring: "You have heard that it was said.... But I say to you." These words indicate a rather more critical stance toward the enscriptured law than the one saying of 5:17–18, taken on its own, prepares us for. It may well be the case that each of the ensuing pronouncements "fulfills" the law. But in cumulative effect as well as in detail, these pronouncements set aside the enscriptured letter of the Mosaic code in order to assert a yet more radical code of holiness and justice above and beyond the enscriptured law. In other words, Jesus, the Matthean new Moses, calls his disciples to practise a critique of the Scriptures which transcends their literal meaning and fulfils instead their "true" intent. Such an interpretation is of course somewhat at odds with the Declaration's claim that "the church may not judge the Scriptures."

2. John 10:35

If those to whom the word of God came were called "gods"—and the scripture cannot be annulled....

This verse belongs to John's account of a disputation between Jesus and "the Jews" in Jerusalem during "the feast of the Dedication" when "Jesus was walking in the temple." At this particular point in the disputation, Jesus is answering his opponents' charge of blasphemy "because you, though only a human being, are making yourself God." He responds, "Is it not written in your law, 'I said, you are gods'?" The quotation does not come from the Pentateuch but from Psalm 82. "Law" here is metonymy for the Scriptures of the Old Testament. The crucial point of the argument is the way Jesus describes these Scriptures: they are "*your* law." Here he is dissociating himself from what his opponents take to be the final authority, even as he exploits one of its texts in order to confound their accusation. The rhetoric of the Johannine Christ at this point has all the marks of irony; he is twisting the assumptions of his opponents to his own advantage. Thus, Jesus' almost parenthetical sally, "and the scripture cannot be annulled," partakes of a certain ironical ambiguity; and to treat it as if it were a plain statement of truth is perhaps to miss the cleverness of the Johannine Christ—and the point of the text.

Such, then, are the two texts cited in Article 6 of the Declaration which, at first sight, appear to support its claims for the authority of the Scriptures. On closer inspection, they are seen to have nuances which put their viability as "proof-texts" in question. But there are nine other citations; and these contain references which are even more ambiguous.

3. Deuteronomy 29:29

The secret things belong to the Lord our God, but the revealed things belong to us and to our children for ever, to observe all the words of this law.

This passage appears to identify "the revealed things" as "all the words of this law." In the context of the book of Deuteronomy itself, "all the words of this law" are *spoken* by Moses and *heard* by the people, not written and read.[12] I will admit, however, that historical-critical analysis will not let this point be pressed very far. The book of Deuteronomy, as we now have it, came into existence as a written code.[13] The phrase "the words of this law" therefore refers both to what Moses was supposed to have spoken and to the actual written text of Deuteronomy.

4. Isaiah 40:8

The grass withers, the flower fades; but the word of our God will stand forever.

5. Isaiah 55:11

So shall my word be that goes out from my mouth; it shall not return to me empty, but it shall accomplish that which I purpose, and succeed in the thing for which I sent it.

In neither of these two passages is it obvious that "the Word of God" univocally refers to a *written* word. On the contrary, "the Word" in question is identified with the Lord's own self, and thus with the personal agency and power of the Lord. This means that, in these two texts, the actual Word of God is what God's own mouth utters or speaks prior to its being written down—and indeed whether or not it is written down at all. So these two passages are not a declaration of the authority of the Scriptures; they are a declaration of the sovereignty of God, and of God's faithfulness and reliability in that sovereignty. The Word of God may be identified with God; but may we identify, simply and without remainder, the God whose Word "will stand fast for ever" with the Scriptures? We need to be careful how we answer. For if we make the latter identification, might not we be saying that there is nothing more to God—that God has no other life and existence, no further sovereignty—than what is written down in the pages of the Scriptures?

6. John 14:26

But the Advocate, the Holy Spirit, whom the Father will send in my name, will teach you everything, and remind you of all that I have said to you.

This text, part of Jesus' "final discourses" in John's Gospel, refers to what can only be called a charismatic event. It is *the Spirit* who "will remind you of all that [Jesus has] said." No mention is made of a written record; even the hint of such a thing would have undercut the point of this saying, which is to assert the living presence and intimate power of the Spirit in those who believe. To be sure, the written record is not excluded *as an instrument* of Spirit-informed remembrance. But it still requires an enormous exegetical—or rather, *eisegetical*—leap to think that this verse means the written word of the Scriptures *alone*. The letter of the text means no such thing.

7. Romans 1:16

For I am not ashamed of the gospel; it is the power of God for salvation to everyone who has faith, to the Jew first and also to the Greek.

The citation of this verse in the context of the Declaration's sixth Article presumes that we can simply identify Paul's use of the term *gospel* with the canonical New Testament. A measure of anachronism seems be at work in such a presumption and in such an identification. For there was no such thing as the canonical New Testament when Paul wrote; and "the gospel" he proceeded to summarize here in his letter to the Romans was originally and, even as he wrote, primarily a proclamation, not a document—that is, primarily *spoken* discourse. Paul committed aspects of his proclamation to writing as occasion arose; but even then, the written statements depended upon the proclaimed gospel, not vice versa. This suggests that "the gospel," the proclaiming of "the good news of Christ," is a much larger phenomenon than the written word of the Scriptures. Since Paul's day it has certainly come to include the Scriptures, but not even today can proclaiming "the Good News" be taken to refer to the Scriptures exclusively. After all, Paul was not in the business of proclaiming "God's Word written"; he was in the business of proclaiming Christ.

8. *Ephesians 1:17–19*

I pray that the God of our Lord Jesus Christ, the Father of glory, may give you a spirit of wisdom and revelation as you come to know him, so that, with the eyes of your heart enlightened, you may know what is the hope to which he has called you, what are the riches of his glorious inheritance among the saints, and what is the immeasurable greatness of his power for us who believe, according to the working of his great power.

In citing this passage, the Declaration seems to be working on the assumption that the term "revelation" in the phrase "a spirit of wisdom and revelation," like the word "gospel" in the previous citation, is synonymous with the canonical Scriptures. It is at least a question whether revelation can be simply identified with the text of the Scriptures *tout court*. One might argue that revelation, like the Word of God which "will stand for ever" (see nos. 4 and 5 above), is as much God's act of self-giving as the information that God gives in, and with, and through, the sharing of the divine Self. But I am not sure that the passage under consideration reaches into that high mystery. The author is talking about the inner illumination of believers ("with the eyes of your heart enlightened"), their subjective appropriation of the truth that God has made manifest in and through Christ. The idea involved here is in the same range as Paul's affirmations, "We have the mind of Christ" (I Cor. 2:16), and "As the truth of Christ is in me" (II Cor. 11:10). Hearing the Scriptures, reading, marking, learning, and inwardly digesting them may well be part of this spiritual process. But "the spirit of wisdom and revelation" is not the spirit of the Scriptures themselves; it is the charism, the gift, which enables believers to carry out the process, to know and understand, to own and hold fast "the truth as it is in Jesus" (Eph. 4:21). So the sense of this passage from Ephesians does not support the assumption which governs the Declaration's citation of it.

9. II Timothy 2:15

Do your best to present yourself to God as one approved by him, a worker who has no need to be ashamed, rightly explaining the word of truth.

Yet once more, the phrase "explaining the word of truth" is too ambiguous in reference to allow a simple identification with the written word of the Scriptures. It might indeed refer to the exposition of the Scriptures; but it might just as surely refer to the divine Word and its human proclamation which are the origin, rationale, and context of the canonical writings.

10. II Timothy 3:14–17

But as for you, continue in what you have learned and firmly believed, knowing from whom you learned it, and how from childhood you have known the sacred writings that are able to instruct you for salvation through faith in Christ Jesus. All scripture is inspired by God and is useful for teaching, for reproof, for correction, and for training in righteousness, so that everyone who belongs to God may be proficient, equipped for every good work.

Here is the scriptural *locus classicus* for the authority of the Scriptures. And yet it is a text that falls somewhat short of the Declaration's purpose. It says nothing about the Scriptures as *judge*; it says only that the Scriptures are "useful" (*ôphelimos*) to a leader of the church like Timothy for the purposes of building up the people of the church in the way of salvation. To be sure, the Scriptures have this *usefulness* because the writings are "inspired by God." But it still remains that they find their usefulness in the hands of bishops and deacons; the text does not accord the Scriptures an independent authority and power, as of a personal agent, to adjudicate those leaders and the church for their faithfulness to Christ's revealed truth.

11. II Peter 1:20–21

First of all you must understand this, that no prophecy of scripture is a matter of one's own interpretation, because no prophecy ever came by human will, but men and women moved by the Holy Spirit spoke from God.

This passage is somewhat convoluted. Yes, the author affirms that it was none other than the divine Spirit who enabled the prophecy recorded in the Scriptures to be *spoken* in the first place. But this affirmation is made in order to issue a warning which implies another affirmation; namely, that it is the same divine Spirit who enables "scriptural prophecy" to be interpreted. Because "prophecy of scripture" was inspired by the Spirit, the same Spirit is needed for true interpretation of that prophecy. This passage implies yet one thing more, which seems to have escaped the drafters of the Declaration: it is not the Scriptures themselves which guarantee their own truth or their right interpretation; it is the Spirit who guarantees the truth of the Scriptures and inspires the believing community to interpret them aright.

In short, the Declaration requires us to assume that a variety of crucial terms—"word," "revelation," "gospel," "word of truth"—can have no other reference but to the text of the canonical Scriptures. I have tried to make the point that we cannot assume any such thing in every instance. In some cases, identifying a term with the Scriptures smacks of anachronism; in other cases, the term is ambiguous in its reference and cannot be bound exclusively to the written text. I have to conclude that the scriptural catena subjoined to the Declaration's sixth Article does not serve the Article's purpose, much less prove the metaphor of magistracy by which it contends that "Scripture under Christ judges the church for its faithfulness to his revealed truth."

The Living Word

Speaking of that metaphor, it is interesting to note that the Declaration, in the catena subjoined to its sixth Article, does not cite two other texts in particular. The first text is John 12:48. The Johannine Christ is speaking about the rejection of his message: "The one who rejects me and does not receive my word has a judge; on the last day the word that I have spoken will serve as judge." The second text is Hebrews 4.12: "Indeed, the word of God is living and active, sharper than any two-edged sword, piercing until it divides soul from spirit, joints from marrow; it is able to judge the thoughts and intentions of the heart."

The absence of these two texts from the Declaration's catena is striking, because they are just the scriptural texts which might have supported the Declaration's metaphor of magistracy. For John 12:48 and Hebrews 4:12 are the sole scriptural texts to assert the power of the divine Word, precisely as word, to *judge*. In John 12:48, it is far from clear whether "the word that I have spoken" possesses and exercises real agency in its own right; it may have no more agency than "a stone that will make people stumble, a rock that will make them fall"[14]—that is to say, the word of Christ will be like an obstruction in the path of the unrighteous, which they cannot avoid and over which their own unrighteousness will cause them to trip. But Hebrews 4:12 is quite unambiguous. The author ascribes to the divine Word, precisely as word, all that the verb *judge* implies—the personal subject's ability to understand and to will, and to exercise discretion and agency with respect to other personal subjects.

The absence of these two texts from the sixth Article's catena might be construed as a tacit admission that citing them in this context would have pushed the Declaration's luck. For when the Johannine Christ talks of "my word," the primary reference is to the spoken word, not the written word. And when the author of the Letter to the Hebrews refers to "the word of God," he or she does not mean "God's Word *written*," but that actual "speech" by which God addresses the human community through the human agency of prophets and teachers of the faith. The latter is the Word of God in the original and primary sense; and in this primary sense the Word of God is truly "living and active." For, as I noted above when discussing Isaiah 40:8 and 55:11, this *spoken* Word of God may be identified with God's sovereign agency and even with God's own life in a way that the Scriptures, as *written* word, cannot be.

We might think that talk about God in terms of speech or living utterance is a metaphorical conceit at best or, at worst, an example of gross anthropomorphism. For language—whether it be spoken, written, iconic, or gestured—is implicated in that ontological ambiguity which Augustine of Hippo considered the fundamental limitation of created existence in general and human existence in particular, our peculiar condition of neither *altogether being* nor *altogether not being*.[15] We have being, we do indeed exist; but we do not possess and (what was crucial for Augustine) enjoy all that we are all at once. Language might be considered a principal locus as well as a major paradigm of this ambiguity. For although we can and do communicate our very selves to one another, yet our communication with each other is not immediate and instantaneous. It is constrained as well as mediated by language—or rather by the particular language, and by the particular dialect of the particular language, that we speak.

This fact of human life poses the chief obstacle to understanding the Word of God as a real event of spoken communication. In classical Christian theology, God is supposed to be "without body, parts, or passions,"[16] and for that reason is also supposed to transcend all constraints, every limitation, and any ambiguity. This means that God must also transcend, not only the particularities of human language and speech, but also the very need of language and speech altogether. Therefore, when the Scriptures identify the word of God with spoken communication, it would seem necessary to assume that they are really using a metaphor.

But is the matter so straightforward as that? Christianity is indeed a religion which confesses the transcendence of God; but it is also a religion which confesses the condescension of this same transcendent God in the person of Jesus. The dynamics of such a confession were adumbrated in the primitive Christian hymn quoted (or composed) by Paul in his Letter to the Philippians:

> Let the same mind be in you that was in Christ Jesus,
>   who, though he was in the form of God,
>   did not regard equality with God
>   as something to be exploited,
>   but emptied himself,
>   taking the form of a slave,
>   being born in human likeness.
> And being found in human form,
>   he humbled himself
>   and became obedient to the point of death
>   —even death on a cross (2:5–8).

Christ, though able to claim "equality with God" simply because his whole existence was "in the form of God," condescended to the level of the rest of humanity and even below it, to the status of a slave—which is as degrading a constraint and limitation on a person's humanity as can be. Moreover, the Pauline hymn views this kenotic condescension of Christ as voluntary, not enforced, as free, not constrained; and Christ's very freedom in enacting such a kenosis serves in the hymn to launch the paschal trajectory of the mystery.

This same understanding received another formulation in Leo the Great's famous *Tome*, the epistle he sent to Flavian of Constantinople in 449. In the fourth chapter of this statement on the christological controversy, Leo declared:

> Invisible in his own divinity, [the Son of God] became visible in our humanity; the illimitable chose to be limited; he who abides before time began to be of time; the Lord of all creation "took the form of a slave," a cover having been cast over the immensity of his majesty; the God who is free of all constraint did not disdain to be a human who is subject to constraint, and he who is deathless did not think it beneath his dignity to be under the power of death.[17]

God (or rather, in the case of the Incarnation, the Son of God) was not constrained or limited even by the principle of divine transcendence and otherness. What at first appears to be nothing more than egregious paradox, the union of two absolute ontological opposites, divinity and humanity, thus becomes an act of divine condescension which reveals the utter freedom of the "three-person'd God." And if the Incarnation reveals the unconstrained freedom of the Almighty to participate really in a condition of constraint, it also attests the whole economy whereby God has participated just as really in the realm of human discourse and "spoken a word" to communities of believers through human witnesses.

But why *speech*? In the ancient world, the world in which the Scriptures were written, there was of course no such thing as telecommunications. Speech necessarily involved the physical presence of the speaker before the one being addressed. Even now, when telecommunications have indeed become a fact of everyday life, speech still involves the actual and particular presence of one to another or others. Presence, of course, is not only relational in nature, but also relative in quality. On the one hand, when we are present somewhere, we are present in the physical sense of displacing a particular amount of space at a particular time; and this "being there" is the precondition, on the other hand, for our *presence to* another. By this I mean our attentiveness in intellectual, imaginative, and moral relation to that other person, or what is commonly called "commitment." The degree or quality of this mode of presence may vary. When conversing with someone on the telephone, for example, you may have a sense that the other person is doodling or shuffling paper while you yourself are speaking, and perhaps you do the same (however rarely and however guiltily) while another person is speaking with you. Nevertheless, you and your interlocutor not only have actual presence in relation to one another by means of voice and speech, in the sense that each of you is particularly "really there" for the other to deal with. You also have particular *presence to* each other, in the sense that each of you is actually communicating with the other. The core of the speech-event, then, is the particular presence of one to another.

If this is the case, we may have a basis for saying that the Word of God functions beyond metaphor and has its meaning in the realm of analogy, where likeness of action is founded upon a likeness of being. The Word of God, considered primarily as speech, is God's living *particular* presence to the *particular* people with whom God has chosen *particularly* to be in covenant and communion. It is this which gives the Johannine identification of the one who "was with God and is God" as the *Logos* its indispensability in trinitarian theology. For the Johannine naming of this name means that the Word who became flesh is the original of the word of God which is God's living, particular presence to the human community of Israel—and that this same Word, by the Incarnation, became the living utterance of God's presence in all the particularity of human being itself.

Given this understanding, the person and paschal history of Jesus Christ must be regarded not only as the unique embodiment and fulfilment but also as the normative definition *quoad nos* of what is meant and signified by "the Word of God." It would seem to follow that the Scriptures, being a set of texts, can be identified with and as the Word of God only in a secondary sense. For the Word of God is primarily as well as finally a person, and the agency by which that person makes God present to and a participant in the life of the people of God.

It is as this presence to the people of God which participates in their history that the Word of God constitutes both the community of Israel and, still more to the point for our purposes here, the community of the church. We are talking about a Word "living and active," possessing creative agency and exercising moral discretion. It is on this account alone that such a word, having created and constituted the people, may be said to "judge" the people for their faithfulness to the truth of the word—or rather, to One who utters the Word into our humanity and to the Word thus uttered who breathes the Spirit into the community of disciples.

The Relation between the Word of God and the Scriptures

If such is the case, what then is the relation between the primary, constitutive Word of God and its secondary form in the enscriptured word?

I have already argued on strictly theological grounds that we cannot presume a simple identity between the two, because the Word of God is primarily the living agency of God's own presence, in a way that no written text can be. But there are other grounds for questioning an identification of the Word of God with the Scriptures. The principle of the Word of God, I have argued, is that God has entered into the particularities of each language so far as to *be present* to the particular culture, society, or community for which that language is the native means of communication and discourse. But no language speaks itself, however much the particularities of its grammar and vocabulary may determine what those who speak it can say to one another and how they can say it. For the one inescapable particularity of any given language is that particular human beings speak it—and speak it to other particular human beings. Hence, to use the prophetical formula, "The word of the Lord came to me"[18]—that is, to a particular person in order to make the divine purpose or judgement known to a group within the nation or even to the entire nation. God entered the realm of human speech and discourse by calling and making specific humans the agents who utter the Word that is the divine presence to a community in its particular circumstances and historical situation.

I do not mean to suggest that this divine speech is immediate, as if God addressed Isaiah directly in fluent Hebrew or John of Patmos just as directly in somewhat less competent *koiné* Greek, such that the inspired authors were

merely secretaries or even tape-cassettes recording exactly the divine dictation. The human agency of these authors remains precisely that, the real
agency proper to human beings in particular historic circumstances. And
though we can indeed say that their proper agency was enhanced or (to use
Austin Farrer's term) supernaturalized, we may not say that it was overrid-
den, short-circuited, or suspended for the duration of the divine communication. On the contrary, a kind of dual agency is involved, God's and the human
messenger's. This duality is intimated in the first two verses of the book of
Jeremiah: "The words of Jeremiah son of Hilkiah..., to whom the word of the
Lord came in the days of King Josiah" (1:1–2). The prophet's message is at once
the Word of God and the prophet's own words. We may acknowledge that
God's agency is, in the Aristotelian terminology native to scholastic theology,
"the first cause" and the prophet's agency "the second cause." Nevertheless,
such an acknowledgement at the very least carries with it the implication that
the human agents of the Word of God were (and are yet) indeed real agents,
capable of exercising discretion with respect to the Word they receive.[19] Their
task is to interpret that Word even as they communicate it, so that the community, in all its particularities (not least its linguistic particularity), might indeed
"hear" the presence of God.

We are therefore bound to take into account the agency of those humans
who mediate the divine Word in the form of written prose and poetry. The
issue is represented at its most acute by Paul's discussion of marriage and
virginity in I Corinthians 7:

> To the married I give this command—*not I but the Lord*—that the wife
> should not separate from her husband..., and that the husband should
> not divorce his wife. To the rest I say—*I and not the Lord*—that if any
> believer has a wife who is an unbeliever, and she consents to live with
> him, he should not divorce her.... Now concerning virgins, I have no
> command of the Lord, *but I give my opinion as one who by the Lord's mercy
> is trustworthy* (7:10–12, 25).

This passage, which deals with questions of morals, is canonical Scripture. It is
therefore, by confessional definition, "God's Word written." Therefore, according to the Montreal Declaration's principles, its precepts ought to be
binding on the church. Unfortunately, Paul's precepts do funny things to the
Declaration's assertion of "family values" and, in particular, its implicit conviction that heterosexual marriage is the norm and "the call to singleness" an
exception. Paul reverses the order: virginity or (in the case of widows and
widowers) the single life ought to be regarded as the norm, he says, and
marriage ought to be regarded as a concession (I Cor. 7:1–9). Of course, the
Essentialists might point out that, on this issue, Paul is speaking on his own

authority, not the Lord's. But do the principles of the Declaration leave room for such a convenient "out"? For if we insist that this passage, being canonical Scripture, is by definition "God's Word written," are we not bound to say that the precepts Paul gives as his own opinion are really *God's* Word? In that case, Paul was lying when he asserted that he was their source—which is impossible, because God cannot lie. But if Paul was telling the truth, then his precepts are not *God's* Word—which, according to the principles of the Declaration, is also impossible, because all the Scriptures, to which this passage belongs, must be the Word of God.

The only solution to our conundrum is to acknowledge the real agency of Paul and all other authors whose writings have been incorporated into the canon of the Scriptures. We must accept the possibility that the Scriptures do not always and in all places communicate the primary Word of God which constitutes the church. It is possible that, instead, the Scriptures communicate the prophets' or apostles' secondary interpretations of that primary Word. Paul's opinion regarding the greater merit of not marrying was a consequence or conclusion he drew from the eschatological terms of the gospel he had received; he was applying the revealed Word to the particular circumstances of his own age. Are we committed to those consequences or conclusions, as if they were the primary, constitutive Word of God, when we live in different circumstances and without the same eschatological pressure? Indeed, the Declaration itself implicitly concedes the shift in circumstances and pressure when it advocates "family values." For the advocacy of such values belongs to, and seeks to perpetuate, a world order in which people "marry and are given in marriage" (Luke 20:34; cf. Matt. 22:30; Mark 12:25)—the very world order which Jesus himself as well as Paul expressly taught cannot be perpetuated because God was about to end it.

So we need to exercise care—far greater care than the Declaration acknowledges—in the use we make of the Scriptures. The canonical writings do indeed communicate the Word of God which constitutes and, yes, judges the community of the church; but not everything contained in those canonical writings does so simply and without qualification. The authors of the canonical writings exercised the agency proper to second causes in their communication of the constitutive Word of God to human communities through human words; and such agency implies that the human authors were active participants in the event, such that their communication of the divine Word involved the interpretation of that Word. Any given interpretation may be the judgement of "one who by the Lord's mercy is trustworthy"; but the truth remains that it is a human interpretation and cannot be identified with the divine Word.

Against this, someone might wish to remind me of II Timothy 3:16: "All scripture is inspired by God." Yes—but is everything in the Scriptures *equally* inspired and thus *equally* binding? The classic "test case," at least for churches of the Reformation, is the Letter of James with its criticism of Paul's teaching on justification by faith alone and its insistence on the necessity of good works. Is James's teaching as fully inspired, and thus as binding, as Paul's teaching? Luther famously answered No, dismissing James as "that epistle of straw" and even going so far as to say, "I ... refuse him a place among the writers of the true canon of my Bible."[20] In other words, Luther proposed "a canon within the canon." He was not the first, nor was he the last. Indeed, the Declaration itself implies such an intra-canonical canon by the way in which it overlooks those sayings of Jesus himself which are at variance with the supreme value it places on marriage and family.[21]

I am far from making this fact, in itself, a cause for criticism. A canon-within-the-canon is, in practice, unavoidable. For the Scriptures are neither so consistent in the theologies they present nor so evidently self-interpreting as to render the office of preacher and scholar redundant. The community of the church, under the guidance of the Holy Spirit, must exercise a prophetical judgement of its own in order to discern in the diversity of the Scriptures what is truly fundamental for communion with the triune God—and what may be negotiable because non-essential to that divine purpose. In short, the church not only acknowledges the authority of the Scriptures; it also acknowledges that some themes and texts have greater authority over others within the canon of the Scriptures. Just as the historic communities of Israel and the church exercised a judicious judgement under the guidance of the divine Spirit in canonizing certain writings, so we in our own day are called and, yes, authorized to exercise the same sort of judgement in order to discern the divine Word through the human words of the Scriptures.

The Model of the Sacraments

To discern the divine word through the human words of the Scriptures. What is this but to suggest that the Scriptures have a sacramental character? For whatever else we may do in the baptismal and eucharistic sacraments, we discern and share in the presence and action of God, Christ, and the Spirit through the actions we do with particular elements, whether water and chrism or bread and wine. In something like the same manner, I suggest, we discern and receive the presence and constitutive action of the Word of God through the writings incorporated into the canonical Scriptures. Thus, the sacramental event may provide us with a useful model by which to understand the relation between the Word of God and "God's Word written."

I should say that I adopt this model on Anglican terms, according to what the Anglican consensus has held about the sacramental event. Historical circumstance as much as theological considerations caused this consensus to focus its discussions of sacramentality on issues of eucharistic doctrine and practice; and from the Elizabethan Settlement onwards, it defined its own position by negotiating a "middle way" between positions which it perceived as extremes. On one side, the Anglican consensus repudiated the Roman Catholic dogma of transubstantiation. On the other side, it repudiated just as firmly (though generally less stridently) those types of Reformed eucharistology which were conventionally labelled "bare memorialism." The reasons why the historic Anglican consensus rejected these two options are worth exploring.

The Doctrine of Transubstantiation

The classic Anglican reasons for repudiating this doctrine were three in number: "Transubstantiation (or the change of the substance of Bread and Wine) in the Supper of the Lord ... [1] is repugnant to the plain words of Scripture, [2] overthroweth the nature of a Sacrament, and [3] hath given occasion to many superstitions."[22] My chief concern here is with the second of these three reasons, that the doctrine of transubstantiation "overthroweth the nature of a Sacrament." It was axiomatic for early Anglican divines (as for most other Reformed theologians) that one reality can signify or represent another reality only so far as it retains its own proper integrity—and, to that extent, remains *other than* the reality it represents. Just as axiomatic for these divines was the *supperliness* of the Lord's Supper. They identified the act of communion (instead of the act of consecration) as the eucharist's *raison d'être*, because it was through the eating and drinking of an actual meal that the faithful shared in the life of Jesus Christ and their souls were nourished by his Body and Blood. But if the doctrine of transubstantiation were true, the bread and wine ceased to be really such. In that case, early Anglican and Reformed divines believed, the liturgical act of communion could no longer signify the mystical event of being nourished by the Body and Blood of Christ. Hence, in their estimation, the bread and wine had to retain their integrity precisely as food—that is, precisely as creatures.

"Bare Memorialism"

If the Anglican consensus rejected transubstantiation because it "overthroweth the nature of a Sacrament," it also rejected bare memorialism because the doctrines thus labelled emptied the sacrament of any objective significance. Such theologies maintained that communion with Christ was "all in the head," a purely intellectual act by which individual believers remembered or reminded themselves of what Christ had done for them. Receiving the bread and wine thus had no real meaning or effect except as a public statement on the part of individual believers that they did indeed remember and have faith in the work of Christ accomplished once-for-all in the past.[23] In short, bare memorialism denied a real reception of Christ's Body and Blood at the communion.

According to the classical Anglican consensus, then, the sacramental model works on two principles: (1) the reality and the continuing integrity of "these thy creatures of bread and wine" precisely as signs, means, and vehicles by which God communicates salvation to human creatures; and (2) the objective reality of the salvation thus communicated, perceived and received by faith.

If we may apply this model and its two operative principles to the Scriptures, it is possible to argue that the Word of God, constitutive and saving, is indeed communicated through the writings they contain. That is to say, the Scriptures are a real sign, means, and vehicle of the divine Word which creates, constitutes, and defines the ecclesial community of the faithful. At the same time, however, the authors and their writings thus contained in the canon retain their own proper integrity as creatures—and that, with all the particularities which go along with created existence. This includes the circumstances of history, with the particular constraints of language, social and economic order, politics, and the various other issues (such as gender and sexual codes) which combine and interpenetrate these constraints. To argue that everything in the Scriptures is equally and indifferently the Word of God is, in fact, to argue for a divine inspiration which transubstantiates the inspired author, so that only the appearance of human authorship remains after its replacement (whether by conversion or annihilation) by the substance of the divine Word. Whatever other churches might maintain, this is not what Anglicans can maintain in light of the witness of their historic consensus.

Conclusion

I have argued that the Word of God does indeed constitute the church and call it into existence and, not only defines what the church is, but also makes it *be* what it is. This Word of God, however, is to be understood in its original and primary sense, as that living act of God by which God makes the divine life present to the believing community through the person of Jesus Christ by the Holy Spirit.[24] This understanding, I argued, would mean that "God's Word written" in the canonical Scriptures should be called God's Word only in a secondary sense. It is not simply synonymous with, nor does it wholly encompass or exhaust, God's Word in the primary sense.

I went on to argue that the relation between the primary Word of God and the secondary enscriptured word may be understood according to the model of the sacraments. If we pursue the argument just established, we have to say that just as "God is not bound by his sacraments," so the Word of God, in the primary and original sense of God's presence uttered into our condition, is not bound by or confined to the canonical Scriptures. The God who utters that Word, and the Word that God utters, always retain the transcendent integrity and freedom proper to the triune life. Nevertheless, following the sacramental model I proposed, we are obliged to acknowledge that the same transcendent God freely wills to condescend and participate in various levels of our condition's particularities, even to the extent that the divine person whom the evangelist calls *the* Word chose to become one of us, with all the corporeal, psychic, and social particularities which being *one* of us necessitates. God, then, works through those qualities which constitute us as creatures; and though this act involves the supernaturalizing of those qualities—so that the inspiration raises the prophets, apostles, martyrs, and confessors above their natural capacities of mind, imagination, and speech—yet these human agents are not deprived of their integrity precisely as creatures. They speak (and write) the Word of God as God enables them to do so, but they also speak (and write) as individual human beings in their particular human contexts. Just as Jeremiah spoke both his own word and "the word of the Lord [which] came in the days of King Josiah," so the writings of the canonical Scriptures communicate the Word of God through the human language, and with the human concepts and imaginations, of those who composed or edited them.

If such is the case, how is it known when a canonical writing "sacraments" the authentic Word of God and when it represents a human interpretation of that word? The answer, I suggest, lies in taking seriously the truth that the church, as the community of the faithful in communion with God through Christ, is itself inspired and "guided into all the truth" by the Holy Spirit. This inspiration of the ecclesial community has its most obvious historical instance in the process by which the consensus of the church, over several generations, established and constituted the canon of the Scriptures. Through this process, as I said, the church did not simply select and discard among the teachings of those writings already canonized, but selected and discarded among those writings whose teachings it would recognize as communicating the genuine Word of God in the first place. The situation thus becomes far more complicated than the Declaration gives any hint of recognizing. We affirm that the Word of God constitutes the church; but we must also affirm that the consensus of the church constituted, and even yet maintains, the canon of the Scriptures. It is by the consensus of the ecclesial community that we recognize and confess the writings thus canonized as attesting and communicating God's Word to the faithful, and it is on the authority of that consensus that we accept such Scriptures as constituting the Word of God which constitutes the church. In a sense, the constitutional functions of church and Scriptures exist in mutual dependence.

In any case, it is not *the Scriptures* which constitute the church; it is *the Word of God* who constitutes the church. This distinction implies a far more basic distinction between "God's Word written" and "the Word of God." We cannot resolve the constitutional character of God's Word, nor can we assert that Word's power to judge the church for its faithfulness to Christ, unless and until we deal with this distinction. In the end, I wonder whether the failure of the Essentialists to observe this distinction does not lie behind their metaphor of magistracy and thus their "attributing unto Scripture more than it can have."

Endnotes

1. Richard Hooker, *Of the Laws of Ecclesiastical Polity* II.viii.7.
2. *Ibid.*, II.1.2.
3. "The Montreal Declaration of Anglican Essentials," Article 6; in *Anglican Essentials: Reclaiming Faith within the Anglican Church of Canada*, ed. George Egerton (Toronto: Anglican Book Centre, 1995), 311. The Declaration subsequently identifies "the Anglican foundational documents" as "the Thirty-Nine Articles, the Solemn Declaration of 1893, and the 1962 Book of Common Prayer" (*Ibid.*, "The New Beginning," 314).
   Of course, the last two documents might be "foundational" for Anglicanism in Canada, but one wonders whether Anglicans from the United Kingdom and the United States of America are bound to consider them "foundational," or indeed whether the Communion as a whole would set them on a par with the historically "foundational" character of the Thirty-Nine Articles.
4. To be sure, the second paragraph makes it clear that the creeds and "the Anglican foundational documents" have no authority in themselves. What authority they have is wholly derived from the Scriptures, whose "trinitarian, Christ-centred, redemption-oriented faith" they embody. This statement is not designed to diminish or marginalize the creeds and documents in question. On the contrary, it is actually designed to guarantee their authority. The Declaration seems to be saying: "These texts must be maintained and asserted as 'Anglican essentials,' without subtraction and without addition, because no other documents embody 'the trinitarian, Christ-centred, redemption-oriented faith of the Bible' as faithfully and authentically as they do."
5. "The Montreal Declaration," Article 6, in *Anglican Essentials*, ed. Egerton, 311.
6. For example, Thomas Cranmer, *A Defence of the True and Catholic Doctrine of the Sacrament of the Body and Blood of our Saviour Christ* (London, 1550),

I.x; John Calvin, *Institutes of the Christian Religion*, IV.xvii.4–5; *The Decades of Henry Bullinger*, trans. H. I., ed. Thomas Harding, The Parker Society (Cambridge: Cambridge University Press, 1852), V.9, 462–463.

7. See Battista Mondin, *The Principle of Analogy in Protestant and Catholic Theology* (The Hague: Martinus Nijhoff, 1963), 85–102. *Similitude*, it should be noted, is not *identity*. A perfection which may be predicated of human being, for instance, can also be predicated of God only insofar as human being is "made in the image, according to the likeness" of God (Gen. 1:26). But as Thomas Aquinas pointed out (*Summa theologiae* 1.90.1), this does not mean that the human soul has the same being as God or is made from God. It means only that the spiritual basis and dimension of human being gave it a likeness to the God who "is spirit" (John 4:24). In other words, the analogy of intrinsic attribution presumes the difference between God and created human being as much as their resemblance.

8. Wilhelm Schneemelcher, "General Introduction, 2. The History of the New Testament Canon," in Edgar Hennecke, *New Testament Apocrypha*, ed. Wilhelm Schneemelcher, Eng. trans. ed. R. McL. Wilson (Philadelphia: The Westminster Press, 1963), 34ff.

9. Lawrence L. Welborn, "Clement, First Epistle of," *The Anchor Bible Dictionary*, ed. David Noel Freedman, 6 vols. (New York: Doubleday, 1992), 1:1054.

10. "But Hermas wrote the Shepherd quite lately in our time in this city of Rome.... And therefore it ought indeed to be read, but it cannot be read publicly in the Church to the people either among the prophets, whose number is settled, or among the apostles to the end of time." Hennecke-Schneemelcher (1963), 45, lines 73–80.

11. *The Articles of Religion*, VI; in *The Book of Common Prayer and Administration of the Sacraments ... according to the Use of the Anglican Church of Canada* (Toronto: Anglican Book Centre, 1962), 700–701 (italics mine); hereafter cited as "CanBCP 1962."

12. See Deuteronomy 5.1a: "Moses convened all Israel, and said to them...."

13. Moshe Weinfeld, "Deuteronomy, Book of," *Anchor Bible Dictionary* (1992), 2:174–175.

14. Romans 9:33, where Paul conflates Isaiah 8:14–15 and 28:16. Cf. Matthew 21:42–44.

15. "Et inspexi cetera infra te et vidi nec omnino esse nec omnino non esse: esse quidem, quoniam abs te sunt, non esse autem, quoniam id quod es non sunt. Id enim vere est, quod incommutabiliter manet." Augustine, *Confessions*, VII.11.17, ed. John Gibb and William Montgomery, 2nd ed. (Cambridge: Cambridge University Press, 1927), 186.

16. *The Articles of Religion*, I; in CanBCP 1962, 699.

17. "... invisibilis in suis, visibilis est factus in nostris, incomprehensibilis voluit comprehendi; ante tempora manens esse coepit ex tempore; universitatis Dominus servilem formam obumbrata maiestatis suae immensitate suscepit; impassibilis Deus non dedignatus est homo esse

passibilis et immortalis mortis legibus subiacere." Leo, *Epistola 28 ad Flavianum*, 4; in Denzinger-Schönmetzer, *Enchiridion Symbolorum, Definitionum et Declarationum de rebus fidei et morum*, 35th ed. rev. (Freiburg im Breisgau: Herder, 1973), no. 294, 103.

18. Isaiah 38:4; Jeremiah 1:4, 11, 13; 2:1; 7:1; 11:1; 13:3, 8, etc.; Ezekiel, *passim*.

19. Austin Farrer, *The Glass of Vision* (Westminster: Dacre Press, 1948), 32–34. Cf. C. H. Dodd, *The Authority of the Bible*, rev. ed. (London: Fontana Books, 1960), 39; and Karl Rahner, *Inspiration in the Bible*, Quaestiones Disputatae 1 (New York: Herder and Herder/Montreal: Palm Publishers, 1961), 12–18.

20. Martin Luther, *Preface to the Epistles of St. James and St. Jude*, vol. 2 of *The Reformation Writings of Martin Luther*, trans. Bertram Lee Woolf (London: Lutterworth Press, 1956), 307. In the Anglican tradition, "high church" principles led George Bull to essay a reconciliation of Paul and James in his *Harmonia Apostolica* (1669); but Calvinist Anglicans in his own day, and a number of evangelical divines later, found his method and arguments an unconvincing gloss on what they took to be the plain meaning of *The Articles of Religion*, X–XIV.

21. For example Matthew 10:35–38, 12:46–50, 22:23–30; Mark 3:31–35, 10:28–30, 12:18–25; Luke 8:19–20, 12:51–53, 14:26–27, 20:27–35.

22. *The Articles of Religion*, XXVIII; in CanBCP 1962, 710.

23. "Sacraments ordained of Christ be not only badges or tokens of Christian men's profession, but rather they be sure witnesses, *and effectual signs of grace....*" Articles of Religion, XXV; CanBCP 1962, 707–708 (italics added).
"Baptism is not only a sign of profession, and mark of difference, whereby Christian men are discerned from others that be not christened, but it is also a sign of Regeneration or new birth, whereby, as by an instrument, they that receive Baptism rightly are grafted into the Church; the promises of forgiveness of sin, and of our adoption to be the sons of God by the Holy Ghost, are visibly signed and sealed; faith is confirmed, and Grace increased by virtue of prayer unto God." *Ibid.*, XXVII; CanBCP 1962, 709.
"The Supper of the Lord is not only a sign of the love that Christians ought to have among themselves one to another; *but rather* is a Sacrament of our Redemption by Christ's death: insomuch that to such as rightly, worthily, and with faith, receive the same, the Bread which we break is a partaking of the Body of Christ; and likewise the Cup of Blessing is a partaking of the Blood of Christ." *Ibid.*, XVIII; CanBCP 1962, 709 (italics added).
"*Catechist.* What do you mean by this word Sacrament? *Answer.* I mean an outward and visible sign of an inward and spiritual grace, given to us by Christ himself, *as a means whereby we receive this* grace, and a pledge to assure us thereby." The Catechism; CanBCP 1962, 550 (italics added).

24. *Cf. Articles of Religion*, VII ("Of the Old Testament"); CanBCP 1962, 701.

5
Humanity Is One and History Is One
Anglican Social Thought and the Montreal Declaration of Anglican Essentials

ANDREW TAYLOR

The Question

At the present time there is controversy within the Anglican Church of Canada about the nature of the gospel and the relation between the gospel and society. Traditionalist Anglicans of different parties have united in order to stake out their understanding of the irreducible theological fundamentals. A line is being drawn within the church.

My basic argument with the Montreal Declaration of Anglican Essentials, the affirmation of Christian "essentials" issuing from the 1994 conference of the traditionalist groups, is that it is rooted in an exclusivist, christological position that appears to discern the work of God's redemptive, sanctifying grace only in Christians, and only within the community of the church. If, as I believe, the church's social teaching ultimately begins in its christology, the exclusivist model found in the Declaration is alarming. I believe such a position restricts our vision of the cosmic scope of God's redemption of the world in Christ, and logically leads to a de-valued estimate of Christ's assumed body, humankind. The dominant characterization of the human situation inevitably centres on the themes of its innate rebelliousness, lostness, and damnation,[1] rather than on the saving truth of the elevation of humankind to "new ground" in the body of "the whole Christ"—the risen Lord and the people. It is my contention that the Declaration's christological first principles do not lay a solid foundation for a radically orthodox social teaching or social activism—

that is, they do not enable us to meditate on the social dimensions of the fact of the Incarnation, what the taking of humankind into God meant and means "for the life of the world." Rather, the exclusivist christology and low theological anthropology in the Declaration erodes the basis for Christian social activism.

Is this impression of an undervaluation of the created world within the Declaration aggravated by its lack of a theological foundation that grounds the order of creation in God's grace? Is this impression exacerbated by the absence of a sacramental theology that would provide a principle for the divine transformation of the material creation—as witnessed to in the eucharistic liturgy of the Christian Offertory, Consecration, and Communion? Does the explicitly political Article 13 in the Declaration appear to be discordant with the foregoing christological articles because of a rudimentary failure to see that the Christ has taken humanity into the very life of God?

With the Cappadocian Fathers, Julian of Norwich, and F. D. Maurice, I propose an alternative theological model of humankind. This model attempts to be true to the God witnessed to in the Scriptures, to the vision of the human being accepted by the undivided catholic church, and to the Maurician Christian Socialism practically applied by the slum-priests from the second generation of the Oxford Movement—a living application of the Christian revelation that has been gloriously demonstrated from East London to Soweto over the past 125 five years.

In this chapter, I will offer the theological outline of an Anglican social teaching rooted in an inclusivist christology. I will take issue with the Declaration's timorous assertion that Christian social action is merely an integral part of our "obedience" to the gospel, arguing that the entirety of the divine revelation constituting the gospel is "social"—the social plan for the alternative society of God's future—and that Christian social action is nothing else than the faithful following of Jesus Christ to advance the common salvation of all. Prophetic Christian social thought hinges on orthodox theological anthropology, and orthodox theological anthropology is grounded in a christology that is universal in its scope. First, however, I will provide an analysis of some of the factors which have contributed to the widely felt need for the "reclaiming" of a traditionalist agenda in the church, in order to prepare the way for my primary discussion of a renewal of the theological foundations for the reinvigoration of Anglican social thought in the Canadian church.

Factors Contributing to the Traditionalist Reaction

The Reaction to Social and Ecclesial Change

If there is a tendency in some sectors of Canadian Anglicanism today to begin the proclamation of the gospel with a bleak assertion of a sinful and damned humanity, why has this preoccupation within preaching and teaching re-surfaced at this historical moment? I will outline a few of the factors that set the stage for this response.

First of all, there has been a strong reaction from different quarters against the Canadian Anglican "establishment," which is seen as downplaying sin in its radical agenda. This assessment identifies two areas of concern. There is a suspicion in the regions about the central church headquarters in Toronto. While there are, no doubt, concrete grievances against the national church, there is also a destructive scapegoating of the national headquarters at 600 Jarvis Street. There is also the old phenomenon of viewing whatever happens in the financial and cultural "metropole" as another instance of urban deca-dence, misuse of the regions' funds, and the breakdown of the traditional moral order. These reactions to the national church are part of an unfortunate if inevitable institutional conflict between the centre and the regions. At the present time, both a political and an ecclesiastical swing towards decentraliza-tion is underway in Canada, a tendency that need not signal the collapse of the Anglican witness to Christian social thought.

There is also a sentiment among conservative church persons that some of the spokespersons for the church have embraced a woolly type of theological liberalism. This view is a caricature, but may contain a corrective to certain tendencies in the contemporary church. It would appear that some church members, not all Anglican or residents of Toronto, are caught up in pop-spiritualities that downplay the historical location of the great acts of God for our redemption as spiritual paradigms of the psyche's journey toward "indi-viduation." While the subjective appropriation of the mystery of our salvation by faith and love is crucial in the development of a personal, formed faith, this tendency can also depreciate the importance of the historical reality of God's redemptive acts. Christianity is a faith grounded in the affirmation that "the Word was made flesh and dwelt among us." We confess as Lord and Christ a man who "suffered under Pontius Pilate." The unique historical claims about salvation history made by the Christian church must not be reduced to myth or archetype. The revelation of the cosmic, risen Christ must not obscure the unrepeatable nature of God's self-disclosure in Jesus.

Another trend in our formerly mainstream church is a sixties-era theologi-cal naïveté, and with it, a celebration of consumerism's successive offerings in psychology and creation spirituality. The apologists for this kind of religion do not appear to see that this type of spirituality can easily become elitist, since it is available only to middle-class people who have the privileges of leisure time, sufficient money, and privacy.

It is important to differentiate between this recreational religion of bored believers and the concurrent, yet theologically and politically distinct, faith and justice movement in the church. The preoccupation of some of the spiritualities in our culture is with psychological or spiritual self-actualization. In contrast, Christians who are active in the faith and justice movement are critical of a psychological fixation with the self and of any creation spirituality that lacks a theology of sin and a structural critique of the dominant political culture. They argue that there can be no true transformation of the self without redemption from the bondage of personal and social sin.

The attitudes of some faith and justice movement leaders to the conventional political norms of middle-class society have also unsettled and angered some church people. The middle class, the primary constituency in the Canadian Anglican Church, is becoming impatient with the plight of the poor at home and abroad, with those living on social benefits, and so on. These Anglicans do not always agree with the interpretation of "the politics of Jesus" urged by some of the bishops, and by the interchurch coalitions on social issues. Neo-conservatives in the church are put off by the strong emphasis on the church's vocation to work for peace and justice in *The Book of Alternative Services*. There is pressure from the powerful to cut costs. The economic conditions imposed by the latest crisis in world capitalism have translated into social attitudes inimical to the project of the solidarity movement in the churches.

Understandably, some politically and theologically conservative Anglicans have felt uneasy in their "radicalized" church of the 1960s, 1970s, and 1980s. The stark reality of the post–World War II erosion of our foundational constituency in traditional Protestant church-going helped pragmatists to see that change in self-definition was essential. Other influences which altered the social context in which Canadian Anglican theology was done have included the liturgical movement, the ecumenical movement, Canadian nationalism, Native land claims issues, liberation theology, the ecological and feminist movements, the charismatic renewal movement, and the new racial, cultural, and spiritual pluralism in Canadian society.

Some, but by no means all, of the political conservatives appear to regret the loss of the old model of church because it has necessarily involved a relinquishment of power and influence by the Anglican Church. Throughout the history of the tenuous Canadian experiment, the Anglican Church has been an important pillar of the dominant culture. We have very often thought of ourselves as the leading element in the community. Anglicanism tried to wield power with gentility. It is hard to face the fact that our benevolent, understated snobbery and *noblesse oblige* hurt and alienated many Canadians who lived their lives closer to society's margins. It is difficult to admit that in most places in Canada we were perceived by many on the outside as an ethnic culture religion of the dominant class—whatever else we managed to be. In any case, the bold resurgence of Anglican social thought since the 1960s, which addressed many new and difficult moral and political problems in the Canadian church context, taxed the loyalties of church people raised in an era of more stable social markers.

For some, it is difficult even now to admit the loss of this old, elitist social role. But it would be uncharitable and inaccurate to leave an impression that the unease within contemporary Canadian Anglicanism is simply a knee-jerk response by old-fashioned reactionaries. There is real upheaval within the church on many fronts.

The Reaction to Liturgical Renewal

There is a gathering storm in the church, symbolized by the divergent visions of social and spiritual reality expressed in the eucharistic rites of *The Book of Common Prayer* (BCP) and *The Book of Alternative Services* (BAS). Liturgical use and the social, sacramental, and soteriological theologies behind these very different liturgies divide church people. (It should be made clear at the outset of this discussion of the discord over the liturgy in Canadian Anglicanism that not all signatories to the Declaration hold the liturgical position of one of the sponsoring bodies of the Essentials' Conference, the Prayer Book Society. There is a plurality of views and uses regarding liturgy among the traditionalist Essentials grouping.)

Whereas it once seemed that all Anglicans, whether archbishops or lay persons, kings or commoners, were obedient to one common liturgy, *The Book of Common Prayer,* the new alternative liturgies in *The Book of Alternative Services* have been experienced by some Anglicans as an imposition, rather than as a liturgical voice that is their own.[2] They experience alienation in the sacred space and time of the liturgy. They feel unable to approach the eucharistic table without the familiar Prayer Book notes of penitence and preparation, confessing "our manifold sins and wickedness."

Anglicans with these concerns about the role of sin and repentance in worship must always be included in the dialogue about our church's ongoing liturgical transformation. However, since members of liturgical churches are deeply influenced by the rites they habitually use, and since liturgies formed in different centuries and political contexts bear the contrasting devotional emphases and social presuppositions of their eras, we must ask which modes of language, models of social values, and analogies of the divine are appropriate to *our* liturgical celebrations in *our* time and place. All liturgical forms of the Holy Eucharist are historically specific cultural products, as well as symbolic vessels for the re-enactment of the original eucharistic action. We must question whether it is good liturgical theology or good social ethics to authorize indefinitely an unrevised 1962 BCP as the official Prayer Book of the Canadian church. On the level of cultural dissonance, there is the concern that this measure can only continue to promote an anachronistic, Constantinian vision of the marriage of church and state, which glaringly contradicts our contemporary experience of life as Christian believers gathered in little flocks within a non-Christian, multi-faith, liberal-democratic state.

The worldview in the prayers of the BCP does not escape placement in a particular time, in a particular set of social relations, and in a specific political ideology. The worldview in the BCP reverences a Tudor social hierarchy of authorities set under the Almighty and the English monarch. The Prayer for the Church Militant asks God to grant these authorities direction under the Queen that they may maintain an impartial administration of God's "true religion and virtue." We see here a definite ideological bias in the political theory of the BCP. This invariable prayer within the BCP rite does not start its thinking about justice "from below," as it were, asking God to direct the struggling poor and their allies in this and other lands that they might uproot the established injustices of our fallen world order. It does not see justice as a social accomplishment that must be fought for in a class society, but as a boon to be obtained within the established social hierarchy of Her Majesty's realm, a realm placed within the larger realm of the great chain of being.

Some today find this social message attractive, *recherché* and romantic, but it is apt to transform Anglicanism into Canada's museum religion. The liturgy must bring the Christian community into an experience of that which is radically "other." However, this other must not be the ersatz otherness of an exquisite social archaism, but the authentic, radical otherness of sacramental participation in the kingdom of God.

Is Cranmerian eucharistic teaching the most appropriate basis for the Christian community's prophecy, proclamation, or service in the world in our era, fast approaching the year 2000? His Prayer of Consecration does not proclaim the fullness of the biblical account of salvation history as found in the primitive liturgies of East and West. Cranmer's eucharistic prayer is a brilliant poetic piece of great solemnity, whether all in one piece as in 1549, cut in three as in the 1552, 1559, and 1662 editions of the BCP, and to be sure, the doctrine of the Cranmerian eucharistic prayer evinces a forensic logic, as a Reformed interpretation of Anselm's feudal model of the atonement. Those members of the Anglican Church of Canada who no longer wish to be restricted to the exclusive use of the Anselmian satisfaction theory in their eucharistic celebrations, nevertheless do not want to disparage Anselm's biblical insight that it is

God who goes before us for our salvation, and who, in Jesus Christ, took on our human nature, and in the substance of our flesh, fought against and overcame sin and death. But many Anglicans who are aware of the more ancient atonement theology of the ecumenical church view Anselm's forensic and extrinsic account of justification, where God mercifully attributes a legal pardon to the human creature, as deficient because it fails to provide an account of the redeemed creature's new life in Christ. The church fathers acknowledged by both East and West taught that in the saving passion and resurrection of the Lord our common humanity was ontologically fulfilled and liberated by God, so that where death had reigned in and over us, there life was now restored.

In the fourteenth-century Western Church, dominated by the Anselmian satisfaction theology of atonement, there was a notable instance of the retrieval of the ancient theology of humanity's ontic union with the Redeemer. Julian of Norwich did not pursue to the end the forensic logic of Anselm regarding the "at-one-ment" of God and humankind. For Mother Julian, Christ does not transfer over to the church the reward he had received from the Father for his sufferings. Rather, Julian insisted, *we, the new humanity, are the reward, honour and crown given by God the Father to Jesus Christ.*[3]

The forgiveness of sin is placed by Julian within the broader frame of God's deliverance of all from death into life in Christ's resurrected humanity. In Mother Julian's insight, as in the ecumenical theology of the church fathers, Christ's combat and victory over evil and death makes us new beings enabled to lead new lives animated by the life of the Holy Spirit. The point is made by Mennonite theologian Rachel Reesor when she states: "In the end, the operative force [in Anselm's model] is not forgiveness [which must be free, not bought]; it is 'just deserts.' The main concern of the satisfaction theory is to deal with our guilt. It does not provide for any radical change in life in the future, since it does not necessarily link sanctification with salvation."[4]

The liturgically traditionalist Anglo-Catholics, who are represented in the new consortium of the right in the Anglican Church of Canada, have either rejected or failed to mention the Anglican tradition's rich heritage in the treatment of the social dimensions of sacramental theology. One thinks of the Anglican sacramental theology expressed by F. D. Maurice, Stewart Headlam, Gregory Dix, Henry de Candole, F. H. Smyth, and Kenneth Leech. Further, the liturgical conservatives of the Anglo-Catholic tradition in the Essentials grouping do not seem to have taken into account the significant renewal in the understanding of nature, grace, and salvation which took place throughout the Roman Catholic Church at Vatican II. The conciliar texts abandoned a "two planes" theology of nature and grace and asserted a unified doctrine of grace.[5]

One wonders to what extent the rejection of the "new" eucharistic rite of the BAS reflects a more fundamental rejection of its foundation; namely, a nondualistic estimation of the human body and of the material creation found in the anti-Gnostic, early Christian writers. In these early Christian writings we find creational and incarnational affirmations that support doctrines of the real presence of Christ in the eucharist, the goodness of creation, the union of matter and spirit in our sensual-spiritual embodiment, and the image of God in all people.

The Reaction to Lesbian, Gay, and Bisexual Persons

Traditionalist Christians react viscerally against the apparent immorality and decadence of the dominant, "secular" culture. Christians of a more radical political stripe should sympathize with this anguished response to the consumer culture of capitalist society, since they share the conservative's horror at the cheapening and exploitation of human life in a society enslaved by the atheistic values of "the free market." The radical Christian, with the conservative fellow-believer, will stand for collective social principles and moral commitments. However, these two agendas, when spelled out in specifics, often stand in stark opposition.

The conservatives in the Anglican Church tend to oppose women's legal right to an abortion in Canada, and a significant portion of their number are activists in this cause. Some within the evangelical-charismatic communities accept a doctrine of male "headship" over women, claiming to find this model of domination in the Scriptures. Some of the traditionalist Anglo-Catholics and evangelicals continue to deny that women can be ordained as priests and bishops. With the Christian new-right across the United States, most conservatives oppose the presence of "practicing homosexuals" in the ministry, and sometimes even in the congregation, unless they renounce their unions. Some evangelicals and charismatics even seem to believe that lesbians, bisexuals, and gay men can become heterosexuals. Radical Christians see an insidious ideological distortion in this allegedly "biblical" agenda. They believe that in the "talk" and "walk" of Jesus of Nazareth, the social meaning of the church's scapegoating of homosexuals is exposed. Conscience, informed by the Gospels, is awakened to the presence of a shameful history of violence towards lesbians, gays, and bisexuals within the church.

Radical Christians are suspicious of the Christian rightists' special preoccupation with the control of sexuality. It seems that this is decidedly not just an issue of the church's obedience to Scripture. From their perspective, this will to control all "deviance" from a "compulsory heterosexuality"[6] indicates a fundamental contempt for "the other," the stranger in our midst, who is revealed in the gospel to be our neighbour in Christ. It is necessary to take account of this psychological drive for enforcement of (heterosexual) order when discussing homosexuality within the church. Will the church have the courage to confront the politics of this will to control in its deliberations over homosexuality? Will the church repent and apologize for its history of stereotyping, abusing, persecuting, and abandoning its homosexual sisters and brothers?

The Appeal to Scripture

Behind conservative Christians' antipathy to difference and choice in human sexuality and procreation stand the critical issues of how the church receives and interprets the Scriptures, and where it locates ultimate authority for faith and morals. Most Anglicans would agree with the Declaration's assertions about the nature and role of the Bible inasmuch as they affirm that the church is a servant of the word of God in the Scriptures, is under the judgement of God as witnessed to in the Scriptures, and must hold as essential to the faith only that which may be proved from the Scriptures.

However, the Declaration begs the hermeneutical question of who interprets the Bible. In fact, the Declaration only articulates one-half of the dialectical tension that obtains between the living church and the Scriptures. It rightly presents the principle of the penultimate authority of the Bible under Christ against all church tendencies to exempt itself from the critique of idolatry contained in the written word. But having made this necessary assertion of the Protestant principle, there is something else that must be said; namely, that the written word of God is not simply equivalent to the uncreated Word of God. The Bible is an inspired book, but also a human cultural artefact. The Scriptures possess an iconic identity with the uncreated Word, but they are also only a mediation of God the Word and, as such, can also obscure the living Word "in the opaqueness of a historical word."[7]

I would appeal to church people for a candid recognition of the potential for ideological corruption of "the word of the Lord" within the scriptural traditions themselves. Scripture witnesses to the divine Word only through its human words. That is to say, Scripture is not immune to the ideological distortion that originates in the fallen world orders of history. Holy war, slavery, and the subjugation of women are not candidly denounced in Scripture. While maintaining their authoritative ultimacy under Christ in the life of the church, the sacred texts are not free from the ambiguity that characterizes all other texts. Therefore the church must not deceive itself that the Scriptures fell from heaven transparent in meaning, and therefore are self-interpreting. The church must interpret them in order to realize its own sacramental identity as the historical embodiment of the gospel, the catholic church of the ages.

Diverging Doctrines of God, Humanity, and Salvation

The Declaration's Lack of a Social and Mystical Theology

A retrieval and a contextualization of the ancient traditions of the church has taken place in the Anglican Church of Canada. This process represents a fusion of the liturgical movement and the interchurch faith and justice movement. I believe the Spirit has been speaking to the churches, and enabling the articulation of a renewed understanding of the doctrine of God—including the retrieval and contextualization of an inclusive christology—and a renewed understanding of human beings in relation to God.

The Declaration, too, is concerned with reclaiming the essentials of Christian faith for the Anglican Church in our time. Yet, in what it affirms, as well as in what it fails to affirm, the Declaration betrays what can only be described as a sectarian mindset; that is, it fails to give expression to the ancient and central teaching of catholic Christianity. Take, for example, the Declaration's implicit understanding of the human creature before God. Rather than proclaiming the solidarity of the human race in Christ, and humanity's elevation to the status of God's own children in the Incarnation, the Declaration is fixated on humanity's separation from God in intrinsic sinfulness and rebellion. Kenneth Leech points out that the great nineteenth-century Anglican theologian F. D. Maurice taught that "all human beings were created in God's image and knit together in Christ, and that baptism was the sacramental recognition and assertion of what was already in principle the case."[8] The church must begin its preaching and professing where Maurice did, telling the good news of the union of the human and the divine in Christ. Any other theological picture of humanity does not faithfully or fully render the revelation of God's graciousness to the world as given us in Christ and the catholic church.

If one begins one's theological anthropology with the assertion that the human race is sinful (save for an inchoate mention of the doctrine of Creation), one will have a theology that is in effect bipartite (Fall and Salvation), rather than tripartite (Creation, Fall, and Redemption). In fact, neither of Cranmer's two versions of his eucharistic prayer contain any offering of the gifts of creation in their benediction of God for his mighty acts for our salvation—in contrast to the old Roman canon's introductory thank-offering of the gifts of creation offered up to God, and the closing thanksgiving for the holy gifts, the "good things" God "ever creates" and gives us in Christ. To the extent that the Declaration places greater weight on a bipartite salvation-schema of Fall and Redemption, it fails to retrieve the even lineaments of primitive Christian orthodoxy. Not surprisingly, but unfortunately, this uneven theological schema marks the preaching and piety of many Canadian Anglican groupings.

The different spiritual factions whose alliance constitutes the Essentials grouping in the Canadian church have not yet articulated the essentially social and universal significance of the acts of God in Christ. I believe this undeveloped social theology is due to their minimization of the doctrine of Creation as well as to their particular, exclusivist christological model.

In Article 4 of the Declaration, the risen Christ is rightly recognized as "the architect of restored human community" but the rest of the Article makes it clear that its framers are referring *only* to the role of the risen Christ vis-a-vis Christian believers. They do not go on to state that, because our common humanity has been taken into the Godhead through the resurrection and the ascension, Christ is already, in fact, the Lord and Saviour of *all* human beings. This clearly indicates the presence of an exclusive christology, "which holds that the supernatural heals, elevates and fulfils the natural only among Christians, only in the church."[9]

It would appear that in the Declaration's view the resurrection of the Lord and the release of the Holy Spirit possess an eschatological significance only for those who have *ratified* their salvation by a penitential disposition of faith and a conceptual assent to the propositions deemed "essential" by their wing of the church (see Articles 2, 4, and 5). This sectarian mindset fails to offer any vision of the cosmic scope of God's redemption. Are the Essentials signatories concerned with the world that is not directly and technically religious? "Life in the Spirit," states Article 5, "is a supernaturalizing of our natural existence." Is there actually, as the Declaration implies, an hermetic entity called the "natural" plane for the unredeemed, and another one called the "supernatural" plane in which only the saved participate? Are the effects of grace in Christians different from the effects of grace in other human beings? Is the salvation of Jesus Christ an inclusive event which embraces the whole creation?

Consider, too, the Declaration's understanding of God. It does not appear to be grounded in a doctrine of the ultimate unknowability of the holy mystery of God. In this regard, the document would seem not to be genuinely traditional, because it does not indicate an awareness of the mystical theology of the *via negativa*, which historically has deeply influenced the Christian tradition of prayer and the church's attitude towards the knowledge of God. In this tradition, the Christian pilgrim enters the spiritual darkness, where theological self-confidence is undermined. In this graced darkness, the pilgrim sees that our conceptual knowledge of God is inadequate, and a new dimension of the holy mystery of God is perceived with the united heart and mind. Nor does the Declaration give evidence of the necessity of conflict and doubt in the life of faith. Thomas Merton wrote: "We too often forget that Christian faith is a principle of questioning and struggle before it becomes a principle of certitude and of peace.... Christianity is not merely a set of foregone conclusions. The Christian mind is a mind that risks intolerable purifications."[10]

Perhaps these crucial lacunae in the understanding of divine and human account for what appears to be the Declaration's manifestly *propositional* model of the knowledge of faith, and its apparently imperious tone towards the world. The framers and signatories of the Declaration do not appear to see, as Irenaeus did, that orthodoxy is based in paradox. The Declaration does not fathom the depths of God's descent into the human condition in order to be with us at the frontiers of existence—in risk and in self-abandonment. I miss within its Articles the insight that the cross is not only the symbol for the suffering of the incarnate God, but is also the symbol and "way" for oppressed and suffering humankind. Anglican theologian Rowan Williams writes:

> To talk of some kind of ultimate or universal orthodoxy as if it meant possessing a theoretical perspective from which the entire human world could be viewed and decisively understood, a system with pigeon holes for every person and situation ... this is in fact the ultimate ideological sclerosis—orthodoxy as a power mechanism.... The test of an orthodoxy, then, is something to do with its potential for authentic comprehensiveness.[11]

The Declaration as written does not embrace this essential comprehensiveness. One senses when reading the Declaration that one is not in the presence of a voice representing a prophetic minority, nor of a mind passionately searching for the truth, but of an intelligence with an inordinate zeal for conceptual tidiness and control. This seeming need to impose an unambiguous order on ambiguous classical texts, traditions, and confessions lends the Declaration a tinge of unpleasant pedanticism.

Christ and Human Society

Whereas the Declaration seems to view explicit profession of faith in Christ as the beginning of God's work in us, the theological anthropology suggested here sees the presence of the paschal mystery going ever *before* us. The grace of the saving passion and resurrection of Christ is present in the "secular" struggles and decisions of ordinary people, whatever their explicit faith-commitment. Christ is the fullness of the revelation of God's grace, implicit by grace in the created world, and within the very structure of the God-ward orientation of the human creature.[12]

What if human life, by virtue of God's freely bestowed grace, is itself "supernatural"? The church is bound to the sacraments, but God's span is boundless and mercifully enfolds the whole world with grace. If this is true, we will see that the whole history of humankind stands under God's forgiving love shown us in Christ. If this is true, then we have no need to create a little world of religion, but our incarnational religion and inclusive christology will create in us a reverent delight in all the events that expand and express our humanity. It will, as well, enable us to mourn for the destruction and distortion sin has introduced into God's beloved world. We will see Christ crucified, risen, and ascended in the lives of individuals, families, movements, and nations. We will celebrate the work of grace in the struggles of the poor and the oppressed to win their human dignity, and to build a participatory society.

The church must celebrate the presence of the wounded, exalted Word in every human being's unexplored, and perhaps undreamed of, orientation to God. As I have stated, I believe this recognition of the ubiquity of God the Word will attune us to the wisdom of the apophatic mystical tradition of the *via negativa*. Thomas Aquinas wrote that we know *that* God is, but not *what* God is. Behind this statement stands the mystical theology of "unknowing," which reminds us that God's being always transcends anything we can think or say about God. Living in relation with such a God puts us in a radical process of transformation, a transformation that entails struggle and doubt. This mystical theology frees us from the presumption of thinking or speaking as if we possess God because we are Christian believers. On the one hand, we "know" God as members of the church who live a life of repentance and prayer in Christ. Yet, paradoxically, as our prayer deepens into the wordless prayer of love, we know that our "knowing" is as nothing that, as yet, "we see in a glass darkly" through the mediations of analogies and words and sacraments.

If the church doesn't have a full doctrine of Creation worthy of the human nature created and assumed in the incarnate Word, what is the result? The Creation accounts in Genesis, as illuminated by Johanine teaching about God the Word and Pauline cosmic theology, speak of humankind's creation and re-creation in Christ. This is a very different theological presentation from the contempt for creation so often heard in biblicist preaching at different times of crisis in church history.

What if a new process has taken root in the created world of history through the taking of our humanity into the very being of God in the Incarnation of the Lord? What would our Christian vocation mean to us and to the world if we were to begin all our actions, reflection, praying, preaching, and teaching grounded in the fact that the divine image within humanity has been restored, and that our flesh and God's spirit are forever joined?

Many patristic authors expounded such an understanding of the dignity of the person, the flesh, and matter in their battle with the Gnostics and others; and Eastern "fathers" in particular were engaged in the explication of this theological anthropology. We are created in the image of God. God did not cease to care for us when we fell into sin, but healed and elevated our nature by the Incarnation and paschal mystery of Christ "taking manhood into God" (Athanasian Creed). Sin is not seen as natural or intrinsic to our humanity, but rather as a parasitic distortion of human creatureliness. Although marred by sin, human nature inclines to God because it has been created and restored in God's image.

Indeed, even within the significantly different mode of theological conceptualization peculiar to Western catholicism, there always remained the affirmation that the grace of God actually changes the human creature. In the scholastic phraseology, "grace perfects nature" that has been distorted by sin.

It isn't that these competing estimates of human dignity are simply a matter of theological taste or consumer preference. Bad theological anthropology is destructive of our esteem for ourselves, the creation, and others. False ideas about creation and incarnation lead to churches and Christians holding low estimates of the person—particularly women, the poor, lesbians, and gays—and low expectations for either personal or social transformation.

Distorted theology that bypasses the cosmic significance of humanity's creation and glorification in the Body of the incarnate One has often produced movements and churches and Christians which approximate the "authoritarian personality" type. It is surely no coincidence that the religious movements in North America that have been most susceptible to the neo-conservative, law-and-order, right-wing agenda have been those of the evangelical-charismatic tendencies. At the same time, there is good reason for the church to be alert to a style of authoritarian liberalism that tolerates all variants of ideas and practices except traditional ones.

It is foolishness to downplay the radical distortion introduced into the world by personal and structural sin. Some "liberal" Christian spirituality would seem to imply that, because "the Word was made flesh," therefore all that can be done in the flesh is to be recreationally "celebrated" or approved. This hedonistic, self-serving notion flies in the face of the orthodox doctrine of the Incarnation, which asserts that the flesh is *healed and elevated* in the Body of God incarnate. Christians are called to revere the dignity of the flesh. The Christian teaching on sin must be embodied, with the other elements of Christian doctrine, in liturgy, preaching, and teaching. Yet, having said that, Anglicans and other catholic Christians who believe in the world-redeeming character of a creational and incarnational faith, will insist with Irenaeus that *our* humanity, that is, *all* human flesh, has been assumed to be transformed by the Lord. This is not an "implication" of the faith; it is an intrinsic dimension of the one gospel. In the same way, there is no "social gospel" apart from this one gospel—the entire work of God for our salvation is social.

The Gospel of Salvation

If we embrace this latter aspect of the faith, we will find that it has consequences in every aspect of our social and political vision, not least for how the
church views evangelism and how it lives with other religions and cultures in
a pluralistic society. In its evangelism, an authentic Christian proclamation of
the gospel tells people the Good News of humanity's essential openness and
inclination towards God in our createdness before speaking of the havoc
wrought by the Fall and sin, and it tells of the re-creation of humanity accomplished by God in the Incarnation and the paschal mystery of Christ.

This theology understands the grace of God to be universally active and
operative. Therefore, its model of relationship between church and the broader
culture is dialogical—a respectful and serious conversation between two entities that have much to learn from each other. God sometimes addresses the
church to chastise its hard-heartedness from within the movements for justice
in the secular culture. The church must not assume that it possesses all the
answers. In its social vocation, the Christian church has too often refused to
risk the creative process of a forthright dialogue with culture, in favour of
retreat to a "fortress church" posture from which it gazes down on the world
in splendid, self-righteous isolation.

At the same time, the apologetic model I am suggesting is conscious of the
dangers that attend any approximation to culture religion. The capitulation of
cultural Protestantism to German fascism in the 1930s, and the support given
by American evangelicalism to the Reagan arms build-up and monetarist
policies of the 1980s, demonstrate that a dialectical approach is necessary.
Therefore the church's dialogue with the wider culture will take the form of a
critical dialogue, a process of mutual debate and questioning, in which the
church has from the start made clear its preferential option for the poor and the
outcast. The church must speak out of its kingdom values and sociological
analysis as an ethical voice for social justice. In this sense, it is a counter-
cultural movement.[13]

This theology of God the Word also honours other cultures' long experience of the presence of the divine because, with Irenaeus, it sees God the Word
as immanent and at home in the world, and in all the true and just activities
and struggles in human life and culture: "The only begotten Word is always
present to the human race; united and mingled with his own creation, as the
Father willed, and becoming incarnate He is Jesus Christ our Lord."[14] God is
not extrinsic to the world, nor an object of the human mind. Rather God is the
source and ground of our being. This theology of God the Word, culminating
in the Incarnation, appeals to hearers to actualize the reality of their "implicit
redemption" by an explicit profession of faith in Christ and sacramental
incorporation into the new family of the church.

In Article 13, the Declaration speaks in positive terms about the Christian
duty to act "in the cause of justice and in acts of compassion," but in the same

Article, the force of this affirmation is muted by the statement that the church needs to work out the "implications" of the Bible's teaching for the ordering of social, economic, and political life. Yet it is in the great acts of God for the salvation of the world that the social and political dimensions—not implications—of the gospel are revealed. It is in our creation as one species-being that we learn that all racism is blasphemy, and that women and men are equal co-creators with God.

St Mary's bold receptivity to God's initiative models the virtues of the age to come. In contrast to this world order's will to control and to coerce, Mary manifests the power of the spirit-born human being, a person who is so God-centred that she can *fully live out* active self-donation and cooperation: "Here am I; I am the Lord's servant; as you have spoken, so be it."

It is in Christ's proclamation of the coming kingdom of God that we learn that redemption is a social, intersubjective phenomenon, where new egalitarian power relationships obtain, and where justice and peace are manifested. God wishes to bestow the kingdom upon us so that our incompleteness will be fulfilled in the intimacy of covenant with God and with others.

In the Lord's resurrection we witness the vindication of a man who was nailed to a cross and scapegoated by the religious establishment of his nation, as well as by the world empire of his day. The dominant political and religious systems violently resisted the incarnational process and continue to do so today, through militarism, cruel austerity measures imposed on the poor nations by First World capital, and by the global promotion of an idolatrous commodity culture. In the resurrection we see, not just the resuscitation of a corpse, but the inception of a cosmic process that will renew the face of the earth and cleanse it from bondage to a fallen political and economic order.

In the outpouring of the Spirit upon the church we see the new humanity already living in the future kingdom of God. Here and now, communication is to be cleansed of its violence, and our words will no longer justify and cloak the covetousness that is killing the nations. This is where a radically traditional Christian theology and discipleship begins, but in the Declaration, the insights in Article 13 into "social action" as "an integral part of our obedience to the gospel" are not persuasively presented as an organic development of the christology in the prior Articles, but as an "implication" that has its place well down the ladder of the hierarchy of truths. In addition, it is one thing to make the modest claim that social action is an integral aspect of our "obedience to the gospel," but quite another to proclaim that *social action is an integral part of the gospel itself.*

Finally one must ask how "salvation" is understood by different parties in the church. I suspect this goes to the heart of our divisions. The theology advanced here argues for an end to the privatization of the gospel of Jesus Christ. This means an expansion of the religious vision in which most Christians were raised, or into which they were converted. We need to recover the

Bible's teaching about the social dimensions of God's salvation. What are we saved from? Into what new reality are the saved incorporated? The theology articulated in this chapter understands the salvation attested to in Scripture as a reality comprehending complete communion with God, with the creation, and with other persons in society. It rejects the idea that God wishes to fish "souls" out of the evil material world. Instead, it recognizes within God's salvation a divine passion for social solidarity. This theology rejects as a spiritualizing mystification the notion of salvation as only a post-grave union with God. In fact, this latter interpretation of God's salvation is based on a misunderstanding of the Bible, where salvation has a deeply social, "this-worldly" content in the Jewish tradition. With blessed Mary, "our sister in the struggle for survival and hope,"[15] whose total assent to God the Word brought us the dawn of God's liberating salvation, the church therefore rejoices that God

> has torn imperial powers from their thrones,
>   but the humble have been lifted high.
> The hungry he has satisfied with good things,
>   the rich sent empty away (Luke 1:52–53, NEB).

As Cyril H. Powles writes, "one important touchstone for judging where God is at work in history today will be to discover where "monarchs are being dethroned and the poor are being exalted."[16] Salvation includes, but is more than, political emancipation from unjust, unspiritual conditions.

Theological pictures of human nature that are obsessed with human sin and guilt will inevitably suffer from and transmit a low estimate of the human being. Without the balance provided by the teaching of the undivided church about the human inclination for God, the freedom of the will, and our incorporation into "the whole Christ, head and members," could it be any other way? It is certainly true that human nature remains wounded among the "regenerate," and that we must continually rejoice that we are saved entirely by God's grace. Nevertheless, catholic Christianity is marked by a deep and wise hope, one which sees the paschal mystery present wherever people transcend selfishness to act cooperatively and compassionately in the midst of hatred and despair. This Christian hope refuses to succumb to the undialectical pessimism of the Manicheans. It will not abandon the world prematurely.[17]

The Declaration's ambiguous messages on the politics of the gospel stand in stark relief beside the recent renewal of social and political theology among a significant number of the post-1970s Anglican evangelical clergy in England, many of whom trained at St John's College, Nottingham. It would also seem to have missed the renewal of social theology among Free church evangelicals such as John Howard Yoder, Ron Sider, Jim Wallis, the Sojourners community, and the signatories of "the Chicago Declaration."

The new spiritual family of the visible church is to be a sign of eschatological salvation. All people are members together of one redeemed humankind by virtue of their union with Jesus Christ, the crucified political criminal vindicated by God in the resurrection. The resurrection of the Lord is a signal of the restoration of the whole world in "the age to come." Because of this, it is wrong and misleading to divide the world into "sacred" and "secular," "natural" and "supernatural." Humanity is one and "history is one."[18] Come, Holy Spirit, creator, and renew the face of the earth. "Come, Holy Spirit, come."[19]

Endnotes

1. See John Webster, "BAS and BCP: Some Thoughts on a Theological Shift," *Thinking about The Book of Alternative Services: A Discussion Primer* (Toronto: ABC, 1993), 87–88, for a discussion of different emphases in the theologies of redemption of the BAS and BCP.
2. Of course this is not a new Anglican problem: English Catholics had a new liturgy "imposed" on them from above by Thomas Cranmer at Pentecost, 1549! Many did not quickly identify with his new rite.
3. See Joan M. Nuth, "Two Medieval Soteriologies: Anselm of Canterbury and Julian of Norwich" in *Theological Studies* 53 (1992), 611–645. Also see Julian of Norwich, *Revelations of Divine Love* (Penguin, 1966, 1974), ch. 22, 97.
4. Rachel Reesor, "Atonement: Mystery and Metaphorical Language," *The Mennonite Quarterly Review* (April 1994), 209–215, esp. 210.
5. See "Lumen Gentium" and "Gaudium et Spes" in *The Documents of Vatican II*, ed. Walter M. Abbott, S.J. (New York: Herder & Herder, 1966).
6. See Adrienne Rich, "Compulsory Heterosexuality and Lesbian Existence," *Signs* 5, no. 4 (Summer 1980), 631ff.
7. I am indebted to Leonardo Boff for his discussion of the "identity" and "non-identity" dimensions of sacramentality in *Church: Charism and Power, Liberation Theology and the Institutional Church* (New York: Crossroad, 1985), 77–79.
8. In Kenneth Leech, *True God: An Exploration in Spiritual Theology* (London: Sheldon Press, 1985), 246.
9. Gregory Baum, "For and Against John Milbank: A Contemporary Reformation Debate"(unpublished manuscript).
10. Thomas Merton, *Conjectures of a Guilty Bystander*, 1968 ed. (New York: Image Books), 1968 edition, 70.

11. See Rowan Williams' article, "What is Catholic Orthodoxy?" in *Essays Catholic and Radical*, ed. Kenneth Leech and Rowan Williams (London: The Bowerdean Press, 1983).

12. I am indebted to three theological currents in my theological anthropology, representing the Anglican, the Western, and the Eastern branches of the Christian tradition. See F. D. Maurice, *The Kingdom of Christ*, 2 vols., 1838 ed., and Kenneth Leech, *True God: An Exploration in Spiritual Theology* (London: Sheldon Press, 1985); Karl Rahner, "Current Problems in Christology," *Theological Investigations*, vol. 1 (Baltimore: Helicon, 1961), esp. 149–200, and *Foundations of Christian Faith*, trans. William V. Dycch, (New York: Crossroad, 1989), introduction and Parts 1, 2; John Meyendorf, *Byzantine Theology: Historical Trends and Doctrinal Themes* (New York: Fordham University Press, 1974, 1979), esp. ch. 10, 11, and Paulos Mar Gregorios, *Cosmic Man: The Divine Presence*, 1st Am. ed. (New York, N.Y.: Paragon House, 1988), esp. ch. 8 and "Concluding Postscript."

13. I am indebted to my teacher, Dr. Douglas John Hall, for the model of dialogue between church and society that I have presented in the foregoing paragraph, as well as for my discussion of the cross as a symbol of human existence.

14. Irenaeus, *Against Heresies*, 3.16.6, in *The Fathers Of The Primitive Church*, edited and with an introduction by Herbert A. Musurillo (Toronto: The New American Library of Canada Ltd., 1966), 139.

15. Rosemary Ruether, "Mary in U.S. Catholic Culture," *National Catholic Reporter* 31, no. 15 (February 10, 1995), 15–17.

16. Cyril H. Powles, *Interpreting the Present Time: History, Bible, and the Church's Mission Today* (Toronto: Anglican Book Centre, 1994), 45.

17. This last sentence is Dr. Douglas Hall's, as found in my class lecture notes: "Principles of Christian Theology, Part II," McGill University.

18. Gustavo Gutierrez, *A Theology of Liberation*, 15th ann. ed. (Maryknoll: Orbis Books, 1990), 86–91.

19. Litany 16, of The Holy Spirit, first petition and response, in *The Book of Alternative Services*, 123.

6
Anglicanism and the Church's Global Mission
A Critique of the Montreal Declaration of Anglican Essentials

TERRY BROWN

Introduction: Mission and Culture

With commendable faithfulness, the Montreal Declaration of Anglican Essentials affirms essential elements of Christian doctrine, worship, and ministry. However, it then interprets them in a narrow cultural and historical way that obstructs the very mission of the church that the document is trying to promote. As such, the document comes across more as a "circling of the wagons" around traditional English or Canadian *Book of Common Prayer* Anglicanism, and the way of life of those who practice it, than as an open and flexible evangelical witness to the world.

As is recognized in the Declaration and the volume *Anglican Essentials*, Anglicanism is a global phenomenon. The healthiest and fastest growing Anglican Churches are often in Africa, Asia, Latin America, and the South Pacific. Especially in recent years, this growth has often taken place with little reference to traditional Anglican formularies such as the Thirty-Nine Articles or even *The Book of Common Prayer* (BCP).

Historically, other factors have been much more significant. One has been the ability of many but, unfortunately, not all missionaries and emerging local church leaders, both lay and ordained, to bring the Good News in culturally appropriate ways to peoples oppressed within their own cultural traditions. Often this ministry has included the building of new communities of love and justice across previous cultural divides. One thinks, for example, of countless women missionaries like Hannah Riddell in Japan in her work with lepers.

The local women they trained worked (and work) in schools, hospitals, and other institutions to provide more hopeful futures for girls in patriarchal societies that often marginalize women. One also thinks of prophetic missionaries, such as John Coleridge Patteson in Melanesia, Frank Weston in Zanzibar, or Roland Allen and R. O. Hall in China; or local leaders, such as Sadhu Sundar Singh in India, Li Tim-Oi in China, or many leaders in the Anglican south today, from well-known bishops to unknown evangelists. One also thinks of religious communities with a missionary vocation, such as the Community of the Epiphany in India, the Community of the Resurrection in Southern Africa, or the Melanesian Brothers in the South Pacific.

The Anglican missionary movement was at its best when it planted the kernel of Christian faith, the love of God revealed in the life, death, and resurrection of Jesus Christ, in situations of injustice and oppression and encouraged it to grow in concrete ways, shaped by the local culture. Such evangelism was highly contextual, responding differently to each particular circumstance, but always embodying the love of Christ in the local situation. It was both personal and corporate, demanding *metanoia*, "conversion," on all levels. In Anglican missiology, the term "indigenization" is often used for this process of rooting Christianity in new cultures. (The term "inculturation" from Roman Catholic missiology is also used.) It is a process that includes the training of local leaders and the reduction of the role of the foreign missionary. The subsequent emergence of local patterns of evangelism, ministry, worship, theology, and community life has enabled the church to grow and flourish.

While early Anglican missionaries rooted their presentation of Christian life, witness, and doctrine in *The Book of Common Prayer* and traditional Anglican formularies, such as the Thirty-Nine Articles, the missionary experience has led to a reduced reliance on these historic standards. Instead there has been an increased emphasis on developing culturally relevant explanations of the merits of Christianity, more culturally appropriate forms of worship, new forms of pastoral care necessitated by new cultural patterns, and an ecumenism that, while strengthening Christian witness, has weakened institutional Anglicanism. The result is that the church has grown in directions very different from the traditions of the original missionaries. These new directions are evident in the development of local evangelism movements and religious communities in Africa, India, and the South Pacific, in the integration of indigenous understandings of the divine into Anglican consciousness, in the radical ecumenism that brought the Anglican Church in India into the United Churches of North and South India and the Anglican Church in China into the China Christian Council, and most recently, the re-thinking of pastoral practices in regard to polygamy and extra-marital sexual relations in parts of

Africa. The outcome of this growth is the strong and dynamic southern Anglicanism of today; some of it, indeed, outside the Anglican Communion.

Unfortunately, the Anglican missionary movement was not and still is not without its problems. At its worst, it was imperialistic, paternalistic, and racist. Missionaries unabashedly associated themselves with colonial political powers, seeing themselves as necessary agents, not just of evangelism, but of "English civilization." While claiming to encourage the development of local leadership, they often reserved the highest positions (the episcopate, financial administration, and the headship of institutions) for themselves, claiming that local people did not have the necessary skills to lead at this level. In some situations, and not only in Native residential schools in Canada, missionaries used their power to abuse and dominate. English colonists often worshipped in their own exclusive white parishes, consigning local Anglicans to "Native missions." Many missionaries were fundamentally suspicious of indigenization, overly attached to their own English or Canadian ecclesiastical traditions, including *The Book of Common Prayer* and the Thirty-Nine Articles, and, fearing syncretism, afraid to make the Pauline leap across cultures. Despite the success of Anglicanism in many southern situations, the colonial legacy of many Anglican missionaries remains and, indeed, in some situations continues to be practiced.

The most creative and successful Anglican mission enterprises were those that took seriously the experience of St Paul in building up the life of the Gentile church. In the first Christian century, as Gentile churches emerged, unwilling and unable to follow the Jewish law as demanded by the Judaizers within the Jewish Christian church, Paul defended the interests of the new Gentile church and in the process ensured the future of Christianity. Gentile Christians were not required to comply with Jewish rites and practices, such as circumcision and the dietary laws demanded by the Old Testament. The conflict between Paul and the Judaizers described in Paul's Epistles and Acts has become a kind of charter for the most creative and successful Anglican missionaries.

In light of the church's ambiguous missionary legacy, it is natural to ask to what extent the Montreal Declaration of Anglican Essentials is able to encourage a Christian mission that takes seriously the hard lessons of the past. Do the so-called "essentials" put forward in this document constitute the Christian kernel that, flourishing, will enrich and transform cultures, including twenty-first-century North American cultures, or does the Declaration have such Anglicizing tendencies that it discourages the growth of a healthy indigenized Christianity? I would argue that the latter is the case.

Mission and the Authority of Scripture

The root of the difficulty is the Declaration's virtually fundamentalist view of the authority of Scripture ("The church may not judge the Scriptures, selecting and discarding from among their teachings"; Article 6), and the affirmation of *The Book of Common Prayer* as a "standard" of Anglican doctrine and "norm" of Anglican worship ("The Book of Common Prayer provides a biblically grounded doctrinal standard, and should be retained as the norm for all alternative liturgies"; Article 10).

Anglicanism has historically affirmed the divine authority of Scripture, interpreted by tradition and reason. Over the past 150 years, Anglicans have come increasingly to accept the usefulness of the historical-critical method in shedding light on the textual origins of the Bible. We have also accepted the competence of modern scientific inquiry to provide us with information concerning the details of natural and cultural history. The results of these investigations have made problematic the use of Scripture as a textbook of obvious, absolute truths touching all aspects of human life.

More recently, contemporary psychological, sociological, political, and economic analyses have been brought to bear on Scripture, often with very creative results. The liberal evangelical and catholic traditions have generally accepted these interventions, sometimes selectively, as long as they did not fundamentally destroy the Christian kernel of the divine revelation of the love of God in the life, death, and resurrection of Jesus Christ. As a result, Anglicans have been able to be less than rigorous (indeed, liberating in a loving way) on issues such as slavery (Eph. 6:5–8), the Pauline submission of women to men (I Cor. 11:1–16; Eph. 5:22–24), the leadership of women in public worship (I Tim. 2:11–15), the dietary laws negotiated at the first-century Council of Jerusalem (no blood and no food that has been strangled; Acts 15:29) and, more recently, Jesus' condemnation of divorce as practiced in his society (Matt. 5:31–32, and so on). This respect for reason and human experience has also enabled Anglicans to live comfortably with the contradictory teachings of different parts of Scripture, written at different times and places by different authors.

The Declaration seems to reject this well-established Anglican respect for a critical approach to the Bible and would push us in a fundamentalist and sectarian direction. From a missiological perspective, such a nearly fundamentalist view of biblical authority is, I believe, seriously flawed. It places Anglican "renewal" in the tradition of St Paul's Judaizing opponents, trying to reassert a complete fabric of culturally bound traditional belief that is neither appropriate nor possible to maintain. This position does not take into account the great diversity, complexity, integrity, and dynamism of human cultures as seen, for example, in their different expressions of religious belief and practice, corporate and personal self-consciousness and identity, social and economic relationships, sexual mores, artistic creativity, and so on. The world's cultures, including contemporary North American cultures, present the church with many values, beliefs, and practices that the Bible does not directly address. The fatal mistake of many Anglican missionaries was to fill the void by importing an Anglicized Christianity as a substitute for encouraging the development of an indigenous Christianity from the kernel of Christian teaching. The Declaration appears to partake of this position.

Mission and the Book of Common Prayer

Similarly, the Declaration's assertion of *The Book of Common Prayer* as a "standard" of Anglican doctrine and "norm" for Anglican liturgical development presents major missiological problems.

Early Lambeth Conferences required young Anglican Churches to use *The Book of Common Prayer* as the basis for the development of their prayer books, while recognizing the need for local adaptation. For example, Resolution 8 of the first Lambeth Conference in 1867 reads:

> That, in order to the binding [*sic*] of the Churches of our colonial empire and the missionary Churches beyond them in the closest union with the Mother-Church, it is necessary that they receive and maintain without alteration the standards of faith and doctrine as now in use in that Church. That, nevertheless, each province should have the right to make such adaptations and additions to the services of the Church as its peculiar circumstances may require. Provided, that no change or addition be made inconsistent with the spirit and principles of the Book of Common Prayer, and that all such changes be liable to revision by any synod of the Anglican Communion in which the said province shall be represented.

Even at this point the Anglican bishops required adherence only to the "spirit and principles" of *The Book of Common Prayer*, not to the liturgical text.[1]

However, a number of other factors have contributed to the further enrichment of the liturgical traditions of these churches. Among these factors are the liturgical movement, both Roman Catholic and Anglican, influences from other Christian churches, and the integration of indigenous forms into the church's worship. The result has been that many, if not most, southern Anglican provinces have moved far away from *The Book of Common Prayer*. The exceptions are provinces where liturgical indigenization was not encouraged (some African provinces, many Canadian Native congregations), those that have suffered extreme isolation (Burma/Myanmar), and those where English missionaries still dominate (the Southern Cone in South America).

The same liturgical movement that came to question the theological and liturgical integrity of *The Book of Common Prayer* left its mark on southern Anglicanism.[2] Indeed, Anglicanism in mission areas was often more open to the liturgical movement because it lacked the historical baggage of the Church of England and its extensions in the English-speaking world. Sometimes liturgical revision was mild (re-ordering of the BCP after the fashion of the 1962 Holy Eucharist in *The Book of Alternative Services*), and sometimes it was much more drastic. Attempts were made (in India, Japan, Melanesia, Papua New Guinea) to incorporate the insights of the liturgical movement and to indigenize simultaneously. Liturgical change was forced upon provinces and dioceses (for example, Tanzania and Sabah) where competing Anglican evangelical and catholic missionaries worshipped in very different ways, whether from the same or different versions of the BCP. In such situations, the liturgical movement offered a welcome middle ground that enabled churches to move from partisan strife to more unified dioceses and provinces.

In India, the liturgical movement, indigenization (including liturgical usages adopted from ancient St Thomas churches of India), and the ecumenical movement came together in different proportions in successive Anglican and United Church liturgies. In the Anglican Church of Papua New Guinea, close theological and pastoral relations with the local Roman Catholic Church mean that the PNG Anglican Eucharistic rite is virtually identical to the contemporary Roman Catholic mass, though a high level of indigenization (song, dance, dress) takes place in its celebration. The Workers' Mass of the Christian Workers Fellowship in Sri Lanka (not an Anglican organization but very much shaped by the Anglican socialist tradition) includes in its catholic sacramentalism elements of Buddhism, Hinduism, and Marxism. In short, global Anglican liturgical observance has become quite diverse, though in basic structure and theology often quite similar, shaped in varying degrees by the Anglican liturgical tradition (including *The Book of Common Prayer* in its various versions), indigenization, the liturgical movement, and ecumenical relations.

Therefore, the Declaration's assertion that *The Book of Common Prayer* "provides a biblically grounded doctrinal standard" for Anglicans, that it "should be retained as the norm for all alternative liturgies" and "should not be revised in the theologically divided climate of the contemporary church" (Article 10) seems out of touch with what has happened across the Anglican Communion over the last century. The horse has already escaped from the barn. As noted above, *The Book of Common Prayer* has often been replaced by a variety of liturgies much more firmly grounded in their respective cultures, while remaining very much "under the authority of Scripture" (to quote the Declaration)—indeed, I would argue, often more under the authority of Scripture than *The Book of Common Prayer* itself.

Ironically, the Declaration echoes Resolution 36 of the 1920 Lambeth Conference. However, the Lambeth resolution comes to a very different conclusion: "While maintaining the authority of the Book of Common Prayer as the Anglican standard of doctrine and practice, we consider that liturgical uniformity should not be regarded as a necessity throughout the Churches of the Anglican Communion. The conditions of the Church in many parts of the mission field render inapplicable the retention of that Book as the one fixed liturgical model."

Later Lambeth Conferences move away from the unity in doctrine and practice provided by *The Book of Common Prayer* to the unity emerging out of Anglican and ecumenical doctrinal and liturgical studies. The 1958 Conference welcomed this development (Resolution 73) and outlined "essential" features of the Books of Common Prayer to be preserved in liturgical revision, noted "other features in these books which are effective in maintaining the traditional doctrinal emphasis and ecclesiastical culture of Anglicanism" that should also be preserved, but finally urged "that a chief aim of Prayer Book Revision should be to further that recovery of the worship of the primitive Church which was the aim of the compilers of the first Prayer Books of the Church of England" (Resolution 74).

To require Anglicans around the world to return to *The Book of Common Prayer* both as a "doctrinal standard" and a "norm for all alternative liturgies" is to turn the clock back to the last century. As noted above, southern (indeed, global) Anglicanism has developed out of obedience to Scripture and is shaped by tradition, including the historic ecumenical creeds. Anglican formularies and *The Book of Common Prayer* have also been very significant. However, still other factors have also been essential, such as indigenization in a great variety of cultures, human reason and experience (including the social sciences), nineteenth- and twentieth-century theological and liturgical scholarship, and ecumenical and interfaith experience. In short, Anglicanism has flourished because it has become very diverse in theology, worship, community life, and pastoral practice, and because it has moved away from initial efforts to impose uniformity on all Anglicans. Indeed, in many places, including Canada, this process has not gone far enough. Rather than accepting and rejoicing in this rich diversity, the Declaration seems to call Anglicans back to a kind of sixteenth-century Anglican fundamentalism in doctrine and worship.

Because of the cross-cultural mission experience, many southern Anglicans would see *The Book of Common Prayer* as a significant theological and liturgical document, a synthesis of both Catholic and Protestant theological themes and liturgical practices. However, they would also see it as quite contextual to sixteenth- and seventeenth-century England in its theological, liturgical, and political understandings. Even where the BCP continues to be used, contemporary biblical and theological scholarship, theological reflection on one's own culture and situation, the experience of life in church and society, and ecumenical relations, all provide more significant input to the shape of Christianity and the church than *The Book of Common Prayer*. The most basic "standards" of doctrine are more likely to be the Bible, the historic ecumenical creeds, the Lambeth Quadrilateral, and *developing* Anglican tradition.

Many Anglicans in the south are concerned with "Anglican identity." What does it mean to be an Anglican in Korea, Melanesia, Southern Africa, Cuba, Chile, or Jerusalem? Because of Anglicanism's unhappy colonial history, the equation of "Anglican" and "English" is usually rejected, and many southern Anglican provinces have removed "Anglican" from their names upon becoming autonomous. Southern answers to the question often mention the *via media* between Protestantism and Roman Catholicism, the liturgical tradition (including its potential for including free worship), the centrality of the eucharist in Sunday worship, the capacity to indigenize, engagement in society, respect for scholarship, inclusion in the Anglican Communion, the autonomy of Anglican provinces within the Communion, stability combined with flexibility, and unity in the midst of diversity. While *The Book of Common Prayer* has contributed much to this emerging consensus, it has been a stepping-off point rather than an ongoing point of reference. Given the context from which the Prayer Book emerged—a classist feudal conflict in a pre-colonial power—and given its theological limitations, it makes little sense to enshrine it as a "standard" of doctrine and "norm" of liturgy in the culturally diverse Anglican Communion today.

Mission and Ecumenism

In addition to indigenization, two other experiences of southern Anglicanism, namely, ecumenical and interfaith relationships, need to be brought to bear on the Declaration. Early Anglican missionaries frequently found themselves isolated in situations in which other religious traditions were dominant. In many of these situations, especially in India and China, Anglican missionaries sought support and built relations with Christians of other denominations, for survival if nothing else. New converts to Christianity were frequently puzzled by and critical of the denominational differences that the missionaries brought, rooted as they were in sixteenth-century European history. These Anglicans, both missionaries and converts, took seriously the biblical injunctions on the unity of the church, especially Jesus' High Priestly Prayer in St John's Gospel. The ecumenical movement, which eventually brought about the formation of the World Council of Churches, has one of its roots in the missionary movement.

In India and Pakistan, this deep Anglican commitment to the unity of the church resulted in the inclusion of the Anglican dioceses in new united churches, comprising Christians of Anglican, Presbyterian, Congregationalist, Methodist, Baptist, Brethren, and Disciples of Christ backgrounds. Not without some controversy, Anglicans, keeping within the guidelines of the 1888 Lambeth Quadrilateral, shed their institutional Anglican identity and joined these united churches (Church of South India in 1947; Churches of North India and Pakistan in 1970). Retention of *The Book of Common Prayer* of the previous Anglican province, the Church of India, Pakistan, Burma, and Ceylon, was not a part of the unification process. Instead, new united church liturgies emerged that drew on all the liturgical traditions represented in the new churches. The united churches in India, Pakistan, and Bangladesh continue to be in full communion with the Anglican Communion but are also very proud that they have been able to move beyond divisive denominationalism to witness to the unity of Christ's church.

In China, the 1949 Revolution placed all Christian churches on the defensive, associated as they were with centuries of Western colonial exploitation of the country. However, many Chinese Christians, including Chinese Anglicans, identified with the basic goals of the Revolution, particularly that of seeking justice for China's oppressed masses. At the same time, because of the churches' colonial roots, there was enormous pressure on all the churches to cut their foreign links. The government expelled foreign missionaries and checked the power of overseas mission boards. Eventually, Protestant Christians disbanded their denominational structures to form the Three-Self Movement (1950) and the China Christian Council (1980). Anglicans, including Anglican bishops, participated actively in this process. Anglican Bishop K. H. Ting, still president of the China Christian Council, was crucial to this process. Because of the strongly evangelical ethos of the Chinese Protestant church, only three of the four sides of the Lambeth Quadrilateral were maintained; it was not possible to continue the historic episcopate for the Three-Self Movement or the China Christian Council as a whole. However, in 1988 the Shanghai Provincial Christian Council (Anglicans were always strong in the Shanghai region) consecrated two bishops with pastoral jurisdiction in Shanghai province. Three Chinese Anglican bishops took part in this consecration. While the China Christian Council is very proud of the post-denominational character of Protestant Christianity in China, Bishop Ting and others continue to identify themselves as Anglican. In this situation, *The Book of Common Prayer* is a thing of the past, heavily associated with British colonialism, and new and more ecumenical liturgies have emerged. Theological reflection has not consisted of ongoing exegesis of *The Book of Common Prayer* but in crucial reflection on living biblical Christianity in a Marxist context.

In Anglican ecumenical relations in India, China, Kenya, Japan, Nigeria, Britain, the United States, Canada, and elsewhere over the past century, the Anglican "essentials" have been summed up in what is commonly called the Lambeth Quadrilateral. This brief summary of the four minimum Anglican requirements in faith, doctrine, sacraments, and church order in ecumenical conversations was approved by the 1888 Lambeth Conference (Resolution 11):

> The Holy Scriptures of the Old and New Testament as containing all things necessary to salvation and as being the rule and ultimate standard of faith.
> The Apostles' Creed as the baptismal symbol; and the Nicene Creed as the sufficient statement of the Christian faith.
> The two Sacraments ordained by Christ himself—Baptism and the Supper of the Lord—ministered with the unfailing use of Christ's words of institution and the elements ordained by Him.
> The historic episcopate, locally adapted in the method of its administration to the varying needs of the nations and peoples called of God into the unity of His Church.

The Lambeth Quadrilateral has been effective and workable because of its simplicity. While various Anglican provinces, dioceses, institutions, and individuals have increased or tried to increase the minimum (biblical inerrancy, additional theological credos, seven rather than two sacraments, specified liturgical forms such as *The Book of Common Prayer*, three or more orders of ministry, and so on), the simplicity of the Quadrilateral has encouraged a high degree of indigenization and diversity and made organic church unity with other denominations possible in some situations. Any *de facto* attempt to add to it, for example, by enshrining *The Book of Common Prayer* as prescriptive of Anglican doctrine as suggested by the Declaration, should be resisted. Indeed, some Anglicans, both in the north and south, feel that the Quadrilateral, especially in its third and fourth affirmations, is too restrictive. Must bread and wine always be used at the eucharist in cultures where both are foreign? Is the presence of the "historic episcopate" (a term itself subject to many interpretations) in another church always necessary for full recognition of the ministry and sacraments of that church? Recent Anglican-Lutheran dialogues have suggested otherwise. However, in general terms, the Lambeth Quadrilateral continues to offer a more than adequate summary of Anglican "essentials" for global Anglicanism and for the Anglican Church of Canada. In light of these developments, it is difficult to regard the Declaration's further theological, liturgical, and pastoral caveats as truly essential.

Mission, Evangelism, and Interfaith Cooperation

Another day-to-day reality for many southern Anglicans is interfaith relations. As with ecumenical relations, the Declaration is silent in this area. While most Christian missionaries openly sought to make converts from other faiths, today, many Christians, including Anglicans, in Asia, Africa, the Middle East, Latin America, and the South Pacific, have had to rethink this strategy. The Declaration generally assumes the uniqueness and superiority of Christianity over other religions and the need to convert adherents of other faiths to Christianity.

Unfortunately, the matter is not so simple. For many southern Anglicans, evangelization was Anglicization (that is, indigenization failed or was never attempted), and they find themselves foreigners in their own lands. Association with the colonial elite, adoption of the English life-style and language, adoption of sixteenth-century Anglican worship, and other factors such as a privileged economic position often separated (and still separate) Asian, African, and Latin American Anglicans from their fellow citizens. The problem is particularly acute in parts of Asia where Christians are a very small, middle-class minority in the midst of Buddhist, Hindu, and Islamic masses.

In these situations, many Anglicans have had to rethink their understanding of evangelism. In some places, where religious nationalism is rife, evangelization of peoples of other faiths (especially Islam and Hinduism) is illegal. In many places (for example, India and Japan) Christianity is perceived as being so Western as to make it unattractive to peoples of other faiths. Concerned for the survival of the church in the midst of persecution, and striving to put Christian values of love and justice above proselytization that is alienating and oppressive, many southern Anglicans are now responding much more empathetically to people of other faiths, especially where those people are oppressed by their own societies or religious traditions. The aim is not proselytization but the unconditional expression of Christ's love in the world.

One can cite many examples of this new direction in evangelism. In India, the majority of Christians are *dalits*, literally, "the broken people," those who were formerly known as "untouchables" or "outcasts," those outside the traditional, four-fold Hindu caste system. They, like Hindu and Sikh *dalits*, are terribly oppressed, isolated, poor, and without land or dignity. Slowly, Christian *dalits* and the church have become involved in relations of solidarity, mutual support, education, and political organization with Hindu and Sikh *dalits*. The aim has not been to proselytize Hindus (which is illegal in India anyway) but to express the love of Christ towards the poor and the oppressed. Likewise, the Diocese of Amritsar (which has Anglican Church of Canada roots) has worked hard at building relations of friendship and mutual support with the Sikh community in the Punjab with little thought of proselytization. In Sri Lanka, the Christian Workers Fellowship brings together Christians, Buddhists, Hindus, Muslims, and Marxists around a common platform of Christ's love for the poor and oppressed against those who would divide these communities for selfish political ends. Similar examples can be cited from other parts of Asia (Christian-Buddhist cooperation on democratization in

Burma/Myanmar and on work for peace in Japan), Latin America (new interest in and respect for traditional Afro-American religions in Brazil, Cuba, and Haiti, and traditional Amerind religions throughout the region), and Africa (close Christian-Muslim relations in many communities despite major conflicts in other situations).

Certainly, older models of evangelism as proselytization still exist, and newer models do not particularly discourage peoples of other faiths from becoming Christians. But the new model, which grows both out of the Christian vision of God's universal love for all peoples in Jesus Christ and southern Anglicans' experience of living in communities and families with peoples of other faiths, is also widespread. Many would argue that it is the best way forward for Christians, especially with the rise of militant religious nationalism in Islam, Hinduism, Buddhism, Sikhism, and Judaism. Should Anglicans join the fundamentalist crowd and aggressively proselytize, as some Anglican charismatics argue, or is the love of Christ better expressed in being the salt and light that keep people of different faiths in loving community with one another? This question, of course, is also one for Canada.

The Declaration, as the product of a gathering that was almost entirely white, middle class, Canadian Anglican, and in its assumption of a proselytization model of evangelism, evades many of these issues. It needs to be said that interfaith issues in the Anglican south are not the formal "interfaith dialogues" of North American or European theologians and their critics, but the day-to-day realities of life: living in a multi-faith community, subject to religious persecution, oppressed along with those of other faiths by Christian elites, respected because one is a Christian, married to a person of another faith, finding one's multi-faith community torn apart by politicians who use religious nationalism for their own ends and, finally, visited by a wealthy Western or Asian evangelist who complains because Christians have not yet converted their Hindu, Buddhist, or Muslim neighbours to Christ. Southern Anglicans are reflecting on all these experiences, and their answers may not always be those we want to hear.

Mission and Feminism

Finally, I want to reflect briefly on three other themes of the Declaration from a missiological perspective: (1) the fear of the marginalization of the biblical masculine nomenclature of the Trinity (Article 1); (2) evangelism and global mission (Articles 11 and 12); and (3) family life and sexuality (Articles 14 and 15).

Historically, part of the indigenization process has involved persons of non-Western cultures and societies translating the images and concepts of

Scripture, the historic creeds, and doctrinal formulations into their own languages. Masculine terms for God present a special problem. While masculine names for the Trinity are clearly part of the tradition—*Abba* was surely a word used by Jesus—they are not taken as definitive of God's nature. Many Asian and Pacific languages lack gendered pronouns. In these situations, Bible translators have usually used gender-neutral pronouns to refer to God rather than awkward constructions such as "one who is male," which comes across as unnecessarily masculine and patriarchal. These translations suggest that English-speaking Christians might well reflect on the limitations of their language in referring to God. Does not our English "he" for God strongly suggest "one who is male"? A good case can be made for the use in English of gender-neutral nouns and adjectives to refer to God. For example, instead of "his love" or "his wisdom," one might speak of the divine love or holy wisdom.[3]

Similarly, the Japanese liturgy has traditionally used *Ko*, the gender-neutral "Child" for "Son" rather than the gender-specific *musuko* ("son"), for cultural and aesthetic reasons. Is the male denomination of the English trinitarian formula really so significant that alternative, equally biblical formulations, should not be used or encouraged? Indeed, the work of developing new contextualizations of trinitarian theology has already been taking place for many years in many parts of the Anglican south, whether in sophisticated academic theology or in preaching in simple parishes.

One might ask if a dislike and fear of contemporary Christian feminism lies behind Article 1 of the Declaration. In their chapter in *Anglican Essentials*, "Refocusing Cross-Cultural Mission in the Anglican Church of Canada," Donald M. Lewis and Tony Tyndale label "radical feminist theology" as a piece of contemporary Western "cultural baggage":

> Today, the "cultural baggage" Western missionaries bring often reflects Western theological agendas that may have little relevance to non-Western Christians.... [O]ne might suggest that the agenda of radical feminist theology and its talk of "Sophia"-worship has more to say about Western theological confusion than it does about the non-Western churches' analyses of their own problems and need for solutions.[4]

This comment is somewhat of a confused mixture. First, it needs to be said that the Sophia or Wisdom tradition is biblical and therefore part of the tradition of all Christians. It is only appropriate that reflection on the Sophia/Wisdom tradition be shared among Christians of the north and south. In the meantime, contrary to the claim made by Lewis and Tyndale, there is not much evidence that northern Christian feminists are interested in imposing their theological agenda on the south. Indeed, the flow of Christian feminist reflection is often in the other direction, from south to north.

Christian women in the south are often forced, quite independently of any foreign Christian feminist input, to reflect on the place of the feminine in the religious traditions of their cultures and on the place of women in church and society. For example, in India, Christian theological reflection cannot avoid the presence of many female deities in Hinduism. In Korea, as in North American Native religious traditions, the shamans were often women. The place of women in these traditions has both liberating (the positive role of the feminine in creation) and oppressive (Hindu temple prostitution) elements. In the process of inculturating the Christian kernel that Jesus Christ is Good News for women, a theme from the earliest years of the missionary movement, it is only appropriate that Christian women and men in Asia, Africa, and Latin America reflect on the feminine in their own religious traditions.

It also needs to be said that all is not well with the situation of women in the church in the Anglican south. Nor can this dissatisfaction simply be blamed on "radical Western feminists." Despite years of teaching by the church, Christian women in the south often suffer terribly. One has only to sit in their kitchens and visit for a while to hear the stories. For example, in many traditional societies, there were clear divisions of work between men and women: men were warriors and hunters; women gardened, looked after the children, and cooked. With the suppression of traditional warfare and less opportunity to hunt, men have much more leisure, but women continue to work very hard. Similarly, more men than women receive the benefits of Western technology. Boys are sent to school for an education and a career; girls are kept at home to help in the house, and remain illiterate. Substance abuse and family violence also destroy the lives of women and children. Sometimes male priests and bishops are themselves part of the problem. Anglican diocesan and provincial women's programs, and women's religious communities and groups, such as the Mothers' Union, have done much to address these issues. Theological reflection, such as that on the Wisdom literature of the Bible or feminine imagery for God, that helps and encourages women in these situations to reclaim their traditional power as bearers of wisdom, should be encouraged.

Partnership in Mission

The Declaration's Article on "The Priority of Evangelism" (Article 11) is quite general and even low-key. The view of evangelism, as noted above, is largely proselytization, for example in its call "for personal training and a constant search for modes of persuasive outreach." There is no discussion of the context of evangelism nor of relationship building. There is some danger here of those being evangelized coming to feel that they are the "objects" of evangelism, a concern also often expressed by southern Anglicans.

The Article on the "Challenge of Global Mission" (Article 12) is also quite general. Again, it puts forward a proselytization model of evangelism, with the weaknesses noted above. What is striking about this Article is what is missing. For the last twenty years, the Anglican Communion has been going through a process of action and reflection on Partnership in Mission through various committees and working groups of the Anglican Consultative Council (ACC). Out of this process has come consensus on an Anglican understanding of mission. This consensus is summed up in "Ten Principles of Partnership" enunciated in 1992 in *Towards Dynamic Mission: Renewing the Church for Mission*, the Final Report of the Mission Issues and Strategy Advisory Group II of the ACC. Summarized by their titles, the Ten Principles are local initiative, mutuality, responsible stewardship, interdependence, cross-fertilization, integrity, transparency, solidarity, meeting together, and acting ecumenically.

The Declaration's Article on global mission and the interpretive essay by Lewis and Tyndale in *Anglican Essentials* (noted above) mention some of these principles, such as mutuality and cross-fertilization, and apply them positively to a proselytization model of global mission. The basic difficulty is that the Ten Principles of Partnership assume a somewhat different ecclesiology than that of the global mission theology of the Declaration. In light of the autonomy of almost all Anglican Churches in the south, the Ten Principles begin with an affirmation (Principle 1) of the primacy of the local church in the work of mission: "'The responsibility for mission in any place belongs primarily to the church in that place' (ACC II, 53). Thus the initiative for establishing a new missionary venture in any given place belongs to the local church. Partnership therefore implies respect for the authority of the local church."[5]

Northern Anglican Churches and mission agencies have for the most part accepted this principle. The Anglican Church of Canada does not send missionaries to do work in primary evangelism unless requested by the local diocese or province overseas. However, the principle is more difficult for individual Anglicans and Anglican mission agencies who regard primary evangelism on a global scale as the highest priority. Such individuals and groups sometimes decide that the local church overseas is not doing its evangelism well and send their own evangelists without asking the local church overseas, or even against its wishes. For example, some Western organizations train foreign evangelists for China, against the clear policy of the China Christian Council, which rejects foreign evangelists. Similarly, charismatic teams from the Diocese of Singapore have sometimes appeared in other Asian dioceses without the knowledge or permission of the local bishop. In India and Malaysia, local Christians have been embarrassed and endangered by visiting evangelism groups that have taken it upon themselves to do primary evangelism without consulting the local church. The Declaration's silence on this issue should be a matter of concern.

The ACC Ten Principles, while not the last word, are an attempt to move beyond paternalistic and colonial patterns of mission and evangelism. They put forward the equality of partners in the north and south. They reject a model in which one group of northern Anglicans has the truth and a group of southern Anglicans does not. They do not assume agreement between partners in the north and south but provide for clear and honest communication. While the Declaration does not in any way explicitly disagree with these Ten Principles, the overall ethos of the document—the declaration of a large number of non-negotiable Anglican "essentials" based largely on English theological, liturgical, and pastoral insights and practices—does not especially reflect the spirit of the Principles, which emphasize mutual listening and learning.

Mission and Sexuality

Many of the statements in the Declaration's Articles on "The Standards of Sexual Conduct" (Article 14) and "The Family and the Call to Singleness" (Article 15) are good: for example, the affirmation of marriage and family life, a positive view of single persons, and the condemnation of homophobia, violence, and sexist domination. However, many have felt that the Declaration's strict limitation of the expression of genital sexuality to heterosexual married couples is unnecessarily harsh, especially for persons of a homosexual orientation.

From a broad missiological perspective, it needs to be said that homosexuality is a reality, not only in European cultures, but in virtually all of the world's cultures. One has only to read anthropological literature from around the world, watch Latin-American films, or read Asian novels to realize that homosexuality is not just a Western "problem." Indeed, much non-Western experience suggests that homosexuality is not a "problem" at all but simply a reality that people live with. Some South Pacific cultures have institutionalized homosexual behaviour, for example, in the traditional *mahu*, transvestites, of Tahiti. As in Canada, homosexual relationships develop among students in theological colleges in the Philippines, Japan, and Cuba. Church partners in the Philippines have learned to live with gay priests and bishops. At least in some parts of Asia, church partners are more relaxed on these issues than we ourselves. Indeed, in many non-Western cultures, one can argue that sexuality is expressed among people of the same gender in many ways and very broadly—for example, holding hands, sleeping together, and other affectionate behaviour—and that within these deep relationships, a certain amount of homosexual activity may take place. Many people regard the moral issues involved as matters of interpersonal responsibility.

Therefore, from a broader missiological perspective, the Declaration's assertion that certain forms of sexual behaviour, namely "homosexual unions," are "intimacies contrary to God's design," comes across as a rather narrow view of the matter. It ignores the quality of the relationship of those who are sexually involved with one another. Advocates of the Declaration's position cite Scripture to support their view, but many would argue that committed, faithful relationships that have a monogamous genital homosexual expression can be defended biblically, just as the abolition of slavery was defended biblically, despite particular biblical passages to the contrary.

The global Anglican forums for the discussion of homosexual relationships have been the last two Lambeth Conferences (1978 and 1988) and meetings of the primates of the Anglican Communion. In the best Anglican tradition, the position of these bodies is moving from "heterosexuality as the scriptural norm" to a much more nuanced and open position. The 1978 Lambeth Conference (Resolution 10) asserted that "while we affirm heterosexuality as the scriptural norm, we recognize the need for deep and dispassionate study of the question of homosexuality, which would take seriously both the teaching of Scripture and the results of scientific and medical research. The Church, recognizing the need for pastoral concern for those who are homosexual, encourages dialogue with them." The 1988 Lambeth Conference (Resolution 64) reaffirmed the 1978 resolution, urged "such study and reflection to take account of biological, genetic and psychological research being undertaken by other agencies, and the socio-cultural factors that lead to the different attitudes in the provinces of our Communion," and called on each province to reassess its pastoral care of persons of homosexual orientation.

In their Pastoral Letter after their meeting in March 1995, the primates of the Anglican Communion went even further:

> Around the world serious questions relating to human sexuality are being faced by the Church. The traditional response to these questions is to affirm the moral precepts which have come down to us through the tradition of the Church. Nevertheless, we are conscious that within the Church itself there are those whose pattern of sexual expression is at variance with the received Christian moral tradition, but whose lives in other respects demonstrate the marks of genuine Christian character. The issues are deep and complex. They do not always admit of easy, instant answers. A careful process of reflecting on contemporary forms of behaviour in the light of the scriptures and the Christian moral tradition is required. We have to recognise that there are different understandings

at present among Christians of equal commitment and faith. We invite every part of the Church to face the questions about sexuality with honesty and integrity.[6]

In these resolutions and statements, we see Anglican bishops, representing their people, grappling with interpreting Scripture in light of tradition, reason, and human experience. I would argue that this is a more genuinely Christian and, indeed, Anglican process than the certainty expressed in the Declaration.

The Declaration is not very clear in its definition of "family." From a southern Anglican perspective, it would be helpful to clarify that "family" is more than the twentieth-century Western nuclear family (two parents with their children) or alternative versions of it (single parents with children). In this area, the Declaration lacks imagination. Anyone who has spent time in non-Western cultures often finds himself or herself adopted into extended families and whole communities that function as families. The Declaration's understanding of family seems to constitute a kind of sacred place apart from the world where men, women, and children can develop. While privacy and intimacy are certainly a part of family life, it has often been this narrow understanding of family that has produced narrow, dysfunctional adults, frightened of the world. The family should also be seen as an outward expression of God's love, hospitable, ministering to the world.

Conclusion

The Montreal Declaration of Anglican Essentials contains much that is good. It is an expression of the deep faith of many Canadian Anglicans. However, as an expression of Anglican "essentials," if such a thing is possible, I find it to be too fixed and detailed in its positions. Its insistence on *The Book of Common Prayer* as a "biblically grounded doctrinal standard," "the norm for all alternative liturgies," and not subject to revision reveals an Anglo-Canadian ethno-centrism that is quite unhelpful from a missiological perspective. It reflects a sectarian Canadian Anglicanism isolated from developments in the Anglican Communion over the past fifty years. While it professes much interest in evangelism, in its theological, liturgical, and pastoral positions, it excludes rather than includes. If Canadian Anglicanism has a future, it has much dying to do for new life to emerge: "What you sow does not come to life unless it dies. And as for what you sow, you do not sow the body that is to be, but a bare seed, perhaps of wheat or of some other grain. But God gives it a body as he has chosen, and to each kind of seed its own body" (I Cor. 15:36–37).

Endnotes

1. See also Lambeth Conference, 1878, Encyclical Letter 1:11–12 [Recommendation 7] and 3:2–7 [Recommendation 10]; LC, 1888, Resolution 10; LC, 1897, Resolutions 46 and 50; and LC, 1908, Resolution 24. All citations of Lambeth Conference resolutions are from *Resolutions of the Twelve Lambeth Conferences, 1867–1988*, ed. Roger Coleman (Toronto: Anglican Book Centre, 1992).
2. For further information on the liturgical movement and the development of Anglican liturgy in the twentieth century see: Donald Gray, *Earth and Altar: The Evolution of the Parish Communion in the Church of England to 1945* (Norwich: Canterbury Press, 1986) and Peter J. Jagger, *A History of the Parish and People Movement* (Leighton Buzzard, England: Faith Press, 1978). See also relevant essays in Cheslyn Jones et al., eds., *The Study of Liturgy*, rev. ed. (London: SPCK, 1993) and Stephen Sykes and John Booty, eds., *The Study of Anglicanism*, London: SPCK, 1988).
3. For a very full discussion of the relation between gendered language and the nature of the Trinity, see Elizabeth A. Johnson, *She Who Is: The Mystery of God in Feminist Theological Discourse* (New York: Crossroad, New York, 1994).
4. "Refocusing Cross-Cultural Mission in the Anglican Church of Canada," in *Anglican Essentials: Reclaiming Faith within the Anglican Church of Canada*, ed. George Egerton (Toronto: Anglican Book Centre, 1995), 276.
5. Anglican Consultative Council, *Towards Dynamic Mission: Renewing the Church for Mission*, The Final Report (London: Mission Issues and Strategy Advisory Group II [MISAG II], 1992), 25.
6. *Anglican World* (Pentecost 1995), 3.

7
Faithfulness and Change
Moments of Discontinuity in the Church's Teaching

GREGORY BAUM

This chapter, written by a Roman Catholic theologian, deals with moments of discontinuity in the development of doctrine. It raises the question as to whether the church, faithful to the gospel, can change its teaching on homosexuality. Anglican readers may find this discussion useful. Many years ago I wrote on the topic of discontinuity to interpret and justify the extraordinary change of teaching introduced by Vatican Council II in reference to Jews and Jewish religion. Since the early days, the church looked upon the Jews as a people who had lost their divine vocation and excluded themselves from the economy of salvation—the old Good Friday liturgy even referred to them as "perfidious Jews." Yet Vatican Council II, responding in faith to the Jewish Holocaust, dared to declare that since God does not repent of his promises, the Jews remain "most dear to God on account of their father," and reminded Christians that they were heirs with Jews of "a common spiritual patrimony."[1] Such moments of discontinuity, I then argued, were the work of the Holy Spirit in the Christian community.

To analyze the movement leading to doctrinal change, I wish to employ the expression "hermeneutical circle," frequently used in philosophy and introduced into theology by Juan Segundo.[2] The hermeneutical circle that interests me here is one that begins with the experience of contradiction. Yet rather than speaking in abstract fashion of the steps that constitute this circle, I shall illustrate these steps concretely with reference to the change in the church's official attitude towards the world religions. What follows is a brief summary of theological arguments elaborated by many contemporary theologians, which will illustrate their methodological approach.

Christian Openness to the World Religions

Step One: Discovering a Contradiction

The New Testament presents the faith in Jesus Christ as the only true religion. There is no other Name in which people can be saved. Christ is the one mediator between God and humans. The Jews who refuse to believe in Jesus choose to remain in their inherited religion, and in doing so, exclude themselves from divine salvation. While the writers of the New Testament had no knowledge of the great Asian religions, they do mention and reject the religious currents existing in the Roman Empire. Without faith in Christ, no one can be saved.

In relying on this teaching, Christians were unable to have respect for the great religions of the world. The church understood itself as divinely sent into this world to convert the nations to faith in Jesus Christ. God's intention for the world, the church believed, was not the flourishing of religious pluralism but the unity of the human family in the one true religion.

In this century, this understanding of the church's mission has been questioned. There have been several reasons for this. First, it is recognized today that the missionaries in the Americas, Africa, and Asia were, for the most part, supported by the empire to which they belonged. In many cases they regarded the colonial conquest of the European powers as part of divine providence, preparing the way for the church's mission. Even when the missionaries helped colonized people and softened the heavy burden imposed on them, they regarded imperial power as legitimate. Second, while the missionaries preached Jesus Christ as saviour of the world, they also brought to other continents cultural elements of Western civilization that had nothing to do with Jesus, cultural elements they regarded as superior. Missionaries tended to look down upon the religions of the colonized. Without fully recognizing it, the evangelizers were agents of empire.

Over the last fifty years, we have discovered the problematic nature of this approach. The mass murder of six million Jews summoned the church to recognize the social impact of the negative image of Jews which its own preaching had created over the centuries. Today, historians agree that the anti-Jewish prejudice present in Christian civilization explains why there was so little resistance to Hitler's ethnic anti-semitism and why even the ecclesiastical leadership tended to remain silent. The Christian church has also been forced to recognize that its role in overseas missions bears a certain responsibility for the hardship that colonialism inflicted on the people. The church offered very little resistance to the brutal conquest of the Aboriginal peoples on the continent we now call the Americas. Latin American Christians today tell us that they continue to wrestle against the patterns of dependency imposed upon them by the European church. The so-called young churches of Africa and Asia have also protested against the imperialistic presuppositions operative in the missionary enterprise: they are currently seeking a more authentic form of Christian faith.

Over the last fifty years, the Holy Spirit has taught us to take a critical look at ourselves. Self-recognition and repentance, we believe, are gifts of God. We have learned to sorrow over the great suffering inflicted upon others, especially if we share responsibility for the cause of this misery. In our day we have been willing to listen to the Spirit speaking to us through events occurring outside the church, in particular, the Universal Declaration of Human Rights made by the United Nation in 1948. In response to this declaration, the church has affirmed human rights on a theological basis and recognized that oppression and other forms of structured exclusion are against God's will and violate Christ's great commandment of love of God and neighbour. The Holy Spirit has forced Christians to acknowledge the contradiction between the church's teaching on mission and the lack of respect for other people's religion, and the tragic historical consequences of this attitude, violating as it does the great commandment of love. I call this "the contradiction between doctrine and love." Can the church go on denigrating Jewish religion after the Holocaust? Not if we want to be disciples of Jesus and imitate his love.

Contradiction, as I said earlier, is the starting point of the hermeneutical circle.

Step Two: The Root Cause

The next step of this hermeneutical circle is the search for the root cause of the church's teaching that has led to the contradiction of love. I have already indicated that the cause is the christology presupposed by the church's exclusionary thinking. Concentrating on the New Testament passages which proclaim that apart from Jesus there is no salvation, the church tended to divide the world into Christians and non-Christians, produced the hostile logic of "us" and "them," and generated a discourse of exclusion that designated certain groups of people as marginal and inferior. The church believed it was being faithful to the gospel when it denigrated Judaism and the other world religions, when it praised Christian cultures as superior to others, without noticing the social and political consequences of these attitudes. But does the Bible commit us to this exclusivist christology?

Step Three: Re-reading the Scriptures

This takes us to the third step of the hermeneutical circle, which consists of re-reading the Scriptures in the hope of finding hints that may help us resolve the contradiction. In the present case, we re-read Scripture to find biblical themes announcing the universality of God's mercy. In the Old Testament, we listen to the story of God's covenant with humanity promised to Noah, the psalms that speak of God's action in the world as creator and redeemer, and the book of Jonah that challenges the parochial understanding of God's mercy entertained by many Israelites. The message is that God's saving love reaches out to the whole of humanity. In the New Testament we pay special attention to St Paul's proclamation of the cosmic Christ in whom the whole of creation has been reconciled, and to the prologue of the Fourth Gospel according to which God's Word enlightens every human being born into this world. In these passages, human beings are understood as standing no longer under the sign of Adam, as subject to sin, but now under the sign of Christ, as sinners subject to grace. The Scriptures, we conclude, provide passages that announce the universality of God's redemptive will.

While the exclusivist christology has been dominant in the church's tradition, there also existed a minority current, an inclusivist christology articulated by the Alexandrian theologians of the third century, remembered in the entire Eastern tradition, accepted by Thomas Aquinas in the Western Middle Ages, endorsed by Frederick Maurice and other Anglican divines in the nineteenth century, and further developed by Karl Rahner and Henri de Lubac in the twentieth.[3]

The third step reveals that Scripture and tradition are more open and more flexible than the customary teaching on "no salvation outside the church" suggests. Divine grace is mediated beyond the church in the wisdom of the ages and in cultures of cooperation and solidarity. But are we faithful to Jesus Christ when we seek the presence of God in other religious traditions? This takes us to the next step.

Step Four: Christian Experience

The fourth step of the hermeneutical circle is critical reflection on contemporary Christian experience. We are willing to listen to the testimony of Christians living among Hindus, Buddhists, or members of other religions, who have experienced a strong spiritual bond with these "outsiders." These Christian experiences are well documented in the literature.[4] We also have the testimony of Christians who have felt a spiritual union with Jewish believers. In these religious experiences, the Holy Spirit confirms the new openness of the church to other religions.

Step Five: A Systematic Theology

The fifth step is the development of a systematic theology that integrates the new insight into the whole of Christian doctrine and thus prepares for the change of the church's official teaching. In the case under consideration, this task has been performed in more than one theological synthesis. Well known among them is the Logos-christology, hinted at in the Fourth Gospel, proposed by certain ancient writers, and fully developed by Karl Rahner and other contemporary theologians, according to which the new covenant has revealed the saving presence of God's Word (incarnate in Jesus Christ) in the whole of creation, mediated in a hidden way in all cultures and religions, and addressing people everywhere in their moral conscience. Logos-christology sees the church as the one and only community where the mystery of redemption, secretly operative in the universe, is revealed, proclaimed, and celebrated, and explicitly summons the faithful to become disciples of Christ. Since this inclusivist christology protects the identity of the church and its members, it has been widely adopted by Catholic and Protestant theologians and greatly influenced the teaching of Vatican Council II. Because of Christ's victory on the cross and the unity of the human family, the Council affirms that every human being, in a manner known only to God, is offered a share in the mystery of Christ's death and resurrection.[5]

Let me recall the five steps of the hermeneutical circle:

1. The discovery of a contradiction between doctrine and love.
2. The search for the root of this contradiction.
3. The re-reading of Scripture and tradition to find hints for resolving this contradiction.
4. A turn to Christian experience as experiential verification of the new perspective.
5. The development of a systematic theology capable of overcoming the contradiction.

These steps constitute a circle because subsequent experiences in the life of the church may again raise uncomfortable questions and demand critical self-reflection. Since the divine Spirit, as we have seen, is operative in steps 1 to 4, we may call this Spirit the interrupting voice in the church, provoking at certain times moments of discontinuity in the church's teaching.

The issue that interests me here is whether the hermeneutical circle lends itself to encouraging the church to change its teaching on homosexuality. Again, I can only offer a summary of the argument, even though extended treatment would be called for.

The Church's Openness to Homosexual Love

Step One

When tens of thousands of homosexuals were put into concentration camps in Nazi Germany, the world did not cry out against this brutality. As the Christian church remained silent in regard to the elimination of the Jews, so it uttered no word to protect homosexuals from a similar fate. Even after the war, when those who had survived the camps returned to their towns and villages, they continued to be regarded as criminals. In subsequent years the historians of the horrors of the Nazi regime rarely mentioned the massive crime against homosexuals. Why this indifference to murder? What is it in our culture that has made us so hardhearted in the face of the suffering of certain groups? In this case it is undoubtedly due to the church's teaching that homosexuality is a perversion, a sin against nature, a manifestation of evil. Even though Jesus summons us to be in solidarity with the despised, the vulnerable and "the least of them," we are ashamed to be seen in public as friends and supporters of gays and lesbians and to defend their dignity and human rights. The murders of homosexuals on our streets accuse us of a certain complicity, just as the violent manifestations of anti-semitism do. An increasing number of Christians see here a contradiction between doctrine and love.

Step Two

What is the root of the contradiction between doctrine and love? Since the Old Testament was composed in an intensely patriarchal society, surrounded by tribes practicing nature religions that included sexual acts in public worship, the Old Testament insisted that man was the head of the family, that sexual life was restricted to marriage, and that sexuality was not mystical but natural, destined like animal sexuality, towards procreation. In this context, homosexual relations were strictly forbidden. Some exegetes believe that the condemnation of homosexual practices in Leviticus was aimed especially at sexual acts performed as part of pagan worship.

Jesus condemned adultery, but apart from this had nothing to say about sexuality. The moral corruption of the Roman Empire prompted the Apostle Paul to reaffirm the biblical tradition, restrict sexual practice to the married state, insist on man as the head of the family, and vehemently reject homosexual practices. All this is well known.[6]

Traditional Christian teaching has confined sexual practice to married life. While in many periods of history heterosexual transgressions, such as prostitution, were tolerated in Christian societies, homosexual relations among men were judged with much greater severity. Not only did male homosexual practices violate the recognized sexual norms, they also debased the very image of the man in patriarchal society. Christian teaching fostered the idea that homosexual relations were foul and perverted, deserving of contempt and punishment on the part of society.[7]

Step Three

Where does the re-reading of Scripture and tradition take us? In the Bible we find only a single hint that fosters a more open attitude towards human sexuality and that might help us to resolve the contradiction between doctrine and love. I am referring to the Song of Songs, the poetic book of the Old Testament that celebrates the ecstasy of erotic love between a man and a woman, without any reference to marriage and procreation. This book embarrassed the rabbis and, centuries later, Christian teachers. In the Catholic tradition, the Song of Songs was interpreted as an imaginative parable of divine love, the love between God and humans, even though the book makes no reference to this. By its detailed description of the beauty, strength, and delight of the lovers, the Song of Songs shows that erotic love transforms ordinary life into the extraordinary and thus brings to light a hidden dimension of God's creation. In my opinion, the message of the Song of Songs stands in judgement over traditional Christian teaching that tended to instrumentalize sexuality and thus relate it too closely to sexuality in animals. This biblical book encourages the church to move towards a more open approach to human sexuality.

The inadequacy of the church's traditional teaching is not only derived from the lack of appreciation of the role played by erotic love in God's creation; it is also due to a lack of attention of what goes on between husband and wife in married life. Since, according to traditional teaching, sexual relations are ethically acceptable only in married life and always reprehensible outside of marriage, this teaching provided no ethical norms for sexual love within marriage. It created the impression that, within marriage, the husband could do with his wife what he wished, that he had authority and she had to obey. Theologians used to say that wives were obliged to pay their marriage debt.

Today Christians find traditional sexual teaching too lax in regard to married love. They argue that, in the sexual exchange, the husband must respect his wife, please her, honour her wishes, and do nothing against her will. What makes sexual love ethical is mutuality. This principle was ignored by the church's traditional teaching. I shall return to this topic further on.

When we study the church's teaching on homosexual relations, we discover that homosexual acts were always regarded as unnatural behaviour, worthy of condemnation. The idea behind this was that every human being was by nature heterosexual and that homosexual acts were therefore irrational and arbitrary. Until the end of the nineteenth century, people did not recognize the existence of homosexual human beings; that is to say, human beings whose erotic, psycho-physical orientation was towards members of the same sex. Over the last one hundred years, courageous men, despised and sometimes persecuted by society, fought for public recognition, eventually to be inscribed in the law, that there existed a minority of men and women whose essential life-orientation was towards homosexual love.

This was new. This was something the biblical tradition did not know. The biblical condemnations of homosexual acts retain their full validity when these acts are committed by heterosexual men, who in the search for greater pleasure engage in sexual experiments with other men. But they have nothing to say to homosexual men who seek spiritual guidance.

The recognition of the homosexual life-orientation is recent. Even the Roman Catholic Church, known for its conservative stance on matters sexual, has acknowledged the homosexual condition as morally neutral and registers no objection against same-sex love as long as it is chaste.[8] What is still condemned is the sexual expression of homosexual love. Why? First, because according to Roman Catholic teaching sexual acts are ethically acceptable only in marriage and then only if they remain open to conception—a position not accepted by the majority of North American Roman Catholics. The second reason is that, according to Roman Catholic teaching, the homosexual condition, while not a moral evil, is an ontic evil, a defect of nature, more wounding than being blind or deaf-mute. Homosexuals are thought to be damaged human beings. While recent Vatican pronouncements defend the human rights of homosexuals and deplore the discrimination and violence to which they are often exposed, these pronouncements are, in my opinion, quite hypocritical since by designating homosexuals as inferior by nature, they strengthen the traditional cultural forces that produce discrimination and violence against these innocent men and women.

If it is true that some people are by nature oriented towards same-sex love, if in other words people do not choose to be gay but discover their homosexual condition as they grow up, often struggling against it until they learn to accept themselves, then the question arises as to how they should live. How should they live as Christians? This takes us to the fourth step of the hermeneutical circle, focusing on Christian experience.

What have we learned in the third step? First, that one biblical book encourages us to move beyond church teaching, exploring the meaning and power of erotic love in God's creation. Second, that traditional sexual ethics is inadequate because it neglected the principle of mutuality; and third, that the human family created by God is made up of a majority of straights, accompanied by a minority of gays.

Step Four

For the first time in Western history, we have today an extended literature written by homosexual men and women in which they reveal their own self-understanding, their experiences, struggles, sufferings, aspirations, and other contours of their inner life. Today we have books, collections of essays, articles, and other testimonies in which gay and lesbian Christians speak to us of their religious experience and tell us what being a follower of Jesus means to them.[9]

What we learn from their testimonies is that, according to their experience, homosexual love can be integrated into the Christian way of life. We are told that, for many of these Christians, it was faith, faith in God, that empowered them to be reconciled to their homosexuality and to accept their same-sex orientation as a gift from the Creator. In this literature, we read that these Christians listen to the gospel, search for spiritual wisdom, explore the meaning of same-sex love and the obligations consequent upon it, and try (as do heterosexuals) to formulate guidelines that distinguish ethical from unethical sexual relations.

According to Roman Catholic theologian John Coleman,[10] with whom I am in full agreement, an ethico-theological evaluation of homosexual love deserves attention only if this self-reflective literature has been taken seriously. Theological research must take Christian experience into consideration. Let me add that this consideration is totally absent in the negative judgement pronounced by the Vatican on the practice of homosexual love.

Step Five

Have we reached a stage where the development of a systematic theology can resolve the contradiction between doctrine and love? In other words, is it possible to develop a theology of homosexuality that does not create contempt for innocent people and generate hatred, discrimination, and violence? We have been encouraged by one biblical book to be open to the meaning of sexual love beyond its role in human procreation. We have recognized the action of the Spirit in the church: making Christians anguish over the contradiction between doctrine and love, enabling them to assume responsibility for and repent of the damaging consequences of church teaching, strengthening them in the painful task of critically reviewing their own tradition, and generating religious experiences among gay and lesbian Christians that affirm their identity and guide them in their search for wisdom and holiness.

The important task now is to develop a systematic theology of sexuality—and of homosexuality in particular—that does not spread contempt. A second requirement of such a theology is that it clearly acknowledge the sharp line drawn by the gospel across people's sexual practices, enabling them to distinguish actions that promote the good from those that undermine and destroy it, thus saving Christians from the commodification of sexuality produced by contemporary, hedonistic culture.

This is not the place to develop a consistent theology of human sexuality that also leaves room for homosexual love. Still, following the German Roman Catholic theologian Stephan Pfürtner, I wish to propose the theological thesis that *"every person is entitled to sexual happiness within the bounds of love, truth and justice."* What does this sentence mean?

By "love" I mean affection and tenderness, respect, mutuality, willing the good of the other, and the absence of exploitation. I have already mentioned that mutuality in sexual relations is a principle that has come to the fore only recently, offering a stricter norm for married love than the church's traditional teaching. Mutuality, non-exploitation, and fostering the good of the other also exclude sexual relations between unequals: doctors with their patients, teachers with their students, adults with adolescents, and so forth. Also excluded are recreational sex or sexual action with another simply in search of one's own pleasure. Seen in this perspective, sexual love always includes a dimension of selflessness, an overriding concern for the happiness of the other, and, if need be, the readiness to make sacrifices for the other's well-being. This idea of love in sexual relations reaches its intrinsic perfection in married life where it creates a lasting union over time and generates children to be loved, cared for, educated, and sent into the world.

By "truth" in the above thesis, I refer to the ongoing self-criticism needed in all human engagements, and especially in sexual relations. According to Freud, destructive drives are often linked to people's sexual desires, and sexual exchanges even in married life are often hidden games where men triumph over women or women cut men down to size. Truth demands that people critically examine their sexual involvement, probe the quality of their love, and humbly acknowledge, if need be, the exploitive dimension in their sexual relation. Since the ethical quality of sexual life depends on the good it creates or the good it destroys, heterosexuals and homosexuals need an abiding dedication to truth in order to detect signs of encouragement or signs of warning in their lives. In theology, detecting these signs is called the discernment of the Spirit.

By "justice" in the above thesis, I refer to the social dimension of sexual love. What is its effect upon others and upon society? People will not want to seek their sexual happiness in mutual love if this involves being unjust to others: the children, the family, or the community. What this means in concrete terms must be decided in the context of the particular culture in which these men and women live. Does divorce unjustly damage the cohesiveness of a traditional society? Is a husband who leaves his wife unjust to the children? Does a priest or minister who engages in a non-conventional sexual relation betray his congregation? These are the kind of questions that must be asked. More than that, the reference to justice calls to mind that the love between two people, even when it is generous and selfless, can create mutual self-absorption, "un égoisme à deux," an indifference to society, a neglect of political responsibility and a non-involvement in urgent matters of social justice. Justice relates sexual life to society.

These brief reflections reveal that the above-mentioned theological thesis on sexual ethics does draw a sharp line, guided by the gospel, across the sexual condition of humanity, distinguishing between good and evil. At the same time, it delivers Christian teaching from the rhetoric of exclusion that generates contempt for homosexuals, legitimates discrimination, and in the long run, kills.

What this thesis implies in detail for homosexual relations I do not know. From reading the literature, I have the impression that gay and lesbian Christians are not yet ready to formulate a set of rules to guide them in their love relations. Relying on the Spirit, they want to live their lives courageously, possibly walking a road as yet untravelled by others, always ready to test the impact of their relationship on their partner and on themselves—whether it fosters the good or undermines it, whether it opens or closes the heart in regard to other people, whether it generates peace or anger, whether it distracts them from God or calls for thanksgiving.

Conclusion

Following a doctrinal development, moved by the Spirit, seeking to overcome the contradiction between doctrine and love of neighbour, the Roman Catholic Church has changed its official teaching on a number of important issues. I mentioned in particular its teaching on Judaism and the world religions. Similar changes have occurred in the Anglican Churches. This process, we noted, was not inspired by the cowardly wish of Christians to become conformed to this world. We saw that the development involved specifically spiritual moments, grace-filled events, such as the church's repentance over aspects of its past life, a new commitment to love of neighbour, the re-reading of the Scriptures, and attention to new Christian religious experiences. This process, I argued, has also taken place in wide sectors of the Christian community in regard to the ethics of homosexual love.

Endnotes

1. See in *The Documents of Vatican II*, ed. Walter Abbot (New York: Herder & Herder, 1966), "Lumen gentium" (On the Church) n. 16, p. 34, and "Nostra aetate" (On Non-Christians), n. 4, p. 664. For detailed commentary, see John Oesterreicher, *The New Encounter Between Christians and Jews* (New York: Philosophical Library, 1986). A corresponding change in the attitude of Canadian Anglican is evinced in the liturgy for Good Friday in *The Book of Alternative Services*. A rubric indicates that "the term 'the Jews" in St John's Gospel applies to particular individuals and not to the whole Jewish people." In places where *The Book of Common Prayer* is used, the third collect for Good Friday with its reference to "the Jews ... and all who

reject and deny the Son ... [out of] ignorance, hardness of heart, and contempt of thy word" is omitted by direction of General Synod.

2. Juan Segundo, *The Liberation of Theology* (Maryknoll, N.Y.: Orbis Books, 1986).

3. For references see Karl Rahner's article, "Salvation: Universal Salvific Will," in the theological encyclopedia, *Sacramentum Mundi*, 5:405–409; Richard McBrien's *Catholicism*, rev. ed. (San Francisco: Harper, 1994), 180–184; and Georg Kraus' article, "Universal Will of God," in *Handbook of Catholic Theology* (New York: Crossroad, 1995), 731–734.

4. General references: *Meeting in Faith and Spirituality in Inter-Faith Dialogue* (Geneva: WCC Publications, 1989); Arnulf Camps, *Partners in Dialogue* (Maryknoll, N.Y.: Orbis Books, 1983); W. Cantwell Smith, *Toward a World Theology* (Philadelphia: Westminster Press, 1981); *Faith in the Midst of Faiths*, ed. S. J. Samartha (Geneva: WCC Publications, 1977).

5. The significant passages are in *The Documents of Vatican II*, "Lumen Gentium," nn. 2, 16; pp. 15, 35; and "Gaudium et Spes" (The Church in the Modern World), nn. 16, 22; pp. 214, 222. For theological commentary on these passages, see *Commentary on the Documents of Vatican II*, ed. H. Vorgrimmler (New York: Herder & Herder, 1967 [Volume 1], 1969 [Volume 5]). For an Anglican perspective, see Andrew Taylor, "Humanity is One and History is One" in this volume.

6. See Marion Soards, *Scripture and Homosexuality: Biblical Authority and the Church Today* (Louisville, Ky.: Westminster/John Knox, 1995); Robin Scroggs, *The New Testament and Homosexuality* (Philadelphia: Fortress Press, 1983).

7. A milder interpretation of the church's tradition is found in John Boswell's *Christianity, Social Tolerance and Homosexuality* (Chicago: University of Chicago Press, 1980), according to which the church became intolerant of homosexual love only in the fourteenth century.

8. The recent *Catechism of the Catholic Church* (1992), while reaffirming that homosexual acts are intrinsically disordered, recognizes that homosexuals have not chosen their homosexual condition, that they must be accepted with respect, compassion, and sensitivity, and not be subject to unjust discrimination. For commentary see Richard McBrien's *Catholicism*, 995–997.

9. See Mel White, *Stranger at the Gate: To be Gay and Christian in America* (New York: Simon & Schuster, 1994); Virginia Mollenkott, *Sensuous Spirituality* (New York: Crossroad, 1993); Chris Glaser, *Coming Out to God: Prayers for Lesbians and Gay Men, Their Families and Friends* (Louisville, Ky.: Westminster, 1991); John McNeil, *Taking a Chance on God* (Boston: Beacon Press, 1988); and Chris Glaser, *Uncommon Calling: A Gay Man's Struggle to Serve the Church* (San Francisco: Harper & Row, 1988).

10. John Coleman, "The Homosexual Revolution and Hermeneutics," *The Sexual Revolution: Concilium*, no. 173 (3/1984), 55–64. See also Gregory Baum, "Homosexuality and the Natural law," *The Ecumenist* 1 (2/1994), 33–36.

8
Reflections on the Anglican Ethos
The Dialogical Middle Way

EILEEN SCULLY

A caricature, if it is a good one, always contains something of the original profile but exaggerates these features in such a way that misinterpretation is almost inevitable. Such is the case with dominant caricatures of Anglicanism: the church that looks to Scripture, tradition and reason; the Tory Party at prayer; the Middle Way; the Way of reasonableness, tolerance and openness. It is to the latter two descriptors that I now turn my attention. My intention in this chapter is to revisit the meaning of Anglican "centrism" as a way of beginning a conversation with the Essentials movement within the Anglican Church of Canada. My hope is to shift the question from "What are the Essentials of Anglican Christianity and how can we reclaim faith in the Anglican Church of Canada?" to "What does it mean to live as a Canadian Anglican Christian and how do we think about our faith?" The bulk of the work here involves the process of shifting between questions, rather than answering them directly.

Another caricature of Anglicanism is the church's ability to embrace diversity, especially doctrinal diversity. And, as in all good caricatures, the facial outlines are there. Our current reality, however, speaks more of increasing polarization and not only within the church, for we must also count the positions of those who have left the church for whatever reason as an expression of basic conflict. Is the descriptor accurate?

First, I would argue that, just as much as we need critically to revisit the relationship between the myths of Canada as a peaceable, tolerant, and generous society, Anglicans would do well to re-examine our own myths of how well we have actually lived out "reasonableness, tolerance, and openness." What can we learn from those times when we have jumped to conclusions rather than listened to all the voices and weighed the issues carefully; when we have acted from prejudice and elitism rather than respect for difference and a desire for mutuality; when we have closed a conversation before it has had the chance even to begin?

Such descriptive myths serve a purpose, and are not arbitrary. They are the expressions of the original intention of a group; as expressions of ideals, or that which we hope to be, they serve as directives. Insofar as they are lived out in community, and not just spoken about, the tradition is kept alive. Note that this is not just a process of handing down something received, but rather appropriating an original intention, living it, moving it along, putting it into new language and symbol forms that appropriately express the original intention and add to it new insights that are judged to be valuable. What of Anglican tolerance for diversity? Is there something in the original intentions of early Anglicanism, worked out in the context of tremendous ecclesial, political, theological, and social conflict and bloodshed, that has something to say to us today? It does us no good to hearken back to a peaceable time that indeed never existed; I propose no Golden Age of Anglicanism; rather, I think we do ourselves a disservice in the present if we fail to include bits of wisdom from the struggles of the past in our discussion of struggles of the present.

In what follows, I wish to offer some reflections on the need to shift the theological question from "What are the Essentials of Anglicanism?" and the process of defining a system of doctrine, to a focus on the question of theological method; to provide a brief overview of some of the inherited wisdom from Anglican theological tradition; and to consider a possible contribution to the conversation about Anglican identity in Canada. The chapter is meant as a prologue to particular explorations and an invitation to continuing dialogue.

Shifting the Question

On Polarization

> There is bound to be formed a solid right that is determined to live in a world that no longer exists. There is bound to be formed a scattered left, captivated by now this and now that new possibility. But what will count is a perhaps not too numerous centre, big enough to be at home in both the old and the new, painstaking enough to work out one by one the transitions to be made, strong enough to refuse half-measures and insist on complete solutions even though it has to wait.[1]

Bernard Lonergan's description offers a particularly potent challenge to Canadian Anglicanism. To be sure, Lonergan employs caricature to describe the extreme positions on a continuum; further, the words *left* and *right* do not presently mean what they did in 1967 when he wrote the article, and I am unconvinced of their appropriateness to today's climate—these are perhaps better avoided. Still, the image is enduring: between nostalgia and novelty, he suggests, there is a more honest dialogical middle ground; eschewing false appropriations of history and ungrounded orientations towards the future, we are called to live fully in the present, in that already-but-not-yet prophetic vocation of those called to live the historically announced, future-driven reign of God in the present.

Note well that the "middle ground" that he is describing here is characterized neither by mediocre compromise or opportunistic lack of commitment. This is no lukewarm place to be. This is not the home to "the nearly soulless/ whose lives conclude neither blame nor praise," as Dante describes those who went wherever the wind blew them, looking only after their own interest. Far from being the haven for those "who have lost the good of intellect" (again from Dante),[2] this kind of centre is the place where the challenge is to exercise intellect to the full.

Further, Lonergan's description is no simple denunciation of the extreme, polarized ends in favour of what some would argue to be typically Canadian, or typically Anglican, more moderate positions. He does not point to moderation as the answer (or, dare I say it, tolerance). I would argue that these so-called "moderate" positions present more complicated problems. As groups on either end of the continuum tend to be isolationist, the real tension today is more commonly seen between those who find themselves a few steps in from the end of each pole, and even between the many who like to see themselves in what they understand to be the centre of the spectrum.

The challenge inherent in this selection from Lonergan is to take the meaning of this radical "centre" seriously. Within the theological enterprise, Lonergan's centre suggests a place where the fullness of tradition meets with the fullness of present wisdom. As such it is no wonder that he describes this as a "*not-too-numerous* centre."

The centre of which Lonergan speaks addresses polarization by a lengthy process of sifting through, weighing and judging what the past and the present have to say to each other. This centre deals with polarization by engaging a process of dialogue, as openly and honestly with the past as with the present. Given the situation in the church today, beyond, as well as within, the borders of the Anglican Church of Canada, is the most important question truly "What are Anglican essentials"? Is it true that our priority is to "reclaim" faith? The questions raised by the Essentials movement clearly highlight the existence of polarized positions within the Anglican Church of Canada; but are the ways in which the questions are answered truly responsible to the tradition that the questioners wish to uphold?

My purpose in writing is not to deal with particular issues raised by the volume *Anglican Essentials*, but rather to offer some initial thoughts that reflect my concerns about how to take up the challenges posed by the Essentials movement, specifically as these pertain to the task of theology. In so doing, I find that much of what I have to offer has already been said, and I have little intention of repeating decades-old discussions between liberal, evangelical, and "orthodox" movements within the Anglican Church—a task for another time, perhaps. In Canada, the Essentials movement has served to highlight the importance of critical engagement by Canadian Anglicans with the same questions that gave rise to expressions of Anglican theological identity in those early centuries, to revisit earlier intentions, and to bring these into full and open dialogue with present situations. Simply put: we *are* in need of a far-reaching, sustained theological discussion of what it means to be an Anglican Christian in Canada today. On this point I am in agreement with the Essentials' intention. But from that point on, we part company. My contention is that the basic thrust of the Essentials movement, while correct in identifying polarized positions within the church, only contributes to further polarization by opting for an affirmation of "Anglican Essentials" that upholds a particular theological system. By so doing, the movement rejects much of the very tradition which it claims to uphold. I would argue that a more responsible theological position is one that takes up Lonergan's challenge to work at the "not-too-numerous centre," a position consonant with the best of Anglican theological tradition and practice. Again, this is no easy, lukewarm place to be.

Doctrine and Community

All Christian doctrine is, in essence, language: symbols that shape and pass on what the community through time has lived and learned, believed and discovered to be their shared meaning and shared value. Doctrine includes, equally, a body of texts and the process of interaction with these texts; indeed without appropriation in liturgy and in praxis, the texts wither as the language is not kept alive. This is rudimentary hermeneutics. It involves the dialectic between what is passed on and what is encountered and lived in the present. Does this mean that I am collapsing doctrine into mere "present experience"? Hardly. To work in the "not-too-numerous centre" means taking belief (what is handed down) as seriously as we take the present situation. It means also taking seriously the present situation and those who work to understand the present situation, and to change the present situation by living the presence of God in the world. In truth, what is demanded of theological reflection on doctrine is to keep a series of dialectics alive: between tradition and present community, between lived story and inherited story, between theological wisdom and knowledge of the past and the wisdom and knowledge of the present; between yesterday's mysteries and today's puzzles. And of course it also means re-reading the past for what has been forgotten, neglected, or left out and judging whether and how forgotten, neglected, or abused treasures can be brought into present discussions.[3]

Anglican Christians affirm the catholicity of our faith: that is, we hold that Christian faith is not bound to any particular time, place, or culture; such is the biblical witness itself, in the life of Jesus and in the struggles of the earliest Christian communities.

> Being in Christ Jesus is not tied down to place or time, culture or epoch. It is catholic with the catholicity of the Spirit of the Lord. Neither is it an abstraction that dwells apart from every place and time, every culture and epoch. It is identical with personal living, and personal living is always here and now, in a contemporary world mediated by meaning, a contemporary world not only mediated but constituted by meaning.[4]

Neither identified with any particular linguistic or cultural form, nor beholden to any particular interpretative framework, the gospel challenges us to bring it anew into every age. Edward Schillebeeckx described the gospel as "the present ever new." He thus draws attention to the fact that grace is both content (Good News of the presence of God's love, forgiveness, and reconciliation) and process (conversion or *metanoia*) shared in community. This "present ever new," he says, is "one of the factors that determine how we put into words the substance or content of belief in Jesus the Christ."[5] Commenting on this phrase, Robert Doran adds,

> The situation plays such a role in Christian proclamation and theology only because Christianity has some genuine *universal* significance that enables it to transcend every concrete historical definition of its essence, even as it always embodies this universal significance in specific and varying forms. "Christianity only stays alive and real if each successive period, from out of its relationship to Jesus Christ, declares anew for Jesus of Nazareth." This declaration is a matter, not of determining first the "essence" of Christian faith, and then in a second moment accommodating that essence to the present situation, but of progressively discovering the universal significance of belief in Jesus precisely as the church humbly and faithfully shoulders the difficulties which that belief entails in the current situation.[6]

All this is simply to repeat major theological judgements from the past thirty (and more) years; the present challenge is to take it all seriously.

The more grounded we are in our history and the more questions we ask of our traditions, the more we will be able to engage with a wider circle of partners today. The more we encounter people of other faiths and cultures, the more we listen to the challenging stories and questions of marginalized and silenced peoples, the greater the perspective that we will be able to bring to Scripture and our traditions. We risk much if we consider the hermeneutical community to consist only of those "under" rule of essential doctrine; to close the hermeneutical community in such a way is to reduce the meaning of the theological enterprise and of doctrine itself. Simply put, the more engaged we are in efforts to live the reign of God in the present in all its fullness and for the sake of the whole world, the more the past opens up for us and the more faithfully we are able to pass on the tradition. What is demanded is the humility and hospitality on the part of those bearers of tradition to create the context for mutuality and open dialogue. This is a difficult task in this age: we cannot be hospitable if our fear of threat dominates, and we need courage and patience to discern where there is real threat, where the threat is only perceived, and where what appears to be threat is actually a gift.

Anglican Method? Some Notes on the Starting Point

My intention in this brief section is neither to provide a comprehensive overview of early Anglican theology nor to enter into the larger debates about the question of Anglican theological identity.[7] Following my previous statements about the "present situation," I wonder what was "the present situation" to the early Anglican Church, and what were the insights and judgements from the "new" situation that shaped the way in which Hooker and others appropriated, lived, and passed on Christian faith. It is my intuition that early Anglican theology has something to teach us about what it means to live in the "not-too-numerous centre."

It is commonly argued that there is no such thing as a distinctive Anglican theology; but that rather than having an identifiably Anglican *system* of theology, we can claim a peculiarly Anglican *method* in theology, identified in terms of our adherence to Scripture, tradition, and reason as vehicles of revelation. A triad of theological authorities alone does not a method make, however, unless we know what to do with these. Nor can the *via media* serve as a methodological approach unless we know the context in which this *via media* was worked out.

The theological context was one of conflict between two poles on a continuum; on the one hand, a decayed sixteenth-century Thomism that had lost much of Thomas' own original intention and method and become closed; on the other, a closed Calvinism. The story is well known: two closed systems, claiming conflicting sources of absolute and external authority (Scripture and Magisterium),[8] operating by deduction and abstraction, each negating the other, came to vicious conflict. Hooker's approach was worked out in the context of conflicting absolutes; between battling perspectives, he pleaded for tolerance and mutual understanding.

Does his approach constitute a distinctive Anglican *method* in theology? Sykes, in claiming that there is a dearth of Anglican systematic theologies and no identifiable Anglican theological method, seems also to be arguing that there ought to be a distinctively Anglican method that upholds a single and distinctive Anglican system of theology.[9] While it is commonly argued that Hooker was the first Anglican theologian, suggesting that he elucidated the first distinctively Anglican theological method, I will argue in what follows that he *began* the process of defining a method. What his work exemplifies is more the spirit, tone, and ethos of Anglican theology. While he followed a particular path of analysis and reflection, the methodological questions were simply not framed with the kind of rigour that we need today—nor was he able to do so at that time. But let us not underestimate the ethos that he defined, however elusive the categories appear to us today: reasonableness, tolerance, and openness.[10]

Reasonableness

The influence of Renaissance humanism on Hooker is most perceptible in his approach to the argument of "probable persuasion." While later British empiricism tended to identify reason with sense-experience, Hooker's understanding of reason was more a matter of "following the argument wherever it leads."[11] Reasonableness, in Hooker's works, does not mean rationalism. When the Cambridge Platonists worked out "probable persuasion" during the time of the Civil War, their approach was a far more self-consciously Socratic one.[12] Was Socratic method *the* method of early Anglican theology? Hardly, but it made a strong mark. Its lasting contribution was induction and persuasion, rather than abstraction, logical proof, and argumentation.

Tolerance

Hooker's wariness of all claims to infallibility is well known. "In this present age," he commented in the *Laws of Ecclesiastical Polity*, "zeal hath drowned charity."[13] The kind of tolerance for which he argued must be understood in the context of what I wish to call his pedagogical-pastoral intention, an intention stripped of notions of mere polite agreement to "tolerate" difference rather than to attack it. In our present context, the word is used too casually to describe groups who, even though they may live in complete misunderstanding of one another, nevertheless tacitly agree not to "bother" each other, but to let the other live their lives in whatever way they choose, so long as it does not touch the life of the other group. When one examines Hooker's appeal to charity and his call for the suspension of judgement and mutual understanding one by the other, the contemporary meaning of the word "tolerance" does not work. The ethos to which he aspired here had more to do with encouraging mutual comprehension as a way to overcome the conflict between systems.

Openness

The openness demonstrated by the early Anglican Church was an openness to new ways of acquiring knowledge and new ways of learning about the world: at first, Renaissance humanism, and then the modern scientific methods of the seventeenth century. Openness itself is the gift; the particular discoveries are only secondary. Likewise, ought we not to be as open to criticisms of Enlightenment thought, modernism, liberalism, and neo-orthodoxy in ways that do not hearken back to a supposed "Golden Age"?[14]

Hooker's process, the way in which he clarified Anglican identity, was dialogical, concerned with the conflicts in the church and in his world. Far from *via media* as compromise between systems, it was a reorientation that questioned the purpose of *closed* theological systems. As Henry Chadwick has clearly put it, "The duty of authority often is not to bring discussion and debate to a speedy end by promptly taking one side or the other, but rather to see that at the end of the affair legitimate options are kept open."[15]

Some Present Challenges

To this point my remarks have been of a rather general nature. The concerns that fuel this long, drawn-out discussion are pressing, however. Do "reasonableness, tolerance and openness" have anything to add to contemporary polarized positions?

I am intrigued by the attention given to the meaning of tolerance in contemporary philosophical discussions.[16] As cultures and ideologies collide, particularly in the academic world, the liberal understandings of tolerance have come under notable stress. To what extent do we tolerate free speech, for example, as a legitimate extension of tolerance of diversity? At what point do we insist that law intervene, and to protect what higher values? Our views have shifted over recent decades. Obviously an ethical imperative towards respect for human dignity and integrity precedes mere tolerance on a scale of values—but on the particularities of that ethical imperative, there is no small debate, both in society at large and in the church.

One approach has been to distinguish between tolerance of diversity in "mutually exclusive and disrespecting cultures" and a more discriminating respect for legitimate expressions of diverse positions: obviously a line must be drawn somewhere. Amy Gutman describes the polarization of two prominent groups in academia:

> In an equal and opposite reaction, essentialists and deconstructionists express mutual disdain rather than respect for their differences. And so they create two mutually exclusive and disrespecting intellectual cultures in academic life, evincing an attitude of unwillingness to learn anything from the other or recognize any value in the other. In political life writ large there is a parallel problem of disrespect and lack of constructive communication among the spokespersons for ethnic, religious and racial groups, a problem that all too often leads to violence.[17]

Toleration, she argues, "extends to the widest range of views, so long as they stop short of ... discernible harm to individuals."[18] To answer the bankruptcy of tolerance, she suggests *respect* as "far more discriminating."

> [U]ndeserving of respect are views that flagrantly disregard the interests of others and therefore do not take a genuine moral position at all, or that make radically implausible empirical claims (of racial inferiority, for example) that are not grounded upon publicly shared or accessible standards of evidence.... Hate speech violates the most elementary moral injunction to respect the dignity of all human beings, and simply presumes the fundamental inferiority of others.[19]

Respect, she argues, comes with the responsibility to engage in dialogue. It "requires a widespread willingness and ability to articulate our disagreements, to defend them before people with whom we disagree, to discern the difference between respectable and disrespectable disagreement, and to be open to changing our own minds when faced with well-reasoned criticism."[20]

Gutman's is one response to the polarized positions that one might face in academia. The moral injunction is a generalized one: to respect the dignity of all human beings. As we face conflict between divergent theological positions, I would suggest that our Anglican heritage of "tolerance" be appropriated along with contemporary notions of what it means to be in dialogue. The most critical dialogue will be between theological tradition and current ethical demands. In the "not-too-numerous centre," it seems that basic human dignity, though a fine starting point, is not nearly enough. Neither is it enough simply to hold up as ideals the ethical and social norms from other eras— "tolerance" is a good case in point; slavery, fourth-century gender roles, heresy trials, colonialism, and so forth provide other obvious examples.

Is what we need most a tight statement of an Anglican system of ethics? What is demanded in the *via media* is rather a creative process of dialogue,[21] beginning not with the conclusions of particular norms, biblical or traditional, but with moving into the inner logic of Jesus' story, by creatively transposing from his context to our own. "Discipleship to Jesus cannot be understood as imitation of what he did, but, as well as accepting his value on the basis of our judgement that his life was utterly worthwhile, discipleship to Jesus involves learning from him how to go on, learning how to determine what we ought to do. We must learn how to integrate our changing practice with our permanent value."[22]

There is an important distinction to be made between essential or permanent values, and essential propositions and norms. Essential values demand *integration with* the present situation; essential norms are far less able to enter into dialogue with the present. If there is a sad commentary to be made about the state of the church today, it is the same comment that I offer to society in general: I fear that many of us are not well-equipped for dialogue, and those ethical-theological challenges that are most pressing risk action delayed and face increasing polarization, not because people are not well-grounded in Anglican "essentials," but because we are poorly equipped for dialogue.

Conclusion

I took up Lonergan's description of the "not-too-numerous centre" as a more-than-somewhat disturbing personal challenge, as one who has known well the attractiveness of nostalgia and novelty. My opening remarks reflected on caricature, and I fear that much of what I have presented here remains at that level; as intended, this paper does no more than provide a few arguments about why it is critical that we examine the question of defining "essentials." My primary concern remains: any definition of doctrine that *identifies* revealed truth with a particular theological system needs to be challenged. I have not argued directly that this is what the Essentials movement is doing, though clearly the tendencies are there; I would be equally concerned about attempts to identify, say, nineteenth-century theological liberalism with doctrinal truth. Indeed, there is much within the Montreal Declaration of Anglican Essentials with which I am in agreement, as I indeed affirm the central credal proclamation of the Christian church. But proclamation is not the only ministry of the church. That to which I object is the closed nature of the statement and the climate of survivalism surrounding its definition.

The "facial outline" that emerges from the caricature of Anglican identity is a *way* that is on its way to developing into a method; further methodological development in the present day needs to take up "reasonableness, tolerance and openness" in a new intellectual and social context. Perhaps "reasonableness" is better understood as the dynamic workings of human intellectual and imaginative integrity; perhaps "tolerance" is better understood as mutuality and dialogue; perhaps "openness" can embrace the human capacity both for generosity and solidarity (openness to others) as well as the willingness to explore new ways of understanding the world, its history and its present. If such questions are to form even a small part of the discussions, the "not-too-numerous centre" may indeed find itself growing.

Endnotes

1. Bernard Lonergan, "Dimensions of Meaning" in *Collection: Papers by Bernard Lonergan*, ed. Frederick E. Crowe and Robert M. Doran (Toronto: University of Toronto Press, 1988), 266–267.
2. The citation is from *Canto III* of *Dante's Inferno*. Virgil is describing to Dante the lot of the Opportunists, those who in life were uncommitted either to good or to evil, but only looked after their own interests, blowing this way, then that, as opportunity arose and situation demanded.
3. I think immediately of the wealth of fine scholarship on women's history, social history, and the work that has been done to re-orient historiography in general.
4. Lonergan, "*Existenz* and *Aggiornamento*," in *Collection*, 231.
5. The phrase is originally from Schillebeeckx' *Jesus: An Experiment in Christology* (New York: Crossroad, 1987). See pp. 575ff for his discussion of present christological problems.
6. From Robert Doran, *Theology and the Dialectics of History* (Toronto: University of Toronto Press, 1990), 108. The internal citation is from Schillebeeckx, *Jesus: An Experiment in Christology*, 575.
7. For an overview of elements of the debate, see *The Future of Anglican Theology*, ed. M. Darrol Bryant, Toronto Studies in Theology 17 (Toronto: Edwin Mellen Press, 1984).
8. Of course the post-Tridentine Roman Catholic Church argued not "Magisterium alone" but Scripture and Tradition; the tendency in practice was, however, for Scripture to be eclipsed by Magisterium.
9. See Sykes, *The Integrity of Anglicanism*, and the discussions of his work in Bryant, ed., *The Future of Anglican Theology*.
10. In my elucidation of these three points in the paragraphs that follow, I am relying on the work of D.R.G. Owen, "Is There an Anglican Theology?" in Bryant, ed., *The Future of Anglican Theology*, 6–12.
11. *Ibid.*, 6.
12. *Ibid.*, 8.
13. The citation is from Richard Hooker, *Of the Laws of Ecclesiastical Polity* (London: Everyman's Library), 1:360. Quoted by Owen in *Ibid.*, 9.
14. Owen presents a colourful picture of the period: "This kind of openness to the new knowledge represented by modern science was in striking con-

trast to the reaction on the continent. In the same century, Galileo was condemned in a notorious trial in Rome, Servetus was burned at the stake in Geneva and in France the works of Descartes were placed on the Index. To experience the atmosphere in England, to which the Anglican thinkers gave expression, was like entering another world. Voltaire, who was present at Isaac Newton's funeral, marvelled that a scientist could be buried in Westminster Abbey, with the honours due a hero." From *Ibid.*, 12.

15. Henry Chadwick, "The Context of Faith and Theology," in *Theology in Anglicanism*, ed. Arthur A. Vogel (Wilton, Connecticut: Morehouse-Barlow, 1984), 27.

16. I am thinking particularly of the work of Charles Taylor. See *The Malaise of Modernity*, CBC Massey Lectures (Toronto: Anansi, 1991); see also Amy Gutman's introduction to *Multiculturalism: Examining the Politics of Recognition* (Princeton, N.J.: Princeton University Press, 1994).

17. See Gutman, introduction to *Multiculturalism*, 21.

18. *Ibid.*, 22.

19. *Ibid.*, 23.

20. *Ibid.*, 24.

21. I am informed by Patricia McAuliffe's use of the language of creativity in relation to ethics. See her *Fundamental Ethics: A Liberationist Approach* (Washington: Georgetown University Press, 1993).

22. *Ibid.*, 160.

Study Guide

PAUL JENNINGS

Questions for Further Reflection

The following questions are designed to aid individual study or group discussion of the papers included in this volume. They were drawn up to help the reader

- identify and focus on some of the main questions raised by the authors;
- become more aware of the larger, complex issues behind the specific positions;
- connect these issues with his or her own understanding, opinions or experience of the church.

The brief Bible studies prefacing each of the chapters are not intended as "proof-texts" but as an introduction to the themes discussed and an attempt to place the contemporary discussion in the context of biblical faith experience.

Foreword *by Michael Peers*

Biblical Opening: *Read Philippians 2:1–13*

Paul urges the church in Philippi to "be of one mind." What does it mean for a church to be of one mind? Does everyone have to have the same opinion? What do we know about Paul's attitude towards differences of opinion? (Compare Rom. 14 & Gal. 2:11–14!)

In your experience, how well does your church community deal with conflicting opinions? Are they welcomed, tolerated, or treated as taboo? What effect does each of these attitudes have on the health of the church?

In the Philippians passage, how does Paul qualify and describe the "one mind" that Christians are to have? Who models this mind for us? (v. 5).

"Work out your own salvation with fear and trembling" clearly cannot mean, in the context of Paul's theology, that we bring about our salvation ourselves. He seems to mean that we must "spell out" the meaning of salvation (which is God's gift) for our own lives, and that this is a very serious business. Can we see the theological discussion in the church as part of this "spelling out our own salvation with fear and trembling"? What would that mean for our attitude towards theological debate?

---

1. How do you feel about public dissension, conflict, or debate in the church about matters of doctrine and ethical teaching?

   • What are the limitations of dissension? (What would a church look like in which everyone taught his or her own view, with no mutual accountability?)
   • What is the necessity of theological debate? (What would a church be like with no room for questioning, for differences of opinion and personal expression?)

2. Looking deeper than the specific issues which divide us, Peers refers to "the generosity of God who created and loves us in our variety" as the ultimate source of human diversity. In what way are our theological opinions and understandings shaped by the specific differences of our created humanness—the differing backgrounds and experiences which make us the individuals we are?

   • How can this theological understanding of created diversity inform the way in which we handle our disagreements?

3. What images does Peers use to describe the unity of the church?

4. How is "unity in diversity" shown in the Anglican tradition? Think of your experience of Anglicanism, as well as what you know of the classical Anglican tradition.

Introduction *by John Simons*

1. Simons points out a fundamental ambiguity in the Declaration: Is it talking about specifically Anglican essentials, or essentials of the Christian faith in general? Which of the "essentials" mentioned in the Declaration would apply to all Christians, and which are obviously uniquely Anglican?

- How do uniquely Anglican essentials differ from the general essentials of the Christian faith? What is the standard of authority in each case (how do we decide what is essential)? Why, in each case, would it seem necessary to adhere to them?
- What is the significance of ecumenical encounters and dialogue for determining what is truly essential Christian faith? How have encounters with Christians of other traditions informed your faith?

2. What purposes do formal statements of doctrine (creeds, confessions, catechisms) have in the history of the church?

- What claims does Simons understand the Declaration to be making?
- What do you understand the purpose of the Declaration to be?

3. What do you feel the church needs in terms of a "declaration of faith" today?
- On what issues would you find a clear definition of the position of the church helpful? Why? On what authority should such a statement be made?
- On what issues would you find a clear statement divisive, intrusive, or premature? Why?

1. "Feminism and the Church" *by Susan L. Storey*

Biblical Opening: *Read Genesis 16:1–16*

Where can we identify sin in this passage? What role do the following factors play in creating the domestic mess:

- the institution of slavery (and the issue of racism)?
- the role and expectations of women?
- Abraham's and Sarah's mistrust of God's promise?
- personal animosities of the various characters?

- How do these factors relate to each other? What is the difference in our understanding if we see them all together or if we isolate one as the "real point" of the story?
- Who is the victim of each of these instances of sin?

In v. 13 Hagar recognizes her experience as an epiphany, a vision of God which enables her to name God anew.

- This kind of experience is otherwise reported almost exclusively of the patriarchs of Israel (Abraham, Jacob, Moses). What does it mean to your faith that it is also reported of a woman? A slave? A foreigner?

- The name she gives God means "The Living One who Sees Me." What does it suggest about her experience of God?
- What does this episode have to say about our practice of naming God?

Why do you think women such as Hagar play such an obscure role in the traditional Christian reading of the Bible? On the other hand, why do you think this marginal tradition was preserved in the book of Genesis at all?

---

1. Storey names patriarchy and androcentrism as the "twin faces" of sexism (p. 20).

   - How does she define "patriarchy"? Where can we identify aspects of patriarchy in the Christian tradition, both past and present? Where do we see parts of the tradition that work against patriarchy?
   - Similarly, how does she define "androcentrism"? Where do we find it in the Christian tradition? Can we find aspects of the tradition which counteract androcentrism?

2. A central concern of feminist theologians is the conviction that the traditional ways of speaking about God, being almost exclusively masculine, subtly reinforce the idea that God is male.

   - What do you think of this concern? Have you noticed this process at work in your own thinking about God, or in the some of the assumptions you hear from others?
   - How do you respond to the counter-claim of some Anglicans that they use the names "Father," "Son," or the pronoun "He" without thinking of God as male?
   - How do you respond to the notion that God is ultimately a male being? How has the church counteracted this widespread misconception?

3. Storey summarizes two different proposals put forward by Gail Ramshaw and Elizabeth Johnson for overcoming the exclusive use of male names for God (p. 21). How do the two proposals differ?

4. How do you feel about the use of feminine images in liturgy to speak about God? What has been your experience of this kind of liturgy? Why is this practice so emotionally charged, even threatening, for many in the church?

5. Storey challenges a view of Scripture and tradition which sees them as absolute authorities to be accepted submissively. "'How can a text that contains so much that is damaging to women function authoritatively in the Christian community as normative of faith and life?'... If the Bible does

teach that God is male and women are inferior, these texts cannot bear 'Good News' for women or function salvifically for them" (p. 22).

- How do you react to this statement? How do you react to a view of scriptural authority that demands we accept everything as God's word, no matter how offensive or hurtful it may be?
- How might we attribute authority to Scripture in a way that takes into account our experiences of oppression and healing? What approaches of feminist exegesis does Storey mention?

6. Storey begins her article by stating that coming to terms with the feminist critique is one of the essentials for the church today. Why does she believe it is essential, and should not be "dismissed and passed over in silence"?

- What are "some of the graces, the gifts to the church, that feminist analysis offers"?

2. "Naming and Glorifying the Trinity"
by John Simons

Biblical Opening: *Read Exodus 3:1–15*

In the course of this important revelation, Moses asks what the name of God is. His concern seems to spring less from his own interest as from the hope that this knowledge will authenticate his sending in the eyes of others (v. 13). How do we use—and abuse—the name of God in religion? What is the meaning of the Jewish tradition that the name of God should not be spoken aloud?

How do you understand God's answer: "I am who I am"? What does it tell us about the relationship of God's self to the various names we use for God?

How successful is the church at remembering that God is ultimately the great "I AM," greater than the names we use in worship and prayer? What do we do to remind ourselves that God's being is ultimately ineffable and inexhaustible?

What is the central content of this revelation to Moses? What is it that God came to tell the people? What is it that we learn about God—before Moses asks for a name?

1. How has your understanding of the Trinity been shaped? What words, images, or explanations come to mind when you hear the word *Trinity*?

    - How do you respond to the suggestion that the church's understanding of the Trinity has been impoverished by the almost exclusive use of the names "Father," "Son," and "Holy Spirit"?

2. Simons writes: "If we take seriously the credal way of speaking about God, then before to the church's affirmation of the Trinity, the Trinity affirms itself. The divine Persons eternally distinguish themselves from one another and recognize the fullness of deity in one another. The church's affirmation of the Trinity ... is fundamentally an entry into this same dynamism of triune life, a dynamism articulated— that is, revealed — in the deeds and gestures of grace as much as in sacred words or privileged formulae" (p. 29).

    - What is the difference between thinking or talking about an idea of God and thinking or talking about *God*, living and real? What consequences does the awareness of God's reality have on the way we think or talk about God?
    - Why does Simons see fit to remind us that the distinctions in the Trinity lie in God's own being and precede our way of understanding them? What could "an entry into this same dynamism of triune life" mean for the church? How does that differ from a merely verbal affirmation of the Trinity?
    - Implicit in the last phrase quoted above is a contrast between two understandings of revelation: (1) revelation as the passing on of special religious information, "sacred words or privileged formulae," and (2) revelation as the story of God's saving action, "deeds and gestures of grace." What is your understanding of revelation? Where do we find each of these understandings of revelation at work in the Christian tradition? What kind of a faithful response do each of these concepts of revelation demand?

3. How does Simons define the "higher righteousness" evinced in Jesus' action and teaching? (p. 32).

    - Where does he see the tension between this attitude of Jesus and the Declaration's call for clear and absolute standards in sexual behaviour and family life? Do you agree? If not, how would you respond to his concerns?
    - Why do you think the church (at least in recent generations) has been so much more vocal in condemning sexual and familial irregularities than other forms of sin (greed, injustice)? The perception of the church

in the minds of many outsiders seems to resemble the proverbial Pharisee more than Jesus' attitude and practice. Is this widespread impression fair?

4. What are the two visions of evangelism which Simons contrasts? (p. 34). What might a eucharistically based evangelism look like?

5. There is an apocryphal story about a little boy who called God "Harold," because he heard everyone pray, "Harold be thy name"! This story might serve as an illustration of the issues Simons raises about the meaning of names (pp. 37–39; note 18).

    • Are "Father" and "Son" just arbitrary names, such as "Harold," which convey no meaning? If not, what are they intended to say about the persons of the Trinity? What other connotations do they carry which do not apply to God? (Simons mentions several on p. 38.)
    • Since any image or expression we use to name God will apply only in part, how can we remain aware of the inadequacies inherent in the way we talk about God in order to avoid being misled by them?

6. One of the difficulties with the traditional trinitarian formula is that it refers only to the relationship of Father and Son, leaving the Spirit tacked on as a poor third. Simons suggests that if we take the full divinity of the Spirit seriously, it will influence and enrich the way we name the two other persons.

    • What does the Bible tell us about the relationship of the Spirit and the Father? (See Gen. 1, Psa. 104:30, Ezek. 37, Judges, Isa. 61, Rom. 8:14–27, among others.) What other ways of naming and glorifying the "Father" and the Spirit might these traditions suggest?
    • What does the Bible tell us about the relationship of the Spirit and the Son? (See Isa. 11, 42 [=Matt. 12:18ff], and 61 [=Luke 4:18ff]; Luke 1; John 14 and 20:22; I Cor. 12:12–27, among others.) What other ways of naming and glorifying the "Son" and the Spirit might these traditions suggest?

7. Simons defines idolatry as:
    – the worship of the creature instead of the creator;
    – an act of unconscious self-deception, by which we worship the work of our own hands;
    – the projection or divine personification of values established in a culture.

    • Do you think that feminine imagery for God—or non-traditional imagery of any kind—could be idolatrous? In what way? Under what conditions?

- In what way (according to Simons) can an exclusive use of traditional imagery for God be idolatrous? (pp. 44–45). What do you think? How can the church guard against these tendencies?

3. "Towards a Biblical Church" *by Paul Jennings*

Biblical Opening: *Read Hebrews 11*

What do we learn about the nature of faith from the examples cited in this chapter? What hopes, struggles, doubts, and decisions are involved in faith? Who was God for Abraham, Sarah, Moses, and the rest? Can you describe your own faith in similar terms?

How does the Epistle to the Hebrews use the scriptural tradition in this passage? In what way are the (Old Testament) Scriptures functioning here as a revelation of God? How might our traditional way of describing the Bible ("God's Word written, inspired and authoritative") apply here?

Verses 39 and 40 contain an unusual and powerful thought: "that apart from us they would not be made perfect." The hope and redemption of the men and women of the Bible is not complete without us. What could this mean for our relationship to the Bible? Do we treat it differently when we realize that it is a story ongoing in our relationship to God?

---

1. What has been your experience of the critical academic study of the Bible?
   - How can it strengthen the faith of the church?
   - How might it also harm or weaken the faith? What are its limitations?

2. How does Jennings define "liberal" and "traditionalist" positions within the church?
   - What understanding of Scripture and of faith as a whole are implied in each of these positions? (pp. 52–53).
   - Where do you see these tendencies at work in the Anglican Church today? Do you believe we have to choose between them, or are they a false alternative?

3. Jennings argues for the discernment of the human voice in Scripture as distinct from the word of God as a crucial element in a theologically

responsible use of the Bible. He suggests that most Anglicans would agree in principle. Why is this distinction observed so seldom or so inconsistently in the practice in the church?

- What are the technical difficulties surrounding this distinction?
- How can this distinction be abused? How can the church guard against this abuse?

4. The central insight of the Reformation tradition is that the primary message of Christianity is the "gospel" (*evangelium*, "Good News") of God's love for us and acceptance of us. If this insight is to be the guiding principle of the church, what role will the Scriptures play?

- How does this differ from the widespread conception of the Bible as primarily a rule book, a guide to correct behaviour or doctrine?
- How does a gospel-centred understanding of how the Bible gives us guidance in ethical questions differ from a legalistic understanding? Compare Jennings' example of an ethic of horseback riding in notes 9 and 10, and Paul's statement in I Corinthians 10:23. How would this distinction apply to one of the real ethical issues the church is facing today?

5. Jennings points out that all our efforts to "make sense" of the Bible ultimately articulate only a foreshortened version of God's truth, a consistency imposed by our limited understanding.

- Can you think of instances in which your reading of Scripture has suddenly given you a new perspective on your faith, or even shaken your previous convictions?

6. Implicit in Jennings' remarks on the relationship of Scripture and doctrine is the notion of a "hermeneutical circle." Doctrine — the traditional understanding of the church—informs the way we read the Bible. We see this clearly if we try to debate with a Jehovah's Witness, who can argue (with some plausibility) that the doctrine of the Trinity is not scriptural. On the other hand, Scripture must continue to inform our understanding of doctrine; if it doesn't, we have replaced the encounter with the living God in Scripture with a rigid and incomplete ideology.

- The church's reading of Scripture traditionally leads to new discoveries which compel us to revise our doctrinal priorities—discoveries which are experiences of God's living voice. How does this come about? What examples come to mind from the history of the church? Where do you see this operating in the church today?
- Why is it important for individual Christians to read the Bible continuously, even if we may be firmly grounded in Christian doctrine?

- "Doctrine should serve to balance and enable our encounter with the Word, not to replace it." Do you see this process at work in the way your church community reads and preaches on the Scriptures?

7. A recent development in the theology of the Bible has been an interest in "narrative theology," based on the insight that faith is more powerfully articulated in stories than in dogmas. How does a biblical story address us differently than, say, a theological argument in the Epistles?

- Using the example of the sacrifice of Isaac, how does our response differ if we read it primarily as a story, than if we read it with an explanation of what it's supposed to mean foremost in our minds? (p. 64) In the same way, how does our understanding of the crucifixion differ? (cf. note 13).
- Jennings speaks of the Scriptures as having a creative authority for our faith. How does this creative authority work in your experience? How does it relate to the "regulative authority" of Scripture as a standard for correct doctrinal understanding?

4. "The Word of God and 'God's Word Written'"
by Stephen Reynolds

Biblical Opening: *Read Hebrews 4:11–13*

How is the Word of God described here? What terms refer to God's living presence? Does the text distinguish between the Word and God's full presence?

What various events and realities does the expression "Word of God" refer to in the Bible? How do these traditions relate to the living presence of God? How do they relate to the Scriptures?

What does the image of God's Word as a sword "piercing to the division of soul and spirit" suggest to you?

The last phrase in v. 12 is variously translated as "judging" or "discerning" the thoughts of the heart (Gk = *kritikos*). What does each of these words imply to you? What is the difference in the meaning of the verse?

When do the Scriptures act as the living, piercing, judging presence of God? When do they not?

---

1. Reynolds analyses the metaphor implicit in the statement "Scripture under Christ judges the church for its faithfulness to his revealed truth."

   • In your experience, how can the Scriptures act as a judge with respect to individual Christians? To the church as a whole?
   • What human agency is necessary in each of these cases to name and interpret this judgement? How can the human authority be abused? How can it be most responsibly employed?

2. What factors does he describe having been at work in the formation of the canon? (pp. 76–77). Try to imagine being a Christian of the first century, before a clearly accepted canon of the Bible had been drawn up. What would be the basis for faith?

3. In his examination of the verses appended to the Declaration's article on Scripture, Reynolds points out that the Declaration seems to assume that the biblical expression "Word of God" refers exclusively to the Scriptures.

   • What associations does the expression "Word of God" have in the Old Testament tradition? In the New Testament? In the practice of the church?
   • What does the word "gospel" (*evangelion*) mean in the New Testament?
   • How do the Scriptures, as "God's Word written," relate to these other manifestations of God's Word?
   • What role does the living presence of God play in each of these manifestations?

4. What is the "canon within the canon" in your community—which books, passages, stories, and ideas play a key role in the worship, preaching, and self-awareness of the congregation? Which parts of the Bible are neglected?

   • What shape does your personal canon have? Make a list of passages which are particularly important to you, which you might give to someone to read who wanted to know what you believe.
   • How is this kind of "canon within the canon" useful? How is it limiting or even dangerous?

5. Reynolds invites us to think about the identity of the Bible in terms of the sacramental model of the eucharist (pp. 91–93).

   • What is Reynolds' argument against transubstantiation of the eucharist—the doctrine that the bread and wine, while retaining their original appearances, actually turn into the Body and Blood of Christ?

- How could we apply these categories to Scripture? What understanding of the relationship between the living Word of God and the Scriptures could we describe as
  – a form of transubstantiation?
  – "bare memorialism"?
  – a genuinely sacramental understanding?
- The sacramental model is rooted in the primary sacrament of the incarnation: God's self-giving to us in Jesus, fully human and fully divine. How can the identity of Jesus help us to understand more clearly the complex questions about the nature of the eucharist and of the Scriptures?

5. "Humanity is One and History is One"
by Andrew Taylor

Biblical Opening: *Read Matthew 12:22–32*

What does this scene tell us about Jesus' relationship to the established religious authority of his day? Why do you suppose the Pharisees are so reluctant to see God at work in Jesus' healings, and indeed ascribe them to Satan?

How does Jesus answer them in vv. 25–29? What criterion does he hold up in order to challenge them to see God at work and not Satan?

Make a list of some of the experiences of healing, of liberation from demons, of the binding of oppressive "strong men" we see in the world today. Think specifically of examples where evil is overcome outside of the church, where the name of Jesus is not spoken.

- How might this text help us to evaluate such experiences in terms of our faith? What might it suggest about the action of God's Spirit in the world?
- How well has traditional theology prepared us to see God's Spirit at work in secular experiences of liberation? Why do you think the church has often resisted or even demonized secular liberation movements?

In v. 32 Jesus says that denying or slandering him will be forgiven, but denying or slandering God's Spirit will not. How might this verse guide us in our relationship with the non-Christian world?

1. Taylor finds some common ground with the Declaration in his critique of some tendencies in the church towards "a woolly type of theological liberalism" (pp. 100–101). What does he say about pop-spirituality's understanding of
    – individual vs. communal redemption?
    – the historical reality of God's redemptive acts?
    – sin (both individual and collective)?
    – our identity as Christians in a consumer society?
    - Do you see these tendencies at work in the church? Where?
    - How does he distinguish the "faith and justice movement" from this "recreational religion"? How does the faith and justice movement differ in its understanding of the four issues named above?
    - These two attitudes towards the faith are often lumped together as the "liberal" wing of the church. Is the distinction which Taylor makes new to you? Is it plain to you?

2. Taylor refers much of the anxiety in the church to the end of the "Constantinian era," the age in which Christianity was the official and dominant religion of our society. He points out that the Anglican church historically had a particular role in Canada as "an important pillar of the dominant culture."
    - What was, historically, the role of the Anglican church in your community? Did it have a clear social profile compared to other churches? Does your congregation today differ socially from local evangelical churches?
    - How do you react to the sentiment often expressed that Canada must remain—or return to being—an officially Christian society? What would this mean for the life and mission of the church?

3. What criticisms does Taylor make of the BCP's political ideology and its theology of the atonement? (pp. 103–104).
    - Do you agree with his comments?

4. Taylor contrasts a "bipartite" theological anthropology (focusing on Fall and Salvation) with a "tripartite" understanding (focusing on Creation, Fall, and Redemption) (pp. 107–108).
    - The Declaration of course does not deny the fact of creation—why does Taylor nonetheless call the position of the Declaration bipartite? How does the Declaration speak about human nature? What consequences does its confession of creation seem to have for its understanding of humanity's present state? What does it seem to say about humanity outside the church?

5. In Taylor's view, how does the tripartite model, starting from the fundamental fact of our creatureliness, affect our understanding of
    – the redemptive work of Christ? (p. 108).
    – humanity outside the church? (p. 108).
    – the nature of sin? (pp. 110–111).
    – the created cosmos? (p. 110).
    – the value of the human person? (pp. 109–110).
    – the social consequences of the faith? (pp. 112–113).

6. How does Taylor understand "salvation"? (p. 113f.).

    *   Why do you think the social, this-worldly aspects of salvation have been so neglected in the Christian tradition, or played off against an other-worldly understanding? Can the two understandings of salvation be reconciled?

6. "Anglicanism and the Church's Global Mission" *by Terry Brown*

Biblical Opening: *Read Acts 15:1–21*

What is the position of the Christians mentioned in vv. 1, 5 concerning the mission to the Gentiles? Try to put yourself in their situation—why would the Mosaic law seem an "essential" of the faith to them?

How does Peter argue with them? What criterion does he cite? (v. 8, 9).

How did the early church, according to the New Testament, deal with the problem of cross-cultural mission?

*   How did they deal with the question of authority?
*   How did they distinguish between the essential message and culturally specific religious traditions?
*   Why was the issue of the Gentiles' freedom from Mosaic law so crucial for Paul? (Compare Paul's account of the same episode in Galatians 2.)

---

1. Brown begins with the observation that "the healthiest and fastest growing Anglican churches are often in Africa, Asia, Latin America, and the South Pacific."

    *   How might this fact affect our understanding of the identity of Anglicanism?

- What spiritual gifts do the churches of the Two-Thirds World (Anglican and others) have to offer the Canadian church? In what ways has your faith been nourished by the witness of these churches?
- What gifts (other than material) do we in the Canadian church have to offer them? How does your answer compare with the answers which might have been given forty years ago?

2. What aspects of "indigenization" does Brown mention as being operative in various Anglican churches? (pp. 118–119).

   - Which of these tendencies are you comfortable with? Which, if any, do you find troubling?

3. What factors, traditions, and attitudes are important to you in defining the identity of the Anglican church as distinct from other Christian denominations?

   - What aspects of the tradition does Brown mention as important to southern churches in defining their identity as Anglicans?
   - How do you react to the decision made by Anglicans in India and Pakistan to form a United church with other Protestant denominations? How important is the survival of the Anglican church as a separate institution to you? What Anglican values do you feel must be preserved as the Christian church continues to evolve?
   - Is the Lambeth Quadrilateral a helpful definition of Anglicanism? Does it say enough? Does it say too much?

4. What are the characteristics of the "imperialistic" or "paternalistic" attitude which plagued the worst of Christian missions? (p. 119).

   - What are the Ten Principles of Partnership which Brown mentions? (p. 131). How do they address the imperialism of the older model? How would you describe the model of the church's role in evangelism which they outline?
   - Traditional missionary practice often unconsciously promoted Western culture, language, dress, and social values as part of the gospel. How do we go about distinguishing the core gospel from cultural accretions in our version of Christianity? What role does an open and equal dialogue with churches in other cultures play in this exercise in self-knowledge?

5. Many Christians, especially in Asian countries, find themselves a small minority beside other religions. And increasingly Canadians, especially in urban centres, find themselves living alongside adherents of other religions.

- What form of evangelism is most appropriate and respectful in these neighbourly contexts? Assuming we feel called to communicate something of our faith, what should we be trying to accomplish?
- What do we as Christians have to learn from adherents of other faiths?

7. "How the Church Changes its Mind"
by Gregory Baum

Biblical Opening: *Read Matthew 15:21–28*

What reason does Jesus give in v. 24 for initially ignoring the woman's request? To whom does he appear to be speaking? *Is* it in fact a direct answer to the woman's request? If not, what is it?

What is the disciples' reaction to the woman? Why would they be so negative? Why doesn't Jesus send her away, if he agrees that her request is inappropriate?

What reason does Jesus finally give for granting her request? What could he mean by "faith" here, since he is speaking to a Canaanite who does not worship the God of Israel?

What do you suppose might have motivated Jesus to change his mind— indeed, to change his principles? What role might compassion have played? The text does not mention it here, but it is mentioned as a factor in many of his healings. Consult a concordance on the use of the word "compassion" in the Gospels (the Greek word means "to be moved in one's gut"). To what extent does Jesus seem to base his decisions on compassion?

---

1. Baum writes consciously as a Roman Catholic theologian, but his central assumption should be familiar to Christians in the Reformation tradition (such as Anglicans): that the church may err in its understanding and application of the gospel, and must thus exercise constant self-scrutiny and willingness to reform (*semper reformanda*).

   - How open should the church be about reviewing its teachings? About admitting it might err? How might this be perceived as threatening to faith? As strengthening faith?

- Baum writes: "Self-recognition and repentance ... are gifts of God" (p. 138). How do you feel about gestures of repentance on the part of the church (for example, the apology to Native Peoples, to the Jews)?

2. Baum calls the church's process of reflection a "hermeneutical circle." What five steps does he outline in this process?

   - What sources of authority does the church consult at the various stages? How are these various authorities balanced?

3. Baum's fourth step is critical reflection on contemporary Christian experience. Why is it important to take seriously the experience of fellow Christians, even if—or especially if—their experience differs from our own?

   - What role should such experience play in our common discernment of doctrinal and moral teaching?
   - What is "critical" reflection? How do we recognize the genuine role that contemporary experience has to play, without descending to the anecdotalism which often seems to pass for theological reflection in the church today?

4. Baum links the condemnation of homosexuality at least in part to the discomfort with sexuality in general within the Christian tradition.

   - How does traditional morality define a "legitimate" sexual encounter? What criteria are most relevant —what questions has the church traditionally asked of a relationship?
   - What questions did traditional sexual morality not ask, or ask only secondarily? What is the importance of joy, compassion, gentleness, quality of relationship, or other criteria to the moral judgement of the church?
   - How might the experience of homosexuals, as well as heterosexuals, help us to form more appropriate standards of sexual ethics?

5. Following a suggestion by Stephan Pfürtner, Baum proposes a sexual ethic based on love, truth, and justice (p. 145).

   - How does he work out the implications of each of these virtues for sexual ethics? What role do these criteria play in your thinking about relationships, or in the relationships of others around you?
   - In what ways is this model of sexual ethics more permissive than the traditional model? In what ways is it stricter?

8. "Reflections on the Anglican Ethos"
by Eileen Scully

Biblical Opening: *Read Romans 11: 25–36*

Paul is writing (don't forget!) as a Christian Jew. In this passage he is facing the fact that the majority of his people have rejected belief in Jesus.

- How does he evaluate this rejection from the point of view of his central theological understanding (vv. 28, 30). (You may want to review his extended argument in ch. 9, 10). How does this judgement compare with our modern ideal of tolerance?

As much as he holds them responsible for this rejection of the gospel, Paul repeatedly refers to it as God's doing (vv. 25, 32; 9:14–18). What conception of God's sovereignty lies behind this paradox? What salvific meaning does he ascribe to their rejection of the gospel? (v. 25).

- What difference might it make in our attitude towards those with whom we radically disagree if we believed that their "bloody-mindedness" was part of God's plan?

Paul's conviction that they had rejected God's salvation might seem sufficient for him to write them off completely—yet the passage leads towards a radical openness to their continued part in God's salvation.

- What is the root of this openness? What implications does it have for (Gentile) Christians' attitude towards Jews?
- How does this openness fit with the "in-tolerance" Paul shows on the issue of their rejection of the gospel? How might Paul's attitude help us to sort out our relationship to other religions, or to other understandings of the gospel?

Why has Paul's openness had so little echo in the shameful history of the church's attitude towards the Jews?

---

1. How does Scully characterize theological existence "in the middle"? In what way are past and present to be brought together?

   - What assumptions do each of the three positions sketched by Lonergan (p. 149) make about the role of tradition? About the historical nature of the faith?
   - Where do you see these assumptions at work in the church today?

2. In her reflections on tolerance (pp. 154ff), Scully differentiates between the classical Anglican virtue (Hooker) and a contemporary "liberal" understanding.

    - In what ways does she see the liberal conception as "bankrupt"?
    - What are the characteristics of Hooker's attitude, and how does it contribute towards a constructive dialogue?

3. In what ways have you heard Anglicanism referred to as a "middle way" (*via media*)? In what respect do you yourself see the Anglican Church this way?

    - What are the dangers of being in the middle? Why can one grow stagnant or self-satisfied there? Do you see these tendencies in the Anglican self-understanding?
    - What opportunities are offered by being in the middle? Why can it be a challenging, indeed essential, place to be? Do you see these tendencies in the Anglican Church?
    - What makes the difference between stagnating or being productive in the middle? If the Anglican Church is to continue to understand itself as the middle way, what attitudes and commitments do we need to cultivate for the future?

Appendix
The Montreal Declaration of Anglican Essentials

"In essentials, unity; in non-essentials, liberty; in all things, charity."
— Richard Baxter, after St. Augustine

As members of the Anglican Church of Canada from every province and territory, and participants in the Essentials 1994 Conference in Montreal, we unite in praising God for his saving grace and for the fellowship we enjoy with our Lord and with each other. We affirm the following Christian essentials:

1. The Triune God

There is one God, self-revealed as three persons, "of one substance, power and eternity," the Father, the Son, and the Holy Spirit. For the sake of the gospel we decline proposals to modify or marginalize these names and we affirm their rightful place in prayer, liturgy, and hymnody. For the gospel invites us through the Holy Spirit to share eternally in the divine fellowship, as adopted children of the God in whose family Jesus Christ is both our Saviour and our brother. *(Deuteronomy 6:4; Isaiah 45:5; Matthew 28:19; 2 Corinthians 13:14; Galatians 4:4–6; 2 Thessalonians 2:13–14; 1 Peter 1:2; Jude 20–21. Cf. Article I of the 39 Articles, Book of Common Prayer [BCP], p. 699.)*

2. Creator, Redeemer and Sanctifier

The almighty triune God created a universe that was in every way good until creaturely rebellion disrupted it. Sin having intruded, God in love purposed to restore cosmic order through the calling of the covenant people Israel, the coming of Jesus Christ to redeem, the outpouring of the Holy Spirit to sanctify, the building up of the church for worship and witness, and the coming again of Christ in glory to make all things new. Works of miraculous power mark the unfolding of God's plan throughout history. *(Genesis 1–3; Isaiah 40:28; 65:17; Matthew 6:10; John 17:6; Acts 17:24–26, 28; 1 Corinthians 15:28; 2 Corinthians 5:19; Ephesians 1:11; 2 Timothy 3:16; Hebrews 11:3; Revelation 21:5. Cf. Article I.)*

3. The Word Made Flesh

Jesus Christ, the incarnate Son of God, born of the virgin Mary, sinless in life, raised bodily from the dead, and now reigning in glory though still present with his people through the Holy Spirit, is both the Jesus of history and the Christ of Scripture. He is God-with-us, the sole mediator between God and ourselves, the source of saving knowledge of the Godhead, and the giver of eternal life to the church catholic. *(Matthew 1:24–25; Mark 15:20–37; Luke 1:35; John 1:14; 17:20–21; Acts 1:9–11; 4:12; Romans 5:17; Philippians 2:5–6; Colossians 2:9; 1 Timothy 2:5–6; Hebrews 1:2; 9:15. Cf. Articles II–IV, the Nicene Creed, BCP.)*

4. The Only Saviour

Human sin is prideful rebellion against God's authority, expressing itself in our refusing to love both the Creator and his creatures. Sin corrupts our nature and its fruit is injustice, oppression, personal and social disintegration, alienation, and guilt before God; it destroys hope and leads to a future devoid of any enjoyment of either God or good. From the guilt, shame, power, and path of sin, Jesus Christ is the only Saviour; penitent faith in him is the only way of salvation.

By his atoning sacrifice on the cross for our sins, Jesus overcame the powers of darkness and secured our redemption and justification. By his bodily rising he guaranteed the future resurrection and eternal inheritance of all believers. By his regenerating gift of the Spirit, he restores our fallen nature and renews us in his own image. Thus in every generation he is the way, the truth, and the life for sinful individuals, and the architect of restored human community. *(John 14:6; Acts 1:9–11; 2:32–33; 4:12; Romans 3:22–25; 1 Corinthians 15:20–24; 2 Corinthians 5:18–19; Philippians 2:9–11; Colossians 2:13–15; 1 Timothy 2:5–6; 1 Peter 1:3–5; 1 John 4:14; 5:11–12. Cf. Articles II–IV, XI, XV, XVIII, XXXI.)*

5. The Spirit of Life

The Holy Spirit, "the Lord, the Giver of life," sent to the church at Pentecost by the Father and the Son, discloses the glory of Jesus Christ, convicts of sin, renews the sinner's inner being, induces faith, equips for righteousness, creates communion, and empowers for service. Life in the Spirit is a supernaturalizing of our natural existence and a true foretaste of heaven. The loving unity of Spirit-filled Christians and churches is a powerful sign of the truth of Christianity. *(Genesis 1:2; Exodus 31:2–5; Psalm 51:11; John 3:5–6; 14:26; 15:26; 16:7–11, 13–15; 1 Corinthians 2:4; 6:19; 12:4–7; 2 Corinthians 3:18; Galatians 4:4–6; 5:22–26; Ephesians 1:13–14; 5:18; 1 Thessalonians 5:19; 2 Timothy 3:16. Cf. Article V, the Nicene Creed.)*

6. The Authority of the Bible

The canonical Scriptures of the Old and New Testaments are "God's Word written," inspired and authoritative, true and trustworthy, coherent, sufficient for salvation, living and powerful as God's guidance for belief and behaviour.

The trinitarian, Christ-centred, redemption-oriented faith of the Bible is embodied in the historic ecumenical creeds and the Anglican foundational documents. To this basic understanding of Scripture, the Holy Spirit leads God's people and the church's counsels in every age through tradition and reason prayerfully and reverently employed.

The church may not judge the Scriptures, selecting and discarding from among their teachings. But Scripture under Christ judges the church for its faithfulness to his revealed truth. *(Deuteronomy 29:29; Isaiah 40:8; 55:11; Matthew 5:1–18; John 10:35; 14:26; Romans 1:16; Ephesians 1:17–19; 2 Timothy 2:15; 3:14–17; 2 Peter 1:20–21. Cf. Articles VI–VIII, XX.)*

7. The Church of God

The supernatural society called the church is the family of God, the body of Christ, and the temple of the Holy Spirit. It is the community of believers, justified through faith in Christ, incorporated into the risen life of Christ, and set under the authority of Holy Scripture as the word of Christ. The church on earth is united through Christ to the church in heaven in the communion of the saints. Through the church's ministry of the word and sacraments of the gospel, God ministers life in Christ to the faithful, thereby empowering them for worship, witness, and service.

In the life of the church only that which may be proved from Scripture should be held to be essential to the faith and that which is non-essential should not be required of anyone to be believed or be enforced as a matter of doctrine, discipline, or worship. *(Ephesians 3:10–21; 5:23, 27; 1 Timothy 3:15; Hebrews 12:1–2; 2 Timothy 3:14–17. Cf. Articles XIX, XX, and XXI.)*

8. The New Life in Christ

God made human beings in the divine image so that they might glorify and enjoy their creator forever, but since the fall, sin has alienated us all from God and disorders human motivation and action at every point. As atonement and justification restore us to fellowship with God by pardoning sin, so regeneration and sanctification renew us in the likeness of Christ by overcoming sin. The Holy spirit, who helps us practice the disciplines of the Christian life, increasingly transforms us through them. Sinlessness, however, is not given in this world, and we who believe remain flawed "in thought, word and deed" until we are perfected in heaven. (*Genesis 1:26–28; 3; John 3:5–6; 16:13; Romans 3:23–24; 5:12; 1 Corinthians 12:4–7; 2 Corinthians 3:17–18; Galatians 5:22–24; Ephesians 2:1–5; Philippians 2:13; 2 Peter 3:10–13. Cf. Articles IX–XVI; Book of Alternative Services, p. 191.*)

9. The Church's Ministry

The Holy Spirit bestows distinctive gifts upon all Christians for the purpose of glorifying God and building up his church in truth and love. All Christians are called in their baptism to be ministers, regardless of gender, race, age, or socio-economic status. All God's people must seek to find and fulfil the particular form of service for which God has called and equipped them.

Within the priesthood of all believers we honour the ministry of word and sacrament of which bishops, priests, and deacons are set apart by the Ordinal. (*Romans 12:6–8; 1 Corinthians 3:16; 6:11; 12:4–7, 27; 2 Corinthians 5:20; Galatians 2:16; Ephesians 4:11–13; 1 Timothy 3:1, 12–13; 5:17; Hebrews 2:11; 1 Peter 2:4–5, 9–10. Cf. Articles XIX, XXIII.*)

10. The Church's Worship

The primary calling of the church, as of every Christian, is to offer worship, in the Spirit and according to truth, to the God of creation, providence, and grace. The essential dimensions of worship are praise and thanksgiving for all good things, proclamation and celebration of the glory of God and of Jesus Christ, prayer for human needs and for the advancement of Christ's kingdom, and self-offering for service. All liturgical forms — verbal, musical, and ceremonial — stand under the authority of Scripture.

The Book of Common Prayer provides a biblically grounded doctrinal standard, and should be retained as the norm for all alternative liturgies. It should not be revised in the theologically divided climate of the contemporary church. The Book of Alternative Services meets a widely felt need for contemporary liturgy, and brings life and joy to many Anglican worshippers.

No form of worship can truly exalt Christ or draw forth true devotion to him without the presence and power of the Holy Spirit. Prayer, public and private, is central to the health and renewal of the church. Healing, spiritual and physical, is a welcome aspect of Anglican worship. *(John 4:24; 16:8–15; Acts 1:8, 2:42–47; Romans 12:1, 1 Corinthians 11:23–26; 12:7; 2 Corinthians 5:18–19; Ephesians 5:18–20; Colossians 3:16; 1 Thessalonians 1:4–5; 5:19. Cf. The Solemn Declaration of 1893, p. viii, BCP; Articles XXV, XXXIV.)*

11. The Priority of Evangelism

Evangelism means proclaiming Jesus Christ as divine Saviour, Lord, and Friend, in a way that invites people to come to God through him, to worship and serve him, and to seek the empowering of the Holy Spirit for their life of discipleship in the community of the church. All Christians are called to witness to Christ, as a sign of love both to him and to their neighbours. The task, which is thus a matter of priority, calls for personal training and a constant search for modes of persuasive outreach. We sow the seed, and look to God for the fruit. *(Matthew 5:13–16; 28:19–20; John 3:16–18; 20:21; Acts 2:37–39; 5:31–32; 1 Corinthians 1:23; 15:2–4; 2 Corinthians 4:5; 5:20; 1 Peter 3:15.)*

12. The Challenge of Global Mission

Cross-cultural evangelism and pastoral care remain necessary responses to the Great Commission of Jesus Christ. His command to preach the gospel worldwide, making disciples and planting churches, still applies. The church's mission requires missions.

Christ and his salvation must be proclaimed sensitively and energetically everywhere, at home and abroad, and cross-cultural mission must be supported by praying, giving, and sending. Global mission involves partnership and interchange, and missionaries sent by younger churches to Canada should be welcomed. *(Matthew 28:19–20; Mark 16:15; Luke 10:2; Romans 15:23–24; 1 Corinthians 2:4–5; 9:22–23; 2 Corinthians 4:5; 8:1–4, 7; Ephesians 6:19–20; Philippians 2:5–7; 1 Thessalonians 1:6–8.)*

13. The Challenge of Social Action

The gospel constrains the church to be "salt" and "light" in the world, working out the implications of biblical teaching for the right ordering of social, economic, and political life, and for humanity's stewardship of creation. Christians must exert themselves in the cause of justice and in acts of compassion. While no social system can be identified with the coming kingdom of God, social action is an integral part of our obedience to the gospel. *(Genesis 1:26–28; Isaiah 30:18; 58:6–10; Amos 5:24; Matthew 5:13–16; 22:37–40; 25:31–46; Luke 4:17–21; John 20:21; 2 Corinthians 1:3–4; James 2:14–26; 1 John 4:16; Revelation 1:5–6; 5:9–10. Cf. Article XXXVIII.)*

14. The Standards of Sexual Conduct

God designed human sexuality not only for procreation but also for the joyful expression of love, honour, and fidelity between wife and husband. These are the only sexual relations that biblical theology deems good and holy.

Adultery, fornication, and homosexual unions are intimacies contrary to God's design. The church must seek to minister healing and wholeness to those who are sexually scarred, or who struggle with ongoing sexual temptations, as most people do. Homophobia and all forms of sexual hypocrisy and abuse are evils against which Christians must ever be on their guard. The church may not lower God's standards of sexual morality for any of its members, but must honour God by upholding these standards tenaciously in face of society's departures from them.

Congregations must seek to meet the particular needs for friendship and community that single persons have. *(Genesis 1:26–28; 2:21–24; Matthew 5:27–32; 19:3–12; Luke 7:36–50; John 8:1–11; Romans 1:21–28; 3:22–24; 1 Corinthians 6:9–11, 13–16; 7:7; Ephesians 5:3; 1 Timothy 1:8–11; 3:2–4, 12.)*

15. The Family and the Call to Singleness

The family is a divinely ordained focus of love, intimacy, personal growth, and stability for women, men, and children. Divorce, child abuse, domestic violence, rape, pornography, parental absenteeism, sexist domination, abortion, common-law relationships, and homosexual partnerships, all reflect weakening of the family ideal. Christians must strengthen family life through teaching, training, and active support, and work for socio-political conditions that support the family. Single-parent families and victims of family breakdown have special needs to which congregations must respond with sensitivity and support.

Singleness also is a gift from God and a holy vocation. Single people are called to celibacy and God will give them grace to live in chastity. *(Psalm 119:9– 11; Proverbs 22:6; Matthew 5:31–32; Mark 10:6–9; 1 Corinthians 6:9–11; Ephesians 5:21–6:4; Colossians 3:18–21; 1 John 3:14–15.)*

The New Beginning

Together we reaffirm the Anglican Christianity that finds expression in the historic standards of the ecumenical creeds, the Thirty-Nine Articles, the Solemn Declaration of 1893, and the 1962 Book of Common Prayer. Respect for these standards strengthens our identity and communion. In humility we recognize we have often been ashamed of the gospel we have received and disobedient to the Lord of the church. God helping us, we resolve to maintain our heritage of faith and transmit it intact. This fullness of faith is needed both for Anglican renewal and for the effective proclamation of the good news of Jesus Christ in the power of the Holy Spirit.

We invite all Anglicans to join us in affirming the above as essentials of Christian faith, practice, and nurture today. In this declaration we believe that we are insisting upon only what is genuinely essential. In regard to non-essentials, we should recognize and respect that liberty and that comprehensiveness which have been among the special graces of our Anglican heritage.

Participants in Essentials 94, with the Sponsoring Bodies:
Anglican Renewal Ministries of Canada;
Barnabas Anglican Ministries;
The Prayer Book Society of Canada.

21 June 1994, Montreal, Canada

Contributors

Dr. Gregory Baum

Gregory Baum is professor emeritus of the Religious Studies faculty at McGill University. He received a doctorate in Theology from Fribourg University in Switzerland (1956), was appointed by Pope John XXIII as a "peritus" (theological expert) to the Secretariat for Promoting Christian Unity at the Vatican Council (1962–65), taught Catholic Theology and Sociology of Religion at St Michael's College in the University of Toronto (1959–1986), and became a professor of Social Ethics at McGill University in 1986. He is the author of several books, including *Compassion and Solidarity*, the Massey Lectures given for the CBC in 1986. His first article calling for new theological reflection on homosexuality was published in *Commonweal* (99 [February 19, 1974], 481.)

The Rt. Rev. Terry Brown

The Rt. Rev. Terry Brown is Bishop of the Diocese of Malaita in the Church of the Province of Melanesia. He served the Anglican Church of Canada in an overseas appointment as Lecturer in Theology at Bishop Patteson Theological Centre in the Solomon Islands (1975–1981), and from 1985 to 1996, he served as Asia/Pacific Mission Coordinator of the Anglican Church of Canada. He holds a doctoral degree in Church History from Trinity College, Toronto.

Paul Jennings

Paul Jennings is an Anglican priest within the Diocese of Montreal. He studied literature at the University of Toronto, followed by studies in Theology in Tübingen, Wuppertal, and at McGill University. He trained and worked in the Protestant church in Germany, and his theological thinking has been shaped by the German Protestant tradition. He is currently rector of the parish of Grenville, Calumet, and Montebello, and is pursuing doctoral studies at McGill. His partner, Elisabeth Bachem, an ordained minister of the Evangelical Church of the Rhine, now serves a United Church parish.

The Rev. Dr. Stephen Reynolds

Stephen Reynolds serves as priest of a three-point parish in the Diocese of Toronto and is assistant professor of Systematic Theology at Trinity College,

Toronto. He is the author of *For All the Saints: Prayers and Readings for Saints' Days* (1994), and contributed his Study Paper in *Thinking about The Book of Alternative Services* (1993). He resides with his wife and daughter.

Dr. J. Eileen Scully

Eileen Scully received a doctorate in Systematic Theology from the University of St Michael's College, Toronto, in 1993. She works as Associate Secretary for Faith and Witness, the theological commission of the Canadian Council of Churches, with responsibilities for ecumenical and interfaith dialogue. She also teaches occasionally at Huron College Faculty of Theology, London, and at St Jerome's College, Waterloo. She is a member of the Church of St John the Evangelist in Kitchener, Ontario, and serves on the Faith, Worship, and Ministry Committee of the Anglican Church of Canada. Eileen and her husband, Eric Duerrstein, live in Waterloo, Ontario, with their sons, Michael and Colin.

John Simons

John Simons is principal of the Montreal Diocesan Theological College and faculty lecturer in Philosophical Theology at McGill University (Faculty of Religious Studies). He holds a Ph.D in Philosophy from Georgetown University in Washington, D.C., and has taught at the University of Alberta and the University of Toronto, as well as at Georgetown. Ordained a priest in 1969, he has been chaplain at the University of Alberta, Vicar of Christ Church Cathedral in Montreal, and chaplain at Trinity College in Toronto. He has also exercised ministries in the Dioceses of Washington and Oklahoma in the Episcopal Church. His publications are concerned with issues in the history of philosophy, metaphysics, and the concept of God.

The Rev. Dr. Susan Storey

Susan Storey came to Canada in 1978 from the United States. She studied theology at Trinity College in Toronto, where she completed Master of Divinity and Doctor of Theology degrees. Earlier, she had earned a Master of Arts in Philosophy at the University of Colorado. She was ordained in 1987 and has served parishes in the Dioceses of Qu'Appelle and Edmonton. Currently she is Priest in Charge at St Thomas' Anglican Church in Sherwood Park, Alberta. Dr. Storey is a contributor to *Partners in the Dance: Stories of Canadian Women in Ministry*, ed. Patricia Bays (1993); and to the consultation of The Churches' Council on Theological Education in Canada, June 1993, in Waterloo, Ont. [A Response to Donna Runnalls], the proceedings of which were published in *Consensus: A Canadian Lutheran Journal of Theology* (21, vol. 1 [1995]).

Andrew Taylor

Andrew Taylor shared a Lectureship in Christian Theology and Ethics with his wife, Rachel Reesor, at Queen's Department of Religious Studies and Queen's Theological College, from 1992 to 1996. He is a Ph.D candidate in Christian Theology at McGill University, under the supervision of the Rev. Dr. Douglas John Hall. He has published in the area of social history, theological book reviews, and poetry. Andrew has been involved in lay ministry in different parishes, as a member of the Montreal Chapter of "the Jubilee Group," and as a member of the formation group of the Montreal chapter of the African National Congress. Both Andrew and Rachel currently teach Theology at a Mennonite Liberal Arts College in Bluffton, Ohio.